Interfaith Theology

A Reader

Interfaith Theology

A Reader

Edited by Dan Cohn-Sherbok

ONEWORLD
OXFORD

INTERFAITH THEOLOGY: A READER

Oneworld Publications
(Sales and Editorial)
185 Banbury Road
Oxford OX2 7AR
England
www.oneworld-publications.com

ISBN 1–85168–276–7

Cover design by Design Deluxe
Typeset by Saxon Graphics Ltd, Derby
Printed and bound in Britain by Bell & Bain, Glasgow, UK

For Lavinia

Contents

Introduction

In modern society with its multiplicity of faiths, there has been a growing interest in the relationship between the world's religious traditions. Increasingly, adherents of the world's major faiths have grappled with the issue of religious pluralism. Some conservative thinkers have espoused a traditional form of religious exclusivism based on the assumption that their own faith contains the one true and final revelation from God. A growing number of other writers, however, have criticized such a stance for its narrowness. Disenchanted with such an absolutist position, they have formulated a modified theocentric approach which affirms the salvific presence of God in faiths other than their own. Although such a model of religious diversity is more open than the traditional exclusivist position, an increasing number of thinkers have argued for an even greater tolerance. In their view, what is now required is a fundamental shift in which the Divine, rather than any specific understanding of God, is placed at the centre of the universe of faiths.

This anthology – drawn from over a hundred theologians and philosophers of religion – is designed to provide a bird's-eye view of the contemporary debate. Directed at students as well as general readers who seek to gain an understanding of the central issues involved in this discussion, this volume contains key readings from Christian, Jewish, Muslim, Hindu and Buddhist thinkers; in addition, it contains an extensive bibliography of major works in the field. Organized alphabetically, the collection begins with the Zen Buddhist scholar Masao Abe, who argues that there must be a conscious recognition of the central differences between Buddhism and Christianity if fruitful dialogue is to take place between adherents of these two religions. In particular, the Buddhist conception of absolute Nothingness is fundamentally different from the Christian doctrine of God. According to Abe, the recognition of absolute Nothingness in Zen is the realization of one's true self and provides the means for true Enlightenment. This is of a different order from faith in God as understood in Christianity. For Buddhists the idea of a self-sustaining God is ultimately inadequate.

The discussion continues with the Swedish Christian theologian Kajsa Ahlstrand's objections to the views of religious pluralists. In her estimation, the pluralist position reduces classical formulations of Christian theology to minimalist definitions of the faith. According to Ahlstrand, the fact that some christological assumptions of Christianity conflict with the beliefs of other faiths is not a sufficient reason to abandon the central tenets of the Christian faith. For Ahlstrand, Jesus should be understood as God's tentative Word in the sense that he is God's universal manifestation of saving truth and grace in a perspective of human brokenness.

Arguing along similar lines, the Muslim philosopher Shabbir Akhtar argues that dialogue must acknowledge the distinct features of different faiths. In his view, responsible religious exchange is important in a pluralistic world – yet he insists that the incompatibility between Islam and Christianity must be accepted. Hence, it must be acknowledged that the doctrinal elements in one tradition cannot reasonably maintain a universality of normative claim upon human allegiance. The presence of competing truth-claims outside one's own tradition of faith is undeniable even if disconcerting. As a participant in interfaith dialogue, one must simply accept that there are irresolvable puzzles which cannot be set aside in discussion.

For the Christian missiologist Gerald H. Anderson, Christians must remain faithful to the tenets of the faith when engaging in dialogue with members of other religions. As he notes, various church organizations have stressed the need for Christians to engage in inter-religious encounter. The church is to work vigorously in this area to affirm that God reaches out to all humanity. Yet Anderson stresses that in doing so one should not pass judgement on what others claim to be their experience of salvation. Rather, the Christian should acknowledge Christ as Saviour. Christ does not become the truth because we experience him as such: he is the truth.

On similar lines, the Christian Islamic scholar, Norman Anderson, argues that Christians must not suppress their beliefs when engaging in dialogue with adherents of other faiths. In his view, the world's religions contain elements of truth which come from God, but there are false aspects as well. Given that God most fully revealed himself in Christ, a large portion of dialogue should be regarded as a preparation for evangelism.

Echoing this view, the Presbyterian African writer, Kofi Appiah-Kubi, maintains that God has most fully manifested himself in Christ. Nonetheless, he is to be found in all faiths. All religions, he states, address the central questions of human life; in an attempt to provide adequate answers, each people has offered different and at times conflicting explanations. Hence he concludes that each religion represents a culturally conditioned response to the gift and illumination of God. In this light, the church's duty in dialogue with African religion and culture should be one of understanding rather than condemnation.

Adopting a different approach, S. Wesley Ariarajah, a Methodist minister from Sri Lanka, maintains that a new framework is now needed for fruitful encounter.

In his view, Christians must be open to God's freedom to act within the experience of other people outside the church. In his view, this calls for the recognition that God is the creator, preserver and provider of all that is. God's love is at work to bring wholeness to all of creation. Hence, religious traditions bear witness to how people in all ages and places have attempted to understand and relate to God. Even as Christians bear witness to God's action in Christ, they should be open to listening and learning about the ways God has been active in the lives of other peoples.

Arguing along similar lines, the Muslim theologian, Hasan Askari, stresses that the Qur'an provides a basis for understanding the concept of apostleship in Islam, Judaism and Christianity, as well as other traditions. In his view, there is an apostle for every community. Such figures as Noah, Abraham, Moses and Jesus stand out as supreme examples of apostleship of God. It is obligatory, he writes, for Muslims to bear witness to all the apostles whose names are mentioned in the Qur'an. As the Qur'anic concept of apostleship is comprehensive of all human communities, it is reasonable to assume that God's apostles have arisen in all lands. According to Askari, the notion of finality can be viewed more as a sign of authenticity rather than as a judgement concerning the validity of other faiths.

The Muslim scholar Mahmoud Ayoub similarly stresses that throughout history God has revealed himself to the prophets in different traditions. Islam, he states, proclaims more loudly than any other tradition that God's disclosure is found within the religious experience of humankind. Human history is the history of divine revelation; it is the history of prophets who in their lives provided a link between the temporal life and the eternal.

Paul Badham, an Anglican professor of theology and religious studies, insists that Christians must acknowledge the presence of God in other religions. From the early history of the church, he notes, the Logos was understood as the presence of God working in all human beings. Thus, to accept the Logos doctrine, it is necessary to view all world religions as inspired by the same divine initiative. According to Badham, the Logos as the universal divine presence is not limited to Christ, but refers to the working of God in other faiths.

Adopting a different position, the German theologian Karl Barth argues that all religions – including the Christian faith – must be judged by God's revelation. In his view, Christianity is true only in so far as it reflects the divine revelation. A statement of faith, he insists, is necessarily a statement which is thought and expressed in faith and from faith, that is in recognition and respect of what is revealed. In this light, the presence and reality of the grace of God differentiates the Christian religion from all other traditions.

The Christian liberation theologian José Miguez Bonino draws attention to the contextual nature of dialogue. To what extent, he asks, is the problem of the Christian's relation to people of different faiths a theological issue? There is a danger, he writes, in abstracting the christological question from the context of religious encounter. We do not meet religions – rather we meet people. In that sense, human encounter precedes and conditions inter-religious debate. Thus, Christians should take seriously the nature and conditions of encounter.

According to the Reform Jewish theologian Eugene Borowitz, even though God has a special relationship with the Jewish people, members of other faiths can be saved as long as they observe the Noachide laws. The Torah, he notes, describes God as making a covenant with Noah, and all humanity. Because non-Jews can be saved by observing the Noachide laws, there is no reason for Jews to seek to convert others. In short, humanity does not need to be Jewish, but God needs Jews and Judaism to achieve his purposes and realize the eschatological redemption of human history.

Focusing on the topic of interfaith prayer, the Anglican theologian Marcus Braybrooke stresses that interfaith worship can unite believers of different faiths. Outlining various types of interfaith worship, he points out that it is possible for believers to enter into the religious experience of different communities of faith. Many Christians who take part in such services will wish to maintain the uniqueness of Christ while balancing this by belief that God has made all people in his image. In his view, all prayer is in the spirit of Jesus Christ who endorses all that is good and true.

The German theologian Michael von Bruck contends that even though Christians are called to missionize, such activity should be reinterpreted in contemporary society. Christianity, he emphasizes, is a missionary religion. Mission is the legitimate expression of Christian witness. Yet missionary activity should not undermine the original experience of the Christian community, the revelation of the unconditional love of God expressed in the person of Christ. Today the universal claim of unconditional love of God in Christ has to be expressed in a totally different way. What is now called for is a recognition of the inclusive character of this divine encounter.

For the German theologian Emil Brunner, the Christian faith is not simply one religion among many. This is not religious intolerance. Rather, it is based on the conviction that God has revealed himself in Christ. Nonetheless, Brunner asserts that there are phenomena in the religions of non-Christians which should be referred back to stirrings of the divine Spirit in their hearts. Referring to Calvin, he maintains that the sense of God is deeply interwoven in all humanity. It must be accepted, however, that Christ is the fulfilment of all religion. As Redeemer, he is the truth which these other religions seek in vain.

In the opinion of the Christian theologian M. Darrol Bryant, Christians do not need to abandon the central tenets of the faith when engaging in religious dialogue. Interfaith encounter, he writes, offers a welcome opportunity to enter into a new relationship with believers in other faiths. Such engagement can deepen and enlarge one's own convictions. Yet such a development must be articulated in the horizon of trinitarian faith. The central claims of Christianity must not be set aside in embarking on this spiritual quest.

For the Jewish theologian Martin Buber, encounter with God involves a special relationship. Human beings, he states, have addressed the eternal Thou with many names. But all names are hallowed, for God is not merely spoken about, but also spoken to. Whoever uses the word God and really has Thou in mind, he continues, addresses the true Thou of his life. This I–Thou relationship is a basic dimension of human existence in the world, and the unifying ground for establishing contact with the Divine.

The Christian theologian John Carman maintains that inter-religious dialogue is a task of Christian discipleship, but distinct from Christian evangelism. In the modern world it is a deliberately planned conversation where discussion has not previously taken place or where it has reached an impasse. It is needed especially where there is disagreement and misunderstanding. Such discussion often takes place among scholars, but there is a need for non-scholarly dialogue as well.

According to the Catholic theologian Teilhard de Chardin, God's presence infuses all creation. In his view, the universe is undergoing an evolutionary process toward higher levels of consciousness. Human progress is possible only by uniting with God, who is constantly involved in the creative process. Imbued with a mystical sense of the totality of all existence, Teilhard argues that human striving will eventually end in ecstasy. Although this mystical quest is formulated in christological terms, his conception of the evolutionary process offers a bridge between Christian thought and other religious faiths.

In the opinion of the Jewish scholar Ellen Zubrack Charry, those who embark on interfaith encounter should search for common anthropological ground. This would involve examining how several traditions assess the human condition. In outlining this endeavour, she emphasizes that the world's religions have previously been exclusive in character, but today religious syncretism is increasingly prevalent. Nonetheless, the world's traditions in their different ways by and large agree that human beings are in pain and that release from pain defined in various ways is available, with sufficient faith and trust.

For the Christian theologian John Cobb, Christian triumphalism must be superseded by a new approach to other faiths. As he notes, Christians today share the world with people of other religions. The most common response to this changed situation is for Christians to regard other religious traditions as inferior since they lack the saving truth of Christianity. Such a stance, however, is profoundly mistaken. Christians today must hear the truth found in other faiths. Only those who have been transformed by appropriation of the universal truth found in other ways, he writes, can proclaim the universal truth of Jesus Christ.

According to the Jewish theologian Dan Cohn-Sherbok, Judaism has always been inclusive in orientation. In this light, Jews must be open to the world's faiths. Adopting a pluralistic position, he argues that Judaism should not be placed at the centre of the world's religions; instead a theocentric model should now be adopted. On this basis, other faiths should be understood as different human responses to the divine reality. In his view, the formulation of a Jewish global interreligious theology hinges on several preconditions: Jewish theologians must learn about other faiths than their own, and they must insist that the theological endeavour occurs within a trans-religious context.

According to the Greek theologian Demetrios Constanteolos, Orthodox Christian theologians have always stressed the continuity of God's revealing truth before as well as after the incarnation of the Logos. In the Christian East, numerous writers developed a positive attitude to other religions based on the belief that non-Christians could be crypto-Christians without knowing it. The universal or cosmic covenant that God made with Noah can serve as the basis for fruitful dialogue between Christians and adherents of other religions.

For the Christian theologian Harvey Cox, inter-religious encounter demands a balance between the universal and the particular. Every religion, he contends, has both dimensions – each faith nourishes its own specific tradition while making universal claims for humanity. Thus, he argues, because each religion embraces both elements, they must be integrated if positive dialogue is to take place. Today, however, there is often a separation between these two visions. Those who glimpse the universal dimension advocate interfaith encounter whereas particularists shun dialogue. In a global society, this impasse must be overcome.

Echoing such sentiments, the Christian theologian Kenneth Cracknell argues that Christians must remain loyal to their faith while recognizing that God is at work within other communities. Christians confess that Christ is Lord and Saviour, yet they must accept that God is active beyond the boundaries of the Christian community. Jesus, he argues, opens doors rather than shuts them; he pulls down barriers between people rather than building them higher. What is now needed is a new inclusivist christology which is open to the spiritual realities of other religions.

The Anglican theologian and expert on Islam, Kenneth Cragg, similarly argues for an openness to other faiths. Other religions, he points out, are no longer remote and academic. Instead, today we live in a global community; other faiths cannot be ignored. Hence, he argues that expositions of Buddhist, Hindu, Muslim or other doctrines can contribute to exploring dimensions of the Christian faith. Further, the Christian themes of finality, authority, truth, mission and ministry should no longer be handled from within; in each case they must be set in the active sphere of attention of the other.

Considering the global context of faith, the Christian theologian Don Cupitt argues that there must be a radical reformulation of interfaith dialogue. Conversations between traditionalists in the world's faiths must be superseded by a new vision of religion in a pluralistic framework. In his view the process of world-cultural assimilation has fundamentally changed the nature of religious life. Past ethnic and religious identities are rapidly being eroded, and those who engage in religious dialogue must become aware of this change in religious perception.

Adopting a different vision of interfaith dialogue, the Dalai Lama seeks to draw together the world's religions in a common religious task. All the different religions, he notes, have a similar objective despite their philosophical differences. Every religion emphasizes human improvement, love, respect for others and concern for suffering. On these lines all religions have the same goal. Given this common ground, the world's religions can act together for the benefit of humankind – the aim of all religions is to help others, and their various teachings support this end.

For the Catholic theologian Gavin D'Costa, the Trinity offers a basis for religious encounter between adherents of the world's faiths. Drawing on the fourth Gospel, he asserts that the notion of the Spirit active in other religions can only be understood in the context of specific Christian engagements with non-Christian cultures and practices. Further, the observation of the likeness of Jesus in others is part of what it means to say that the Holy Spirit is present in the world. The Spirit in the church allows for the discernment of Christ-like practice in others.

The Buddhist scholar Gunapala Dharmasiri adopts a more critical approach to inter-religious dialogue. Assessing Christian doctrine, he contends that Christian theological doctrines are misguided. Outlining the Buddhist critique, he contends that there are no grounds for believing in a disembodied soul. While human beings long for continued existence after death, there is no evidence to support traditional Christian belief. In his view, the notion of the soul becomes absolutely meaningless when it is subjected to analysis.

Approaching the issue of religious diversity from an ethical standpoint, the Christian theologian Tom Driver argues that the pluralist stance is the only acceptable one. What is at stake, he writes, is Christianity's self-understanding, its place in history and its understanding of God. Pluralism, he continues, is a demand now laid upon Christians. In the past Christians were anxious to subdue alien cultures – such triumphalism must now be discarded. Instead, Christians must listen and learn from members of other faith traditions.

Arguing along similar lines, the Catholic theologian Francis Xavier D'Sa maintains that religious absolutism is no longer relevant in a pluralistic world. In his view, religious exclusivism is a major hurdle in interfaith encounter. By now, he writes, it is obvious that no absolutist claims can be upheld within the human realm. Given the nature and function of religious language, an ecumenical attitude is the only sensible way of understanding religious pluralism. In place of absolutist doctrines, believers must seek to enrich their understanding by gaining knowledge of other religions.

For the Jewish scholar Randall Falk, Jews are obliged to bear witness to God's truth to all people, even in dialogue. In his opinion, the Jewish nation has been chosen by God for a special mission of glorifying the name of God throughout the world. The ultimate goal of this quest is the acknowledgement by all humankind of the universality of one God. Jews have thus always considered their witness to the sovereignty of God and the supremacy of his law as enabling the Jewish people to serve as co-workers in the establishment of God's kingdom.

The Jewish scholar Ze'ev Falk maintains that although Scripture is critical of religious diversity, there is an alternative tradition within the Jewish faith which perceives that the Divine, known among the Jewish nation as their God, is the same God revered by other nations under different names.

The Asian Christian writer Anthony Fernando stresses that Christian mission needs to be reformulated in the modern world. Although he regards Jesus as unique, Fernando argues that missionary activity should not focus on enlarging the Christian community. Rather, the aim should be to diffuse knowledge of Christ. True missionary activity liberates individuals from their suffering by awakening them to the ideals that make life worthwhile. Missionaries adopting such an approach should feel no fear of preachers in other religions. Instead, they should join hands with them and collaborate in proclaiming the importance of religious values in contemporary society.

For the Christian theologian Joseph H. Fichter, the end of the colonial era has brought about major changes in the Christian view of other faiths. Today non-Christian religions have grown in strength and prestige. As a result, all forms of Christian ethnocentrism should be repudiated. Given that in the Third World and to some extent the Second World, people are avid for Westernization but unconcerned with Christian values, it seems unlikely that Christianity will ever become the universal world religion.

For the Christian theologian Durwood Foster, contemporary society has undergone momentous change. As a consequence, the encounter with other faiths has become a religious imperative. One of the major challenges facing Christians today is the need to overcome parochial bigotry in response to the universalizing love of Christ. The most important motive for dialogue with other faiths is that the God whom Christians worship is the one who creates, upholds and wills to redeem all that is.

Addressing the issue of salvation in Judaism and Christianity, the Christian scholar Helen Fry maintains that salvation is possible outside the church. Today a central challenge facing Christians is how Christianity can make theological space for Judaism. Recently church statements have rejected any form of coercive proselytism. Instead, the churches have affirmed the validity of God's covenant with the Jews. Although many Christians continue to believe in the necessity of mission to the Jewish community, there is a growing awareness that such activity is no longer viable. In her view, Christians should seek to help Jews to be better Jews rather than seeking to convert them.

The Taoist and Buddhist scholar Charles Wei-Hsun Fu proposes a functional concept of truth based on Buddhist teaching. Taoism and Buddhism, he points out, are frequently misunderstood as putting forward their own special truth-claim in competition with those of other religions. This, however, is a mistake. In his view, the substantive approach to truth should be replaced by the functional approach. In this way all truths claimed to be objective should be seen as no more than human projections.

Recounting the early development of his religious thought, the Indian politician and thinker, Mahatma Gandhi, described the impact the *Gita* had on his religious thought. Similarly, he was drawn to Jesus' Sermon on the Mount. In addition, Gandhi was deeply influenced by a variety of texts drawn from other faiths. The study of different religious traditions, he explained, shaped his own religious perception.

Anxious to draw parallels between Hinduism and Christianity, the Hindu theologian Ramchandra Gandhi contends that there are important connections between Christian and Hindu doctrine. In the crucifixion, resurrection and ascension of Christ, Vedic teaching reveals and renews itself. No Vedic scholar, he states, should suffer any anxiety in accepting Christ as a sacrifice and symbol.

In the opinion of the Christian theologian, Langdon Gilkey, there are a number of serious implications of religious pluralism. In the past Christians were well aware of the diversity of faiths. But this knowledge raised few problems. The only effective way to salvation was through Christ. Today, however, religious dialogue demands openness to alternative religious conceptions. In this process religious symbols tend to be seen as only relatively true. Yet, Gilkey remarks, believers do wish to differentiate between inauthentic and authentic religious values. Ecumenical tolerance, however, makes such a task extremely difficult.

The Christian missionary Arthur Glasser discusses how Jesus would have perceived the issue of religious pluralism. Although there is no evidence in the Gospels that Jesus expressed a view about non-Jewish religions, he did not question the witness of Scripture against gods other than the God of Israel. His constant emphasis on the goal of the kingdom of God led him to conclude that his people should make disciples of the peoples of every tribe and tongue.

Critical of the pluralist position, the Christian scholar Paul J. Griffiths argues for an acceptance of the uniqueness of Christian doctrine as a prerequisite for the Christian engagement with other religions. The universalist and exclusivist claims within the Christian tradition, he states, should serve as the basis for interfaith discussion.

The Orthodox Christian theologian Stanley Harakas stresses that Orthodox Christians can be enriched by religious dialogue even though they hold to the central tenets of the faith. Even though ecumenically committed, he holds to the fundamental belief that Jesus Christ is the Son of God, the second person of the Trinity. Further, it is his desire that all peoples accept Jesus' saving power. This is not meant to be a denigrating attitude toward persons of other faiths. Basing himself on Logos theology, he contends that God's image can be found in all human beings.

Adopting a radically different stance, the Christian writer David Hart argues that religious doctrine is ultimately based on human perception. In his view, religious beliefs are shaped by cultural and social conditions. It is not surprising, therefore, that the world's religions differ from one another in the most fundamental ways. A non-realist understanding of religious diversity, he argues, should enable individuals to appreciate other traditions and cross over into them once they understand that faiths are not closed revelations but collections of diverse insights, teachings and practices.

Addressing the issue of religious truth, the Christian theologian Monika K. Hellwig argues that the closer interaction between peoples of different religions demands a wider ecumenism. Because all religious language is analogical, no human language can contain the whole truth. Today, she contends, interfaith encounter offers hope for the human situation. Because Christians believe in the universal salvific will of God, it must be accepted that God is self-revealing to all those who search in good faith, no matter how their understanding of God is expressed.

According to the Protestant philosopher of religion, John Hick, there must be a revolution in our understanding of the world's faiths. In his view, in order to make sense of the idea that the great world religions are all inspired and made salvific by the same transcendent influence, we have to go beyond the historical figure of Jesus to a universal source of all salvific transformation. Christians may call this the cosmic Christ or the eternal Logos, Hindus and Buddhists may call it the Dharma, Muslims may call it Allah, Taoists may call it the Tao, but it is the same ineffable reality.

The former African missionary Eugene Hillman contends that wider ecumenism demands a re-examination of christology, ecclesiology, and missiology. In a religiously diverse world, the meaning of Christianity should be expressed in culture-specific and historically conditioned terms. Today, the church must go beyond itself, emptying itself of power, riches and alien influences. It must open itself to various modes of human existence. Dialogue with other faiths should be mutually enriching, holding the promise of a fuller life for all humankind.

The Christian scholar William Ernst Hocking similarly argues that a person's faith can be deepened by contact with believers from other traditions. In his view, all religions contain a common core. An effort is now required to discern the substance which underlies the profusion of religious expression to apprehend the generating principle of religious life and of each particular form. By self-understanding, he writes, a religion can apprehend the essence of all religious life.

Considering the nature of Buddhist–Christian dialogue today, the Buddhist scholar Kenneth K. Inada argues that Buddhacentrism can serve as the basis for interfaith encounter. This is not meant to counter Christocentrism, but rather to create an ideal situation in which dialogue partners can act as equals. This is not a new proposal, since the evolution of Buddhism is a manifestation of such centrism. Buddhism appeared initially in the context of ideological pluralism, and its doctrines were framed within the prevailing philosophical and religious context. Thus, Buddhism has always been resilient enough to expound its teachings in a variety of ways in accordance with the Buddha's own many-sided approach.

In comparing other faiths, the Muslim scholar Muhammad Iqbal emphasizes that there are important differences between different religious traditions. In assessing the Muslim view, he highlights the fact that Islam looks upon the universe as a reality and consequently recognizes all that exists. Sin, pain and sorrow are real, but Islam teaches that evil is not essential to existence. The universe can be reformed, and the elements of sin and evil can be eliminated. All that is in the universe is God's, and the seeming destructive forces in nature can become sources of life. Human beings are the makers of their own destiny.

Assessing the validity of other faiths, the Jewish scholar Louis Jacobs contends that even though Judaism possesses more truth than other religious traditions, the Jewish faith has always recognized that God reveals himself to others in different ways. Regarding salvation, he stresses that as long as non-Jews follow the Noachide laws, they can enter eternal life. Hence, it matters not at all if a person is brought up in this religion or another, or in no religion at all, provided he or she leads an ethical life.

The Sri Lankan Buddhist scholar K. N. Jayatilleke offers a Buddhist view of other faiths. In his opinion, Buddhism is tolerant of other religions, but not relativist. Here he cites the concept of the Buddha as one who discovers truth rather than as one who has a monopoly of truth. This leaves open the possibility for others to discover aspects of truth, or even the whole truth, for themselves. Nonetheless, Buddhism does not value all religions as equal. Some types of religion are viewed as unacceptable, whereas others are seen as containing the essential core of beliefs and values central to religion.

Assessing Muslim–Christian encounter, the Protestant scholar David Kerr states that Christians should accept that God's revelation is universal, and is evidenced in nature and human history. In his opinion, God has left no people without witnesses to his divine presence. Thus, Muhammad should be seen as manifestly a sign 'in the way of the prophets'. The Qur'an witnesses to the universality of divine revelation, reiterating many of the fundamental perceptions of Scripture.

According to the Catholic theologian Ursula King, interfaith dialogue has important implications for theology. Each tradition, she argues, needs to explore the implications of religious pluralism for its own theological thinking. From the Christian side, theologians need to assess traditional teachings in the light of the encounter with other faiths. Interfaith encounter, she continues, can lead participants to the realization that each religious tradition has received a valuable glimpse of the total vision, and in dialogue believers can complement each other's insights. Today Christians have to learn to live in and respond creatively to a new context of religious complexity.

Emphasizing the significance of liberation, the Catholic theologian Paul F. Knitter contends that religious dialogue must now take place in the context of liberationist aims. Praxis, he notes, is both the origin and confirmation of theory and doctrine – all Christian beliefs must be reconfirmed in the lived experience of religious truth. Thus, in devising a means of grading religions, a preferential option for the poor is of paramount importance. The soteriocentric criteria for religious dialogue contained in the preferential option for the oppressed thus offers believers a tool with which to examine critically and possibly revise traditional Christian belief.

For the Christian theologian Hendrik Kraemer, each religion should be seen as a living, indivisible unity. It is only for the sake of scientific analysis that religious systems are broken up into concepts. Concerning missionary activity, he asserts that the disposition and attitude of the missionary is crucial. What is vital is that those who engage in missionary work should have a genuine interest in the whole life of the people among whom they work. It is only in this way that true contact can be made and the way paved for Christ.

The Catholic theologian Hans Küng similarly stresses the crucial importance of ethical concern in modern society. In his view, the various religions affirm a common moral code. Despite their different systems of dogma, the various faiths foster human well-being. In different ways they promote fundamental maxims of behaviour which are grounded in absolute principles. According to Küng, this common ethical ground amongst the world's faiths offer hope to all humanity.

In the view of the Catholic theologian Karl-Josef Kuschel, Christians must remain faithful to New Testament teaching. It is the duty of Christians to affirm New Testament beliefs. Similarly believers in other religious communities will seek to uphold the tenets of their faith. This adherence to religious doctrine does not make dialogue impossible; on the contrary, by witnessing to their own traditions, those engaged in encounter will be able to learn from one another and gain an understanding of the nature of others' convictions.

For Christopher Lamb, a scholar of Buddhism, interfaith dialogue should focus on moral teaching in the world's faiths. Citing the case of Buddhism, he notes that moral conduct is perceived as the foundation of the religious life. Thus, Buddhism's contribution to inter-religious dialogue is its preference for leading an ethical life over adherence to religious doctrine. In the future, he states, there should be an awareness that faith is not ultimately defined in mythological or credal terms.

For the Christian theologian John Macquarrie, Jesus should not be viewed as a full revelation of God because the infinite cannot be fully comprehended in the finite. Christian dogma, he states, never claimed that the whole of God was incarnate. Rather, it was the Word who is said to have been incarnate. Yet, in Macquarrie's view, Christ is definitive in the sense that he defines the true nature of a human being and the nature of God.

According to the Asian Christian scholar John Mbiti, Jesus is being reinterpreted in numerous ways in both Asia and Africa. There are numerous examples of this multiplicity of redefinition of Christ. While some inherited christological symbols remain the same, others are recast in ways that provide religious significance for those who would otherwise remain outside the Christian community. Such flexibility of interpretation provides a means whereby the Christian faith is being reconstructed in the context of a pluralistic world.

The Hindu scholar Kana Mitra argues that religious pluralism has been a central feature of Hinduism through the centuries. Hindu theologians, she notes, have proudly proclaimed that Hindu thinkers recognized religious diversity from the earliest history of the faith. As a result, they formulated comprehensive theoretical interpretations of religious pluralism through the various periods of Hindu spiritual development.

Stressing the importance of God's kingdom, the Christian theologian Jürgen Moltmann maintains that dialogue with other religions must be based on God's special promises. A central goal of the faith, he argues, is to awaken faith in Christ. Nonetheless, mission has another object as well. Its aim is to infect all people with hope for the world. In the new world situation in which all religions find themselves, the struggle to alter the whole atmosphere of life should be pursued vigorously. This ecumenical quest to create a better world should focus on the major problems facing modern civilization.

According to Moojan Momen, the Bahá'í Faith asserts that it is not possible for humans to gain a complete awareness of the nature of ultimate truth. This is because the world's religions reflect different cultural and social conditions. As a consequence of this understanding of the world's faiths, members of different religions must accept the tentative character of their respective religious traditions.

The Hindu Bithika Mukerji focuses on God-realization as the aim of all religions. In the sphere of religious commitment, she writes, no dogma can operate because God has infinite ways of disclosing himself. Thus variety is a matter of celebration. The wealth of human outpourings of the heart is immeasurable, and no limits can be sought to channel it in one direction. No-one can legislate for another as to the true image of God.

Emphasizing the importance of mutual respect, the Islamic scholar Seyyed Hossein Nasr argues that there are grounds for Christians and Muslims to co-exist. While recognizing that Islam rejects various Christian doctrines, he stresses that within the Islamic world there are those who realize that the destinies of Islam and Christianity are interconnected. God, he writes, has willed that both religions exist and that there are different ways of salvation for millions of human beings. The enemy of both religions, he argues, is modern agnosticism, atheism and secularism.

The Anglican theologian Michael Nazir-Ali focuses on the nature of the church's dialogue with other faiths. Such encounter, he argues, should be based primarily on the recognition that men and women everywhere are created in the divine image. Thus, dialogue with people of other faiths should take place because of this common ground. Regarding mission, he maintains that dialogue should serve as the starting-point for Christian witness. Unless Christians understand the beliefs and cultures of others, they will not be able to witness to people authentically as Christians.

The Anglican theologian Stephen Neill maintains that Christians must remain loyal to the faith in inter-religious encounter, but are nonetheless able to learn from other traditions. Christians, he states, must approach other faiths with humility. They should expose themselves to the full force of these faiths in all that they have that is most convincing. They should rejoice in their beauty. They should listen with respectful patience. If Christians put their trust in Christ, they should not be fearful of such engagement.

According to the Anglican missionary Lesslie Newbigin, Christians today have a responsibility to proclaim the Gospel to all people. In this light, they should reject religious pluralism and acknowledge Christ as Lord of all. However, Christians should co-operate with people of all faiths and ideologies in projects which are in accordance with God's purposes. In his view, the contribution of the Christian to interfaith dialogue is to recount the Christian story.

For the Jewish theologian David Novak, Jews and Christians can proclaim normative truths about the human condition without surrendering their respective religious convictions. According to Novak, general revelation is manifest in universal moral principles which are accessible to human reason. Although the Jewish and Christian communities should not legislate this minimal human morality, they can provide it with an overall ontological context. Nonetheless these religious communities must insist that such moral principles, though necessary for authentic human community, are not sufficient for human fulfilment. This can only be commanded through revelation.

The African Christian theologian Joseph Osei-Bonsu maintains that the traditional concept of salvation only through Christ should be abandoned in the contemporary world. This belief, he states, hinders good relations between Christianity and other religions. The rigid application of this principle would mean that in modern society at best only one-third of the world's population will attain salvation and the remaining two-thirds will be damned. In his view, it makes no sense to believe that when righteous non-Christians die, they will be sent to hell just because they did not belong to the church.

In the view of the Sri Lankan Buddhist thinker Mahinda Palihawandana, inter-religious dialogue can bring about positive change. The Christian critique of what has been perceived as Buddhist pessimism, for example, can serve as a catalyst for a re-examination of various Buddhist doctrines. In Palihawandana's estimation, no-one can forecast what such reconsideration will bring, but it is likely to lead to religious revitalization. Through encounter, religions can strengthen one another.

The Catholic theologian Raimundo Panikkar similarly contends that religious truth can emerge from dialogue. Pluralism, he states, is not an attitude which posits that there are many true religions or many authentic Christs with different names. Rather, truth itself is pluralistic rather than plural. The pluralistic attitude is the fruit of the experience that we are not masters of truth; instead we can decide about truth in each particular case through dialogical discourse.

The Hindu thinker and professor of politics Bhiku Parekh contends that interfaith dialogue, based on sympathy for one another's tradition, can promote self-critical awareness. In his view, dialogue can be based on a desire to understand other faiths. But it can also arise from the search for critical self-understanding and acknowledge that no religion contains the entire truth about the nature of the Divine.

According to Geoffrey Parrinder, a professor of comparative religion, interfaith dialogue offers new opportunities for spiritual growth. Today, he notes, religions face a totally new situation; never before have adherents of different traditions been in such close contact. No longer is religious isolation feasible. The one world in which we live provides a framework for religious encounter on the deepest level. In the context of such diversity, the cosmic Christ can be seen as inspiring and embracing all faiths.

In confronting the question whether there are other saviours in the world's faiths, the Christian theologian Peter Phan contends that Jesus' uniqueness should not be abandoned. Nevertheless, Christianity cannot claim to possess absolute truth, due to the ineffable nature of the divine Mystery, the historically conditioned character of human understanding and language and the limitations of the human intellect.

For the Sri Lankan Catholic theologian Aloysius Pieris, the core liberative dimensions of the world's faiths are of central significance. The core of any religion, he argues, is the liberative experience that gave birth to that faith and continues to be available to the faithful. It is through recourse to this foundation that a religion can resolve its recurrent crises and is able to regenerate itself when facing new challenges. This core experience in all religions, he points out, tends to be interpreted in a variety of ways so as to form various philosophical, theological and exegetical traditions.

The Egyptian Muslim thinker Sayyid Qutb maintains that the message of Jesus has been corrupted. As a result, the Christian faith is unable to serve as a means of conveying God's will. If the Christian ideal had remained that expounded by Christ, it would correctly have expressed God's intentions. But when the followers of Jesus were persecuted, they altered the text of Scripture. Paul's conception of Christianity, he continues, was adulterated by residues of Roman and Greek thought. This was a catastrophe which has infected Christianity through the centuries. In addition, Christianity's ascendency in the Roman Empire brought about further corruption of the faith.

For the Anglican theologian Alan Race, the 'scandal of particularity' is a theme running through Christian history. As an evocation of the absolute uniqueness of Christ, it has functioned as a rallying call to the faithful. Yet, there is now a need to reconsider this doctrine. Today new encounters between people of different traditions are demonstrating how each religion provides a living context for religious expression. Further, historical and philosophical currents of thought have demonstrated how religious truths are more humanly constructed than previously imagined.

Considering the christological claims about Jesus, the Muslim scholar Fazlur Rahman argues that even though Muslims cannot accept the doctrine of the incarnation, they should regard Jesus as a divinely appointed messenger. According to Islam, he embarked on a divine mission from his birth. Jesus, he writes, fulfilled this role, but the concept of the incarnation and the Trinity are far removed from God's revelation. The Qur'an assigns to Jesus only the position of a prophet.

The Catholic scholar Karl Rahner contends that Christianity should regard members of other religions as in some sense anonymous Christians. It would be wrong, for example, to regard adherents of other faiths as in no respect touched by God's grace. If, however, such persons have experienced the grace of God, then they have already been given revelation in a true sense. For this grace accompanies their consciousness subjectively, even though it is not known objectively.

The Jewish writer Stuart E. Rosenberg stresses that the Holocaust is the outgrowth of Christian teaching. This terrible legacy, he argues, should serve as the background to current Jewish–Christian dialogue. In the modern world, he notes, there are a growing number of faithful Christians who are now willing to confess that after Auschwitz the central moral test and religious question for Christianity is the survival of the Jews. The Jewish community, he insists, must continue to raise troubling questions about the Christian involvement in the destruction of millions of Jews during the Nazi period.

The Jewish theologian Franz Rosenzweig focuses on the relationship between Judaism and Christianity. Both the Jew and the Christian, he argues, are engaged in the same religious quest, to realize God's plan for humanity. Yet God gave the Jews eternal life by kindling the fire of the star of his truth in their hearts. Christians, on the other hand, pursue the rays of that star of his truth for all time. Therefore Jews espy the true image of the truth; Christians, however, follow the rays but do not see it with their eyes. The entire truth thus belongs neither to Christians nor to Jews.

Assessing the role of women in the world's religions, the Christian theologian Rosemary Radford Ruether argues that women have been denied their rightful position. By and large, she states, not only Judaism, Christianity, Islam and Buddhism, but even ancient tribal religions have not allowed the Divine to be experienced in a way defined by women. Today, however, the situation is being reversed. Feminism, she states, should engage with adherents of the world's faiths in an attempt to discover new possibilities for women's spirituality.

In the opinion of the former Archbishop of Canterbury, Robert Runcie, Christianity can be transformed through its contact with other faith traditions. Given the experience and witness of the Christian faith, encounter with other religions can deepen and enrich Christian understanding. For Christians, Jesus will always remain the primal source of truth. Nonetheless, Christians should recognize that other traditions reveal aspects of God which can enrich and enlarge the Christian understanding.

According to the Christian theologian Stanley Samartha, Christian exclusivism is no longer relevant in our global society. Currently, he notes, there is considerable hesitation on the part of many Christians to re-examine the basis of their exclusive claims concerning Christ. Such resistance, he argues, must be overcome. In religious experience, he points out, mystery and meaning are related. Without a disclosure of meaning at particular points in history, there can be no human response to mystery. Thus, it is only to be expected that the great religious traditions have responded differently to the mystery of God.

Adopting a different approach, the Hindu scholar Dayananda Sarasvati is censorious of various features of both the Hindu and Christian faith. In his opinion, modern humanity needs a universal religion, based on Hindu teaching. Such a faith should be grounded on universal and all-embracing principles. This religion, which he refers to as the primeval eternal religion, transcends the various creeds in different faiths.

The Catholic scholar Henri le Saux attempts to provide a synthesis of Christian and Hindu thought. If the Christian experience of the Trinity provides new vistas of meaning, he states, then Hindu concepts can greatly assist the Christian in his or her own meditation on the central mystery of the faith. No single theological language will ever be able to express all that has been revealed concerning God. Thus, it is to be expected that the divine preparation of India will lead Christians to contemplate the divine mystery in new depths.

Advocating the mystical way, the Jewish scholar Zalman Schachter maintains that mysticism can play an important role in the encounter between faiths. In his view, there is a universal religion which transcends the various religious world's faiths. Mysticism, he declares, provides human beings with a means of reaching different levels of spiritual experience. The language of the mystics provides a means whereby believers can discover ultimate reality.

According to the Christian theologian Robert P. Scharlemann, even when Christ is understood as the exclusive revelation, the non-Christian is as much a part of this revelation as the Christian. The plurality of religions is therefore not a deficiency, but a fulfilment of the meaning of Jesus being the Christ. In his view, an exclusively understood Christianity requires the acknowledgement of other religions as equal participants in truth and salvation.

In the view of the Christian theologian Christoph Schwobel, both the exclusivist and the pluralist stance are deficient. Instead, he advances a Christian basis for interfaith dialogue based on the acknowledgement of both universality and particularity. The understanding of the universality of God which is grounded in the particularity of God's self-disclosure in Christ, he argues, should be the foundation for interfaith dialogue.

According to the Christian writer Waldron Scott, evangelicals have an important role to play in the encounter with other faiths. Evangelicals, he points out, make up a greater part of the Protestant missionary element of the church. As such, it would be advantageous for ecumenically-oriented leaders to interact with evangelicals. However, such interaction will not take place unless there is a willingness to listen. The specific contribution evangelicals could make to this enterprise will be based on witnessing to the biblical tradition.

As the Muslim scholar Ahmed Shafaat notes, Muhammad's goal was to draw Muslims, Christians and Jews together into one *ummah*, united in the worship of God. The prophet Muhammad, he states, actually described the community consisting of these three groups as an *ummah* when in Medina he attempted to create a multi-religious society. In the light of this, we can see a religious significance in the historical links between the three groups. Their histories are part of the same process of revelation and linked by the divine will.

Adopting a christocentric model of the universe of faiths, the Christian scholar Ingrid Shafer contends that all religious absolutes are embraced by Christ as the universal ultimate. In her view, by accepting the incarnation one can allow a confluence of the religious stream of the rivers of Abraham with the rivers of India and China.

In the opinion of the Christian scholar of religions, Ninian Smart, there are a number of central dimensions of the world's faiths including the ritual or practical, the doctrinal or philosophical, the mystical or narrative, the experiential or emotional, the ethical or legal, the organizational or social component, and the material or artistic. The phenomenology of religion, he states, seeks to draw out these varying patterns which take different forms amongst the various traditions. This taxonomy of the sacred clarifies what are the major concerns in the different cultures of humanity.

In the view of Huston Smith, a scholar of world religions, there appears to be no way to adjudicate between the claims of the different traditions. Nonetheless, he contends that the world's faiths offer a unique perspective on the nature of reality.

For the Christian scholar Wilfred Cantwell Smith, modern Christian theology must take into account the various religions of the world. Human beings have yet to learn their new task of living together as partners in a context of religious and cultural plurality. In his view, the quest to construct world fellowship beyond religious frontiers is of vital importance. It is his belief that God reaches out to all human beings everywhere, and speaks to all who will listen.

Encouraging tolerance of others, the Jewish scholar Norman Solomon outlines an inclusivist position which recognizes the spiritual validity of other faiths. Rejecting any form of relativism, he contends that it would be a mistake to gloss over the differences between different religions. From a Jewish perspective, the covenant of Noah offers a pattern for Jews to seek from others not necessarily conversion to Judaism, but instead faithfulness to the highest principles of justice and morality.

Outlining various approaches to inter-religious dialogue, the Christian scholar Mary Ann Stenger urges Christians not to abandon the Christian notion of Christ as final revelation, but to relate that belief to ultimacy beyond any finite expressions. The direction toward ultimacy in all religions, she believes, is a structural commonality. We can only work out of our own traditions, she states, but we must continue in conversation that is based on the search for truth. In this process core beliefs like the final revelation in Christ should not be abandoned, but instead interpreted anew.

In the view of the Christian theologian Marjorie Hewitt Suchowcki, religious pluralism is the only viable approach within a feminist context. Justice, she stresses, should serve as the focus of dialogue amongst the world's religions. Yet, it should be accepted that justice should not be granted a universally acceptable content. We must look to the meaning of justice in every tradition: using justice as an overarching norm means that the primary visions within each religion of what societal life should be in an ideal world serves as a source of judgement.

Affirming the need for inter-religious dialogue in the modern world, the Catholic theologian Leonard Swidler argues that inter-religious and interideological dialogue is the most suitable matrix within which theology should currently operate. The answer as to why truth should be pursued by means of dialogue is based on the shift that has taken place in Western civilization. Previously the notion of truth was largely absolute; recently, however, it has become de-absolutized. Today those engaged in interfaith encounter should abide by a number of rules of engagement. In this context, Christians should not take a condemnatory attitude toward non-Christians, particularly those who belong to other religions.

For Mohamed Talbi, a Muslim professor in Tunis, Christians and Muslims must engage in dialogue regardless of the obstacles. For Muslims such encounter is first and foremost a vital re-establishment of relations with the world at large. In his view, it must be admitted that there are several ways to salvation. Because God's plan is beyond human comprehension, we must accept our differences and disagreements. Dialogue between faiths, he maintains, is about gaining knowledge of the other and seeking a deeper understanding of truth.

According to the Christian theologian John V. Taylor, Christians must overcome their previous isolation and engage in encounter with other faiths. We should conceive of each religion, he writes, as a people's particular tradition of response to divine reality. In his view, God's self-revelation and self-giving is consistent for all, but different peoples have responded in various ways. Every religion is, he contends, a historically determined tradition of response to what the Spirit of God has disclosed.

For the Christian theologian Paul Tillich, ultimate concern is an essential feature of all religions; thus Christians should engage in discussion with members of other faiths. When embarked on interfaith exchange, Christians should judge their own faith when it judges others. The aim of inter-religious exchange should not be to lead to the triumph of one religion but to penetrate into the depths of one's own faith to a vision of the spiritual presence which is found in all traditions.

The historian Arnold Toynbee argues that Christianity should rid itself of its absolutist claims. In his view the Christian faith should be purged of its triumphalist nature. It has been a mistake for Christians to view their own faith as unique. Intolerance should give way to an acceptance of the spiritual integrity of other traditions.

For the Jewish scholar Leo Trepp, the belief that non-Jews can be saved has been a fundamental element of Jewish theology. Although Judaism perceives itself as unique among the religions of the world, there are certain guidelines which are viewed as providing a framework for righteous living. These laws – the Noachide commandments – serve as the basis for determining who amongst non-Jews merits eternal reward.

According to the Christian theologian Ernst Troeltsch, Christians should accept that other groups living under different cultural traditions have experienced God in different ways. Since all religions have a common goal in the unknown, so too do they share common ground in the divine spirit which continually presses the finite mind onward toward further light and consciousness. This is a spirit which indwells the finite spirit. Its final aim is to attain ultimate union with the Spirit.

The Hindu scholar Vivekananda was a follower of Ramakrishna and devoted himself to preaching a version of his thought. Here he argues that the Orient is superior to Western countries in religious affairs. Christ, he argues, was an oriental religious figure. He was intensely practical, and sought to bring about a change in religious awareness amongst his followers.

For the Christian theologian Hendrik Vroom, it is incorrect to characterize religions in terms of a single basic conviction. Further, each tradition has an idea of the transcendent, of humanity, and of the world. Yet such conflicting beliefs do not eliminate the fact that adherents of different faiths share common ground.

In the view of the Christian theologian Keith Ward, religions in the modern world find themselves in a similar situation. If they insist on a self-contained finality and completeness, they will fail to appreciate the truth that other religions have discerned. Adherents of the different faiths must not give up what is distinctive in their own traditions, nor seek some minimal highest common factor in all religions. Rather, they should accept the provisional character of their own conceptual schemes.

According to the Christian theologian Rowan Williams, the doctrine of the Trinity should serve as the foundation for interfaith exchange. In his opinion, the goal of interfaith encounter should be to find a way of working toward a mode of human co-operation. For Christians, the aim should be to engage with other traditions in the formation of the children of God after the likeness of Christ. In his view, the Christian should invite the world of faiths to find in the narrative of Jesus and his community that which unifies the quest for human integrity.

Adopting a different stance, the Jewish writer Sherwin Wine argues that all religions, including the Jewish faith, should be understood as human creations. Today, he states, there is a general shift away from a belief in God's activity in the world to an acceptance of the human origin of the world's traditions. Despite this shift in perspective, he writes, it is still possible for individuals to identify with their own religious tradition.

The Jewish writer Michael Wyschogrod adopts a different position. In his view, Christians should acknowledge the election of the Jewish people by God. In spite of the differences between these two faiths, both Judaism and Christianity view the Bible as the word of God – hence the church is inconceivable without Israel.

Israel remains the people of election, and the church should be seen as a body of the faithful which has joined itself to the Jewish nation.

For the Buddhist scholar Seiichi Yagi, Christian absolutism is a misguided notion. Today it must be replaced by an acknowledgement that spiritual treasures are found in other faiths. In his opinion, the concept of treasure-in-vessel clarifies how spiritual truth is found in the world's religions.

Masao Abe

The Zen Buddhist scholar Masao Abe was Professor of Philosophy at Nara University of Education, and subsequently taught at the Claremont Graduate School in California and at the University of Hawaii. In 'Self-Awakening and Faith – Zen and Christianity', he points out a number of important distinctions between Zen Buddhism and Christianity.

The dialogue between Zen and Christianity has been becoming more serious and important during the past decade or so. Those of us involved in it are pleased with this development because we maintain that such a dialogue is necessary for the development of mutual understanding between East and West.

To make this sort of dialogue effective and fruitful, we have to be very frank and open, as well as sincere. To be frank, I find it necessary to clarify the difference rather than the affinity between Christianity and Zen. Of course it is necessary for such a dialogue to elucidate both affinities and differences between the two religions. It is rather easy to point out the affinity between Christianity and Zen, because both of them are equally in their essence, religions. So, naturally, there are some kinds of similarity. However, the emphasis on similarity, although important, does not necessarily create something new. On the other hand, an attempt to disclose the differences, if properly and relevantly done, promotes and stimulates mutual understanding and inspires both religions to seek further inner development of themselves. I hope my emphasis on differences in this talk is not understood as a rejection or exclusion of Christianity from a Zen point of view, or as a presumption of the superiority of Zen to Christianity. My point is to reach a real and creative mutual understanding. My understanding of Christianity is, however, insufficient and limited, so I hope you will correct me later, my discussion being completely open to your criticism.

To simplify the point to be discussed in connection with the theme, 'Self-Awakening and Faith – Zen and Christianity', I will try to contrast some central motifs in Zen and Christianity: the difference between Christianity and Zen could be formulated in the contrasts of God – Nothingness, Faith – Enlightenment, Salvation – Self-Awakening... .

This realization of absolute Nothingness is in Zen the realization of one's true Self. For the realization of absolute Nothingness opens up the deepest ground of one's Subjectivity which is beyond every form of subject–object duality, including the so-called divine–human relationship. Enlightenment takes place only through the realization of absolute Nothingness which is beyond every form of duality. This is not faith in the divine mercy nor salvation by a divine other power, but Self-Awakening – the Self-Awakening of true Self. In the realization of absolute Nothingness, the true Self awakens to itself. This Self-Awakening is not something to be sought for sometime in the future or somewhere outside yourself, but it is originally and already realized in yourself, here and now. If Enlightenment is something to be sought for somewhere outside yourself or in the future, that so-called Enlightenment will not be true. It is not absolute Nothingness, but rather a sort of somethingness which would be realized beyond the present now and outside the here. So Zen always emphasizes that you are originally in Enlightenment. You are already inseparable from Self-Awakening.

On the other hand, if I am not wrong, the affirmation of the absolute oneness of God is taken for granted in Christian thinking. When a scribe wanted to know if Jesus was in agreement with the biblical tradition, he tempted him by asking about the greatest commandment in the Law. Jesus answered by quoting the Old Testament passage about loving God with all the heart, soul and mind, mentioning the classical biblical confession: 'Hear, O Israel, the Lord our God, the Lord is one' (Mark 12:29). The scribe then said to him, 'You are right, teacher, you have truly said that he is one and there is no other but he' (Mark 12:32). In Christianity God is the one and only living god. He is father, creator, judge and ruler of the universe and of history... .

From a Buddhist point of view this idea of a self-sustaining God is ultimately inadequate, for Buddhists cannot see the ontological ground of this one and self-sustaining God. This is the reason why the Buddha rejected the traditional Upanishadic view of Brahman as the ultimate power of the universe and proclaimed that everything without exception is transitory and perishable, nothing being unchangeable and eternal. The idea that everything is transitory is inseparably connected to the idea of independent co-origination. So again, from this point of view we have to ask: What is the ground of the one God? How can we accept the one God as the ruler of the universe and history? The Christian might answer this question by stressing the importance of faith in God, this faith being nothing but the 'assurance of things hoped for, the conviction of things not seen' (Hebrews 11:1). (pp. 172–5)

Masao Abe, 'Self-Awakening and Faith – Zen and Christianity', in Paul J. Griffiths (ed.), *Christianity Through Non-Christian Eyes* (Maryknoll, NY: Orbis, 1990).

Kajsa Ahlstrand

The Christian theologian Kajsa Ahlstrand received a BD and Dr. Theol. from the University of Uppsala, and worked in the Church of Sweden Research Department. In 'What's So Special About Jesus?', she points out some of the theological difficulties with the pluralist position.

The pluralist position in the theology of religions has the advantage that it respects the integrity of the religious traditions of the world. Its new interpretations of the Christian doctrines of incarnation, redemption, christology, ecclesiology, sacramentology and trinitarian theology, however, are more often than not embarrassingly shallow. The problem is whether it is possible to combine classic Christian theology in all its richness with a positive view of the many religious traditions of the world. Must the christological formulations of the Creed – 'one Lord, Jesus Christ, the only Son of God, eternally begotten of the Father, God from God, light from Light, true God from true God, begotten not made, of one being with the Father' – be reduced to 'Jesus is an inspiring example in our struggle for justice, peace and the preservation of the earth' if we want to maintain good relations with those who do not belong to the Christian tradition? I don't think so. I am convinced that self-respect is a prerequisite for respect of the other.

It might very well be that some of the christological assumptions of the Christian tradition are incompatible with fundamental assumptions of other religions, but I cannot see that as a good enough reason to abandon the Christian conviction. I do not demand of the others that they abandon their convictions just because they are contrary to my beliefs. The reinterpretation of christology, then, is not primarily induced by a desire to please believers outside the Christian community, but rather by the insight that the traditional christological formulations do not convey sufficient insight into the person and work of Jesus, whom the Christians call Christ, for people from different contexts and different religions to recognize God's liberating and life-giving Word and presence in this Jesus today. (p. 19)

My own christological reflection, informed by Christian kenotic christology as well as by insights from Saivism, Buddhism and Western Atheism, is to see Jesus as God's tentative, particular and rejectable Word. I do believe that Jesus is God's universal, decisive, and indispensable manifestation of saving truth and grace, but that he is so in a perspective of human brokenness. Because the oppressed of today are the oppressors of tomorrow, because the atrocities we see around us are committed by human beings like ourselves, there can be no 'us' and 'them' when it comes to the ability to inflict pain and suffering. In Jesus, divine reality, the ineffable mystery, became one of us.

Much has been said about Jesus as Omega – in this century from J. N. Farquhar's Christ as the crown or fulfilment of Hinduism to Knitter's description of him as God's decisive, universal and indispensable Word. But he is Alpha as well as Omega. He is the beginning, 'the most newly born among us', as Paul Claudel put it. God is not only infinitely greater than our thoughts, God is also smaller, to use a halting metaphor. In Jesus, God became vulnerable, particular and rejectable. In fact, say the evangelists and apostles, God was wounded and rejected in Jesus. If this was possible then, it is still possible. We can reject Jesus.

The God I am looking for is the desecrated God, the one who identifies not only with the unjustly oppressed but with the most despicable creature: the oppressor. This was what Jesus did when he caused scandal by socializing with tax-collectors. And this Jesus, testify his followers through the centuries, was somehow God.

The incarnation means that God has become vulnerable and rejectable. It is not self-evident that everybody wants to accept a convicted and executed Jewish criminal as God's true Word. How do we handle the fact that although many Hindus and Buddhists love and respect Jesus, there are also those who say that he is indeed a very bad example: he ate meat and drank wine and allowed himself to be killed. (pp. 22–3)

Even if there are many true revelations of God, are there also many 'lives that kill death', many resurrected Lords who shall come again to judge the living and the dead? Is it only Jesus Christ or are there many 'Returners'? Mythological as the eschatological language is, it is when it comes to eschatology that pluralist christology is challenged. If Christian eschatology is reduced to an action programme for the betterment of the world, a christology that sees Jesus as example and inspirer is all right, but if a *lokuttara* dimension is allowed for, it becomes more difficult to maintain a pluralist christology. The inclusivists will say that the Buddha Maitreya, the Messiah and Kalkin will remember what it was to be a landless Jew in the Eastern Mediterranean region. What will the pluralists say? Is pluralism provisional or ultimate? If it is ultimate, is there also a plurality of ultimate goals? Does that not imply a plurality of gods? A consistent pluralist christology questions monotheism. (p. 24)

Kajsa Ahlstrand, 'What's So Special About Jesus?', in Leonard Swidler and Paul Mojzes (eds), *The Uniqueness of Jesus: A Dialogue with Paul F. Knitter* (Maryknoll, NY: Orbis, 1997).

Shabbir Akhtar

In his discussion of religious pluralism, the Muslim scholar Shabbir Akhtar argues that dialogue must recognize the distinct features of different faiths.

I do not wish to deny the importance of responsible exchange between members of different faiths. But it must be responsible: well-informed, cognizant of the tensions, ready to acknowledge rift and difference, concerned to record realities. And this is indeed a tall order. Will Christian–Muslim dialogue endure into the next decade? My own view about the future of such dialogue – a view denigrated by some as unduly pessimistic – is, I believe, surely realistic. I myself find it difficult to attend an interfaith conference without thinking that religious exchange will indeed endure into the next century – but merely as a fashion. It could be that religious liberalism of the kind exhibited in dialogue may not survive the currently widening ideological rift between the Crescent and the Cross in many parts of the globe. If it does survive the trial, it is most likely to do so, like modern optimism, by relying on increasingly unclear generalities.

It is not recent scholarship alone that has noted the deep, perhaps irresolvable, doctrinal incompatibility between Islam and Christianity. The problem had already been felt and recorded as early as the seventh century. In fact the Qur'an itself invites Christians to a prayer duel (*mubahilah*) in the larger attempt to break the deadlock. According to this arrangement, sometimes known as 'trial by imprecation', the contending parties invoke the wrath or adverse judgement of God expecting it to 'fall' immediately and visibly on the dishonest, guilty or otherwise misguided party. The trial by imprecation can also be invoked by one individual against an alleged religious imposter or heretic... .

That method of imprecation is, whatever its merits in the age of revelation, clearly unsuited to our current circumstance. Given the silence of God today, the deadlock between any given faith, such as Islam, and its rivals, is not so easily broken. To be sure, there may well be an intellectual process transpiriting beyond death in which the ambiguities and doctrinal statements of this life are finally resolved and broken just as the moral imbalance of mortal existence will, according to ethical theism, be eventually and satisfactorily rectified in a world yet to come. But this view, even supposing it to be coherent and true, still leaves all the important theological puzzles on our hands. Why does God allow many large portions of mankind to remain in doubt, hesitation, or even outright error concerning matters of moment? The Qur'an sternly warns us that confession of the monotheistic credo after death may not suffice to escape damnation: we had better find out while we are still living. If so, isn't God morally obliged, so to speak, to make clear, especially in an age of confusion, his existence, will and purpose for men on earth?

As the various doctrinal deadlocks in Christian–Muslim debate become increasingly prevalent, the critique of the religious rival is likely to become purely moral. Each faith has an associated normative outlook; Christians and Muslims naturally argue that the ethical scheme associated with their faith is superior to all other such schemes. It is felt that religions can sometimes be ranked for plausibility in terms of their moral, as opposed to purely metaphysical, appeal. Such a shift of focus is, it might be argued, a welcome one indicating the direction in which a possible resolution of the Christian–Muslim deadlock lies.

The theme of interreligious dialogue is likely to occupy the centre of theological concerns in this and the coming century. Many characteristically modern religious puzzles are generated by a growing realization that the doctrinal elements in any one given faith cannot reasonably maintain a universality of normative claim upon modern human allegiance. The presence of authentic religiosity outside one's own tradition of faith seems undeniable if religiously disconcerting. Indeed, enlightened opinion among theists – Jews, Christians and Muslims – is more or less unanimous that scripture contains irresolvable puzzles with respect to the existence of plural pieties. (pp. 173–5)

Shabbir Akhtar, 'Christian–Muslim Dialogue in the Twentieth Century', in Dan Cohn-Sherbok (ed.), *Many Mansions* (London, Bellew, 1992).

Gerald H. Anderson

Gerald H. Anderson, a Christian missiologist, has served as Director of the Overseas Ministries Study Centre in Ventnor, New Jersey. In 'Religion as a Problem for the Christian Mission', he points to the changes that have taken place in the Christian understanding of other faiths in recent years. In his view, Christians must hold firm to their belief in the centrality of Christ while remaining open to new theological developments.

Since 1968 a good deal of momentum has developed. This has been generated largely through the efforts of the Vatican Secretariat for Non-Christian Religions, and through the programmes of the World Council of Churches on 'Dialogue with People of Living Faiths and Ideologies'. Especially important are the twenty-one centres for study and dialogue with persons of other faiths in Asia, Africa, Latin America and the Middle East that are affiliated with the World Council of Churches.

These centres have a fourfold emphasis:

- To help the churches to deepen their commitment to Jesus Christ and to rediscover the content and practice of mission in situations of cultural and religious pluralism;
- to provide them with guidelines for their actual engagement with people of different faiths and ideologies with whom they are in daily contact and through whose co-operation the work of social renewal and nation-building must go on;
- to examine the relationship between the Christian faith and other faiths, not just on the conceptual level but in the context of Christian communities living in dialogue and shared humanity with their neighbours of other faiths; and

- to see how the church's confession of Jesus Christ as Lord and Saviour and as the initiator of a new humanity may, at the same time, be related to the common humanity which we all share with people of other faiths and ideologies. (pp. 108–9)

The plea of W. Cantwell Smith through the 1960s was...for the church to 'work vigorously, and work on a large scale, in order to construct an adequate doctrine' that will avoid 'the fallacy of relentless exclusivism' and affirm 'the kind of God whom Jesus Christ has revealed him to be' – namely, the God who 'reaches out after all men everywhere, and speaks to all who will listen'... .

I have several problems with Dr Smith's proposals. First, I am uncomfortable with discussion of religions in terms of truth and falsity and I do not think it necessary to employ these categories ... in order to speak of religions as such. As a missionary, as a seminary professor, and as a pastor, I don't think I have ever claimed that Christianity is true. I do affirm what Jesus said of himself: 'I am the way, and the truth, and the life; no one comes to the Father, but by me' (John 14:6)... . I would affirm with D. T. Niles that 'it is outside the preacher's competence or commission to pass judgement on what others claim to be their experience of salvation; his business is only to invite them to acknowledge Jesus Christ as their Saviour'.

Second, while I am persuaded by Dr Smith that our contemporary concept of religion(s) is a relatively modern and Western systematizing process, I am not convinced that this therefore makes the concept unfeasible, or that his 'alternate theoretical framework for interpreting to ourselves the religious history of man' has fewer problems. What I do realize is that we Western Christians must be increasingly open to Third World refinements, revisions and reconceptualizing of our Western concepts... .

Third, I am troubled by Dr Smith's emphasis on a personalized – almost privatized – conception of revelation and religious truth. 'Christianity' he says, 'is not true absolutely, impersonally, statically; rather, it can become true, if and as you or I appropriate it to ourselves and interiorize it, insofar as we live it out from day to day. It becomes true as we take it off the shelf and personalize it.' This is an important corrective against embalmed faith. On the other hand, Christ does not become the truth when or because we experience him as such. The kingdom of God is not a democracy and Jesus Christ – as Lord and Saviour – is not going out of office if we do not vote for him. (pp. 109–11)

Gerald H. Anderson, 'Religion as a Problem for the Christian Mission', in Donald G. Dawe and John B. Carman (eds), *Christian Faith in a Religiously Plural World* (Maryknoll, NY: Orbis, 1986).

Norman Anderson

Norman Anderson, previously Director of the Institute of Advanced Legal Studies at the University of London, argues in Christianity and the World Religions *that it is an error to believe that those who wish to participate in fruitful dialogue should suppress their beliefs. Through dialogue, he maintains, the Christian can learn from non-Christians, but there should be no attempt to create a syncretistic faith. Christians should continue to engage in mission while accepting that other faiths contain divine disclosures.*

Turning from individuals to other religions as such, what view should the Christian take of non-Christian religions – other than the Old Testament Judaism – as systems which profess to mediate salvation? Many different answers have been given to this question; but, broadly speaking, three main views have been – and still are – held by Christians.

First, there are those who, impressed by the element of truth that can be found in most, if not all, other religions, and by the devotion and virtue of some of their adherents, regard them as a sort of *praeparatio evangelica* – as indeed, all Christians would say of Old Testament Judaism... .

Some who take this view would ... explain the elements of truth in other religions in terms of an original revelation which has never been wholly lost or forgotten. Others, again, would discern in them the work of Christ himself, as the eternal *Logos* and the 'light that enlightens every man'... .

The second view which has been taken by Christians about other religions is the diametrical opposite of this: namely, that they do not emanate in any sense from God, but from the devil. Prominence is given, therefore, to the darker side of their ethical teaching, and the least acceptable elements in their theological concepts... .

The third view sees these religions as not so much divine revelation, nor yet Satanic deception, but as human aspiration – as man's attempts (whether more or less enlightened) to solve the mysteries of life. Among those who take this view there are two possible attitudes with regard to Christianity itself. Some would regard it as no more than the nearest approximation to ultimate truth, man's highest attainment in the age-long evolution of religion. Others would go much further than this, and believe it to be the one and only divine self-disclosure (with Judaism, of course, as forerunner), in which God himself came down from heaven, as it were to reveal himself to man, while all the other religions represent human attempts to climb up to heaven to discover God.

I cannot, myself, opt for any one of these three views *simpliciter*, for there is, I believe, some truth in each. The non-Christian religions seem to me to resemble a patchwork quilt, with brighter and darker components in differing proportions. There are elements of truth which must come from God himself, whether through the memory of an original revelation, through some process of cross-fertilization with some other religion, or through that measure of self-disclosure which, I cannot doubt, God still vouchsafes to those who truly seek him... . But there are also elements which are definitely false, and which I, for one, believe come from 'the father of lies' – whose primary purpose is not so much to entice men into sensual sin as to keep them back, by any means in his power, from the only Saviour. Yet, again, there is much that could best be described as human aspirations after the truth, rather than either divine revelation or Satanic deception. (pp. 169–72)

There are, however, many people today who insist that the very nature and spirit of dialogue are completely destroyed if either of the parties has 'any covert thought for the conversion of the other'. Dialogue, they assert, is simply and solely a matter of sharing – a means of getting to know one another better, of gaining a greater understanding of the faith by which each lives and of exploring some of the pressing (and even agonizing) problems that face us all, in the contemporary world, in the light of what each of these faiths may be able to contribute to their solution. As so often, there is both truth and error, as I see it, in this assertion. It is perfectly true that the primary aim of dialogue is not evangelistic, in the ordinary sense of that term, but that it serves a number of other worthy and useful purposes. It is also true that a large proportion of dialogue could best be regarded as a preparation – a clearing of the ground – for evangelism, rather than its consummation. And it is even more pertinent to remark that a reference to some 'covert' purpose for any Christian activity has a distinctly dubious ring.

Do missionary societies provide equipment and personnel to heal the sick, to prevent the spread of dread diseases, to dig wells, distribute food and erect shelters for those afflicted by drought, famine or earthquakes, only to exploit physical needs for spiritual purposes? (pp. 188–9)

Norman Anderson, *Christianity and the World Religions* (Leicester: Inter-Varsity Press, 1984).

Kofi Appiah-Kubi

The Presbyterian African theologian, Kofi Appiah-Kubi, has served as Theology Secretary of the All-Africa Conference of Churches. In his view, although God has most fully manifested himself in Christ, he is nonetheless to be found in all faiths.

These various religions and cultures share in common the existential questions about humankind, about the meaning and source of life, the source and meaning of pain and joy, happiness, suffering, disease and health, and finally, death and life after death. Where does humankind come from; and where is it going? In an attempt to answer these questions it would seem to me that each and every group of people within their culture and religion may have different methods, but the ultimate goal should be the same; that is, fuller realization of the meaning of life, and God as the ultimate source and reality of life. Thus it can be argued that each religion and culture may represent the traditional way of response of the people to the gift and illumination of God. This, in fact, happens within a particular cultural and linguistic milieu or context.

The story of the evangelization of Africa is too well known to be repeated here, except to say that many of the early missionaries behaved as though they were the source rather than the channel of the gospel. From either ignorance or pure pride of ethnocentrism, they saw Africa as a blank slate on which anything could be written. Africa and its people were seen as living in a religious void. They were therefore denied any religious heritage at worst, and at best the religious heritage they were credited with was rendered pagan, devilish, primitive and altogether dangerous. The evangelizers thus felt that they were bringing Christ to Africa in their luggage. They really forgot that God through Christ was already at work in Africa before the advent of the white missionary. Hence the use of such terms as 'Bringing Christ to the heathens', 'Planting Christianity in Africa', and so forth.

In this particular instance it would seem to me that the church in Africa has failed in its duty to translate divine revelation into every language, to bring it within the range of all cultures, so that all creatures of God can gain contact with their Redeemer in a manner suitable to the mentality and feelings of each one.

As with one culture, religion is inextricably linked to the whole of life whose personal and communal activities it animates. The feeling of wholeness is an important aspect of African life. The celebrations of ritual ceremonies take place in common and for common good. The spirit of solidarity plays a cardinal part in this and the existence of the individual cannot be conceived outside the frame-work of one's integration in society. Religion therefore acts as a unifying factor in African culture. It is like the soul, which keeps the whole body healthy. The Lordship of Christ over all religions and cultures is understood by Africans through their concept of God. To the African, there is no watertight distinction between God and Christ. God and Jesus are linked together. Jesus is, because God is. Hence most of the attributes of Christ are indeed attributes of God... .

The church's duty therefore in dialogue with African religion and culture should not be one of condemnation but of understanding and fulfilment. The church should learn to understand Africa; and learn to address Africans as Africans – by always bearing in mind that God's self-disclosure is, in the first instance, to the whole world and that each race has grasped something of this primary revelation according to its capability. This is not to create gods for every race but to emphasize the all-embracing power and quality of God (and therefore of Christ) as the Creator, Father, King and Judge of all possible religions, cultures and indeed the whole world. (pp. 120–2)

I must confess that I have an uncomfortable feeling at ecumenical meetings where, on the one hand, we seem to say that other religions share in the Lordship of Christ and must therefore be accorded due respect, but on the other hand, we emphasize that Christianity has the pure truth which must be proclaimed to all peoples, at all times and in all places. This is what my people call 'Selling the dog and still holding its tail.' Church statisticians tell us that by the turn of the century Africa will be the most 'Christian continent' in the world, with about eighty-five per cent of the population baptized. What does this mean to us? What is the function of African theology in the church's evangelistic thrust? (p. 127)

Kofi Appiah-Kubi, 'Response' in Gerald H. Anderson and Thomas F. Stransky, *Christ's Lordship and Religious Pluralism* (Maryknoll, NY: Orbis, 1981).

S. Wesley Ariarajah

S. Wesley Ariarajah, formerly Director of the WCC Sub-Unit on Dialogue with People of Living Faiths, argues in 'The Need for a New Debate', that a new framework is needed for interreligious dialogue.

The hope for an interpretation of Jesus appropriate for our witness today lies in our ability to come up with a new framework that both sets out what we believe God to have done in Jesus and remains genuinely open to being surprised by God's freedom to act within the life and experience of other people and outside the history that has shaped our faith.

Does this mean that we go in the opposite direction and openly deny that there is any uniqueness in Jesus or that God might have done something decisive, indispensable, universal, and so forth, in the Jesus event? There is no need to do this, because it is possible to come to an understanding of who Jesus is in which these issues and words become pointless and irrelevant. It is interesting that most of the interpretation of the life and ministry of Jesus in third-world contexts pay little or no attention to the issue of uniqueness. The minjung theologians of Korea, for example, when thrown into jails and tortured for taking sides with the dispossessed, awoke to the fact that Jesus identified himself with the brokenness of the people and met the fate that befell them. They recognized that to follow him is to participate in their misery (*han*) and to be willing to pay the price for so doing. Such an understanding of Jesus may be challengingly relevant to all peoples and all times, and to enter that discipleship might be life-transforming to anyone. But the very spirit that undergirds this interpretation rules out the possibility of using such words as decisive, indispensable, and so on. The uniqueness issue was not consciously dropped; it had become irrelevant and meaningless both to their understanding of who Jesus was and to their witness to him.... (pp. 32–3)

A wider framework needs to take account of several aspects, including the following:

1. God is the creator, preserver and provider of all that is; nothing is outside God's love and care.
2. In our experience we know that the world is not what God intends it to be. God's love, compassion and justice, however, are all at work to bring wholeness to the whole creation.
3. Religious traditions witness to how people in all ages and places have attempted to know, understand and relate to God, or to grasp the meaning of life, sometimes without using God language.
4. In our experience we also know that all human attempts to relate to God and live a life that God intends have been ambiguous; all religious life participates in this ambiguity. But all of them also give undeniable witness to people's life with God and to God's life with people.
5. Christians have, in and through the life, death and resurrection of Jesus, come to a knowledge and understanding of who God is, how God deals with us and what God requires of us. To be a Christian is to be caught up in this profound reality and to accept the discipleship to which this knowledge calls us.
6. This discipleship is exercised in the world in the way we relate to God, ourselves and others. In so doing, we believe that we participate in God's rule, which will in its own time bring fullness of life to all creation.
7. As Christians live with others they witness to the one who called them to this discipleship. Even as they give an 'account of the hope that is in them', they are open to listening and learning about the ways God has been active in the world and in the lives of other people.
8. As people who have come into the discipleship of God's Reign we participate wherever we discern the Spirit of God to be active to bring wholeness. We are also open to inviting all who stand for the values of the kingdom to work with us, despite religious labels, in seeking to fulfil God's will for the world. (33–4)

S. Wesley Ariarajah, 'The Need for a New Debate', in Leonard Swidler and Paul Mojzes (eds), *The Uniqueness of Jesus: A Dialogue with Paul F. Knitter* (Maryknoll, NY: Orbis, 1997).

Hasan Askari

A leading figure in dialogue between Islam and other religions, Hasan Askari, formerly Professor at Selly Oak Colleges, Vrije University of Amsterdam, The American University of Beirut and Osmania University, argues that the Qur'an offers a framework for understanding the concept of apostleship in the Abrahamic faiths and in other traditions.

The principle that for every community there is an apostle is applied to all 'messengers'. In the Qur'anic prophetology, Noah, Ibrahaim, Moses and Jesus stand out as supreme examples of the Apostleship of God. Let us consider a few Qur'anic verses in this connection.

(1) Say ye: 'We believe in God and the revelations given to us, and to Abraham, Isma'il, Isaac, Jacob, and the Tribes, and that given to Moses and Jesus, and that given to all Prophets from their Lord: We make no difference between one and another of them: and we bow to God (2.136, 3.84).

(2) We have sent thee inspiration, as We sent it to Noah and the Messengers after him: We sent inspiration to Abraham, Isma'il, Isaac, Jacob and the Tribes to Jesus, Job, Jonah, Aaron and Solomon, and to David We gave the Psalms. Of some Apostles We have already told thee the story; of others We have not – and to Moses spoke direct; – Apostles who gave good news as well as warning, that mankind should have no plea against God: for God is exalted in Power, Wise (4.163–5).

(3) We gave Moses the Book and followed him up with a succession of Apostles; We gave Jesus the son of Mary clear signs and strengthened him with the Holy Spirit (2.87).

(4) This is the Book (Qur'an); in it is guidance sure, without doubt, to those who fear God; who believe in the unseen, and are steadfast in prayer, and spend out of what We have provided for them; and who believe in the Revelations sent to thee, and sent before thy time, and have assurance of the Hereafter (2.2–4). ...(pp. 93–4)

It is obligatory upon the Muslims to bear witness to all the Apostles whose names are mentioned in the Qur'an. As the immediate addressees of the Qur'an were either the disbelievers of Mecca or the People of the Book (Jews and Christians), only those names of the Apostles figure in the Qur'an which were familiar to them. But as the Qur'anic conception of *risala* (apostleship) is comprehensive of all human communities and as it is not reasonable to hold that God did not at all send any of His Apostles to such vast communities like those of China, India, Africa and the Americas, the Muslim theologians are agreed in principle that there were God's Apostles in every land at different times. This again based on the Qur'anic text:

> We did send Apostles before thee: of them there are some whose story We have related to thee, and some whose story We have not related to thee (40.78).

This is why in the Tradition the number of the Apostles sent to different lands and communities is as large as 124,000. (p. 96)

The question of finality requires to be stated in some other way so as to have a unified understanding of God's Revelations, and this depends how far we are prepared to work with different points of departure: for instance, (1) as for God there is no such thing as past and future, and all the Apostles are contemporary to Him (and is it tenable to ask whether they also are in some sense 'contemporary' to one another?) and hence, to argue from the point of view of revelation in time and raise questions of 'finality' is sometimes to run the risk of not fully realizing that 'time' is in the view of God. (2) When we come across such expressions as 'I am the Way', is it not rewarding to ask what the subject implies here – if it is the ego of the Prophet, he has put it beside God which is religiously impossible, and if not, he has then passed away, and the subject here points to God himself, for in truth He alone can say that He is the Way; (3) 'finality' may be viewed more as a sign of authenticity and certainly of truth with respect to one or another claim, and not essentially a judgement of the other; and (4) the question of finality is a risky thing from another point of view; any undue stress on it will lead one to prejudge the freedom of God. (p. 102)

Hasan Askari, 'The Qur'anic Conception of Apostleship' in Dan Cohn-Sherbok (ed.), *Islam in a World of Diverse Faiths* (London: Macmillan, 1991).

Mahmoud Ayoub

Mahmoud Ayoub served as a Research Associate at the Centre for Religious Studies at the University of Toronto and the Muhammadi Islamic Centre in Toronto. In 'The Word of God and the Voices of Humanity', he argues that throughout history God has revealed himself to prophets in different traditions.

Islam proclaimed more loudly than any other religious tradition the word of God in human voices. 'There is not a community', the Qur'an insists, 'but that a warner had come to it.' The number of prophets is put by Islamic tradition at one hundred and twenty-four thousand. Human history therefore is according to Islam the history of Divine revelation. It is the history of prophets, men who in their lives and vision provided not only models for the rest of humanity to emulate, but also the link between temporal humanity and Divine transcendence. They are in reality a bridge between this world and the next, between man and God. The Qur'an tells us that 'To God do we belong and to him we shall return.'

If then we are to return to our divine origin without faltering along the way or losing our direction in labyrinths of our own making we need guides, human guides who have themselves trodden the way before us. These are the prophets and friends of God. Their task is, according to Islam, to awaken us to that innate state which is implanted in us by God. It is our original state of purity... 'In which God created humankind, and God's creation cannot be altered.' Such a universal exemplar and guide is Abraham whose long journey from doubt to faith and from faith to certainty is graphically reported in the Qur'an.

Abraham ... rejected the idols of his people and left his home and kin in search of God. Like so many of us, he first mistook the majesty of God's creation for God. Soon, however, he discovered that the moon and sun were transient, they rise and set and he 'did not like those that set'... .

Thereafter, it was God's initiative to guide his friend from a faith of knowledge to the dynamic faith of certainty. Abraham received word from his Lord, that is he became a prophet. More directly still, Abraham witnessed how God revives the dead, and thus his heart was put at rest. He thus became the intimate friend ... of God. Armed with this certainty, Abraham was then able to assume the difficult tasks of human leadership. God declared him to be '... a leader (*imam*) of humankind'.

Abraham thus became the father of faith for Jews, Christians and Muslims. Even the Brahmans of India were claimed to be sons of our father Abraham. For later Muslim piety, Abraham and his wife Sarah are the loving guardians in paradise of the souls of innocent children... . There is yet one more instance which gives Abraham the status of the archetype of faith. His unquestioning acceptance of the divine command to sacrifice his son was the supreme test of faith. This acceptance of, or submission to, the Divine will is what Islam means. Abraham was a true Muslim (submitter) to God. Therefore, it was to his pure faith that the prophet Muhammad was sent by God to call us all back. In fact, the Qur'an argues that Abraham was a man of pure faith, a true Muslim before institutionalized religion, Judaism, Christianity or Islam, came into being. This is to say Abraham's faith, to which we must return, was prior to and higher than all our doctrines and creeds. His faith was free from all idols, even those of religion. Islam brings into sharp focus this aspect of Abraham's life as a model and guide for all people of faith. Abraham was the first idol breaker. He first broke the idols made by human hands, the statues which his people worshipped. Then he broke the idols of God's creation, the sun and moon to which he refused to bow down. Finally he broke the idol of family love, and with it love of anything other than God. (pp. 61–3)

Mahmoud Ayoub, 'The Word of God and the Voices of Humanity', in Hasan Askari and John Hick (eds), *The Experience of Religious Diversity* (Brookfield, Vermont: Gower Press, 1985).

B

Paul Badham

Paul Badham, born in 1942, has taught at the University of Wales, Lampeter, where he has been Professor of Theology and Religious Studies since 1973. In The Contemporary Challenge of Modernist Theology *he argues that Christians must acknowledge the presence of the Divine in other religions.*

For the earliest Christians the expression the Logos was understood to refer to the concept of a universal presence of God working in all human beings. Hence to accept the Logos doctrine it is necessary to see all world religions as inspired by the same divine initiative. This was most clearly spelt out by Archbishop William Temple when he wrote in his *Readings in St John's Gospel*:

> All that is noble in the non-Christian systems of thought, or conduct, or worship is the work of Christ upon them and within them. By the Word of God – that is to say by Christ – Isaiah and Plato, and Zoroaster, and Buddha, and Confucius conceived and uttered such truths as they declared. There is only one divine light; and every man in his measure is enlightened by it.

Temple's use of the word 'Christ' is confusing but as this passage makes clear he identifies him so totally as the 'Word of God' (or Logos) and in doing so assumes the stoic understanding of the Logos as a universal divine presence in human beings, rather than something limited to the historical Jesus. Instead it refers explicitly to that working of God which in Temple's view inspired not only Jesus, but also Plato, Zoroaster, Buddha and Confucius and by implication all other great religious thinkers as well. And to make this claim is to make a monumental shift in attitude from the exclusivist Christian position which had become normative over most of the Christian centuries. The revival of the Logos doctrine was thus of immense importance. Hick sees that the use of Logos terminology is dynamic:

> If selecting from our Christian language, we call God-acting-towards-mankind the Logos, then we must say that all salvation within all religions is the work of the Logos and that under their various images and symbols men in different cultures and faiths may encounter the Logos and final salvation.

In fact the Logos terminology provides Hick with a foundation of thought which goes quite as far as the view which came to be expressed in his Gifford lectures, *An Interpretation of Religion*, namely that all religions are human responses to a single divine Reality.

Such a perspective is supported by the theory which has come to be known as 'degree christology'. This claims that the presence of God in Christ was similar in kind (though different in degree) to the presence of God in all human beings. Taking up the implication of the stoic understanding of the Logos it identifies this with 'the light that enlightens everyone who comes into the world' though in practice recognizing that in most human beings the light is obscured by selfishness and sin. However the more saintly the person the more the divine light is perceived. For Christians Christ represents the peak of this development. But to make such a claim does not absolutize the divine presence in Jesus Christ in such a way as to treat as irrelevant the awareness of divine Reality disclosed through the lives of others. By contrast the view that God was present in Christ in a way which was different in kind from God's presence elsewhere carries the implication that Christianity is different in kind from other faiths. Such an attitude leads to an arrogant sense that all truth about God is to be found within the Christian tradition and any insights that other faiths may have are valid if and only if they agree with what Christianity teaches. Dialogue becomes pointless when one side believes it has all the answers. However a full acceptance of all the implications of the Logos doctrine and a degree christology means that the most that can be claimed in relation to Jesus is that his life and teaching gives us insight into the character and personality of God in the same way if to a greater degree than that of other religious teachers. These doctrines take for granted that the prophets of the Hebrew Bible and the saints and doctors of the church as well as Plato, Zoroaster, Confucius, and Buddha and leaders of other great religious traditions including Muhammad, Guru Nanak and Shinran were also channels of that divine spirit which Jesus also embodied. (pp. 140–2)

Paul Badham, *The Contemporary Challenge of Modernist Theology* (Cardiff: Wales University Press, 1998).

Karl Barth

Karl Barth, born in 1886, studied in Germany and was Professor at Gottingen, Munster, Bonn and Basle. In 'The Revelation of God as the Abolition of Religion', he argues that all religions including Christianity must be judged by God's revelation.

In our discussion of 'religion as unbelief' we did not consider the distinction between Christian and non-Christian religion. Our intention was that whatever we said about the other religions affected the Christian similarly. In the framework of that discussion we could not speak in any special way about Christianity. We could not give it any special or assured place in face of that judgement. Therefore the discussion cannot be understood as a preliminary polemic against the non-Christian religons, with a view to the ultimate assertion that the Christian religion is the true religion. If this were the case our task now would be to prove that, as distinct from the non-Christian religions, the Christian is not guilty of idolatry and self-righteousness, that it is not therefore unbelief but faith, and therefore true religion; or, which comes to the same thing, that it is no religion at all, but as against all religions, including their mystical and atheistical self-criticism, it is in itself the true and holy and as such the unspotted and incontestable form of fellowship between God and man. To enter on this path would be to deny the very thing we have to affirm. If the statement is to have any content we can dare to state that the Christian religion is the true one only as we listen to the divine revelation. But a statement which we dare to make as we listen to the divine revelation can only be a statement of faith. And a statement of faith is necessarily a statement which is thought and expressed in faith and from faith, i.e. in recognition and respect of what we are told by revelation. Its explicit and implicit content is unreservedly conditioned by what we are told. But that is certainly not the case if we try to reach the statement that the Christian religion is the true religion by a road which begins by leaving behind the judgement of revelation, that religion is unbelief, as a matter which does not apply to us Christians but only others, the non-Christians, only in so far as we recognize ourselves in them, i.e. only as we see in them the truth of this judgement of revelation which concerns us, in the solidarity, therefore, in which, anticipating them in both repentance and hope, we accept this judgement to participate in the promise of revelation. At the end of the road we have to tread there is, of course, the promise to those who accept God's judgement, who let themselves be led beyond their unbelief. There is faith in this promise, and, in this faith, the presence and reality of the grace of God, which, of course, differentiates our religion, the Christian, from all others as the true religion. This exalted goal cannot be reached except by this humble road. And it would not be a truly humble road if we tried to tread it except in the consciousness that any 'attaining' here can consist only in the utterly humble and thankful adoption of something which we would not attain if it were not already attained in God's revelation before we set out on the road.

We must insist, therefore, that at the beginning of a knowledge of truth of the Christian religion there stands the recognition that this religion, too, stands under the judgement that religion is unbelief, and that it is not acquitted by any inward worthiness, but only by the grace of God, proclaimed and effectual in his revelation. But concretely this judgement affects the whole practice of our faith: our Christian conceptions of God and the things of God, our Christian theology, our Christian worship, our forms of Christian fellowship and order, our Christian morals, poetry and art, our attempts to give individual and social form to the Christian life, our Christian strategy and tactics in the interest of our Christian cause, in short our Christianity, to the extent that it is our Christianity, the human work which we undertake and adjust to all kinds of near and remote aims and which as such is seen to be on the same level as the human work in other religions. This judgement means that all this Christianity of ours, and all the details of it, are not as such what they ought to be and pretend to be, a work of faith, and therefore of obedience to the divine revelation. What we have here is in its own way – a different way from that of other religions, but no less seriously – unbelief, i.e. opposition to the divine revelation, and therefore active idolatry and self-righteousness. It is the same helplessness and arbitrariness. (pp. 13–15)

Karl Barth, 'The Revelation of God as the Abolition of Religion', in John Hick and Brian Hebblethwaite (eds), *Christianity and Other Religions* (Oxford: Oneworld, 2001).

José Miguez Bonino

José Miguez Bonino has served as Dean of the Graduate School at the Protestant Institute for Advanced Theological Studies in Buenos Aires, Argentina. He argues in 'The Uniqueness of Christ and the Plurality of Humankind' that religious dialogue must be understood from within the context in which it occurs.

I wonder to what extent the problem of the Christian's relation to people of different faiths is primarily a christological question, or indeed, a theological question, or even a religious question. Christians, to be sure, have to try to clarify for themselves the theological issues that arise out of their dealings with peoples of other faiths. In fact, we should be equally concerned with theological issues which arise in our dealing with peoples of our own faith. But is it not really a prior question to try to understand the conditions in which we meet people? It is the danger of abstracting the christological question from the context of the totality of our relations that makes me uncomfortable. I'll try to explain what I mean.

1. It is an obvious fact that we do not meet religions but people. In that sense a human encounter precedes and conditions any dialogue ... the dialogue on who Jesus Christ is seems to be 'abstracted' from the conditions and the manner of the encounter. Thus, it takes the nature of a conversation between religions rather than a dialogue between people. Naturally, abstraction is a necessary step as we look back to understand any human encounter or as we look forward to it. But the abstraction, to be useful, has to abstract from the totality of the experience, including its personal, historical, cultural and socio-logical elements.

2. The encounter takes place in the framework of some context which we share. Even in a very elementary – but not insignificant – sense, we meet to dialogue in a room, in a place, at a time. More profoundly, though, we 'theologians' of one or another faith or religion carry with us a 'people' who confess that faith, who carry its tradition, who have inculturated that faith, and who live it every day – consciously or unconsciously – in their habitual ways. More and more, these different 'constituencies' live in the same continents, under the same govern-ments, within a social and economic structure, and in fact they shape and are shaped by all these factors. Increasingly, the context and its problematics are global. From such situations different kinds of issues and problems become central and crucial for all. A common context, therefore, is not an external reality but a commonality that – at least in part – is constitutive of encounter and consequently enters into any dialogue in which these peoples may engage... .

3. For us Christians the point has to be pushed one more step. Ever since the fourth century almost all our religious encounters have taken place from one place: the place of power. Whatever we say about 'our' Christ, even in the most modest and conciliatory ways, is said by those who have the power – economic, political, military – to make their claim stand. It is not so much the uniqueness of Christ, or Christ's universal claim that offends and repels: it is our uniqueness, our universal claim. Early Christians were able to make extraordinary claims about Christ because they made them 'from below' and supported them by their martyrdom and not by their legions... .

Certainly we cannot walk out of our skin. We cannot unwrite the history of Christianity in the world and begin again as a small persecuted sect. Sometimes people have called for a moratorium on all missionary and evangelizing activity. It might not be a bad idea to stop all organized – ecclesiastically planned and strate-gically directed – mission and evangelization and let the faith of Christian people in the world move freely 'as the Spirit'. But we cannot realistically expect such a thing. What I think is possible is that we take seriously the nature and conditions of the encounter and try to relate dialogue to these conditions. (pp. 109–10)

José Miguez Bonino, 'The Uniqueness of Christ and the Plurality of Humankind', in Leonard Swidler and Paul Mojzes (eds), *The Uniqueness of Jesus: A Dialogue with Paul F. Knitter* (Maryknoll, NY: Orbis, 1997).

Eugene Borowitz

Eugene Borowitz, Professor at the Hebrew Union College – Jewish Institute of Religion in New York, argues in 'A Jewish Response: The Lure and Limits of Universalizing Our Faith' that while God has a special relationship with the Jewish people, members of non-Jewish religions can be saved if they follow the Noachide laws.

Traditional Judaism has a reasonably well-defined attitude to non-Jewish religions. The Torah describes God as making a covenant with Noah and thus, through Noah and his children, with all of humanity. The rabbis made this covenant the basis of their authoritative rulings about the religious status of non-Jews. They and all the Judaism that flowed from them considered the covenant with Noah to be real and continuing. Rabbinic Judaism thus believes all people know what God wants of them and can achieve their salvation. But as the Torah story of Noah immediately makes clear, humankind regularly violates its covenant responsibilities to God. The rabbis generally believed that the children of Noah were obligated to carry out seven root commandments: not to blaspheme God, or worship idols, or murder, or steal, or be sexually degenerate, or cut limbs from living animals, and positively, to set up courts of justice. Even as the descendents of Noah built a tower to enter heaven and gain a name, so the rabbis saw most of humanity behaving sinfully and thus deserving of God's judgement.

The Torah understands the covenant with Abraham as a compensation for the sinfulness of humanity. The covenant with Noah is not abrogated by God. Rather God establishes a special covenant so that the divine rule may be properly established among people. Covenant being essentially a relationship of obligation, the Jews fulfil God's special purpose by living in special intensity under God's law. They proclaim the reality of God's rule by doing the commandments, personally and communally; by example, they set a standard for humanity.

Proselytizing has little role in Judaism. People do not need to be Jews: they need only be pious Noachides. So the Jews have no command to convert anyone. They do accept converts and, in love of their faith, occasionally seek to have others adopt it. The rabbis acknowledged that unconverted individuals among 'the nations' could be fully righteous and thus 'saved'. The comment, 'The pious among the gentiles have a share in the life of the world to come', may be taken as the standard Jewish attitude. The rabbis, like the Bible, were, however, spiritually pessimistic about human collectives and freely speculated that they would not survive the post-messianic judgement day. In our own time, the experience of the Holocaust, perpetrated by a nation steeped in Christianity and a leader of modern culture, has reinforced those traditional attitudes. While still hopeful about individuals we are sceptical if not cynical about claims for the goodness of human nature, the progress of civilization, or the way institutions will transform humanity.... .

Yet for all this doctrine, the only gentile religion the rabbis directly dealt with was idolatry. Succeeding generations have had to fill in Judaism's judgement of other religions. With regard to Christianity this involved a consideration of whether it was not another form of idol worship. Its use of icons, its veneration of saints, and particularly its doctrine of the Christ as a person of the triune God, seemed the equivalent of idolatry.... . Islam being radically monotheistic caused many fewer problems. Most Jewish thinkers today see pious Christians and Muslims as fulfilling the Noachian covenant, and thus as 'saved'. A minority opinion remains that their worship is the equivalent of idolatry; also some modern Jews have tried to give these religions a more than Noachian status, in line with their own claims, but no such view has gained even substantial support. This is as far as the Jewish theory of other religions has gone. In sum, humanity does not need to be Jewish but God needs Jews and Judaism to achieve the divine purposes with humanity. This sense of the Jews as chosen and special but only instrumental to the establishment of God's kingdom is so great that some rabbis can see the ultimate disappearance of Jewish distinctiveness at the conclusion of the eschatological drama, though most love the Jewish people too much to believe that God would do without them, even in the life of the world to come.... . (pp. 59–61)

Our particularism may ... need some special limits and I can suggest four that faiths might insist upon. First, we can limit the role of our particularity, applying it only to ourselves, as in the Jewish assertion that only Jews, not all people, need to serve God in the specifically Jewish way. Second, one may adopt the liberal religious stance and acknowledge that one's sense of religious truth, while great enough to stake one's life on, is not absolute. One must then allow room for others with a different sense of truth. Third, whether one can accept the liberal stance or not, one may recognize that religion today stands under the moral judgement of its secular critics. For pragmatic reasons, then, we must not act so as to discredit our claims to serve a universal God. Such a concern for what others think would undoubtedly change as we found ourselves in a position of power, precisely when we need the greatest restraint. Perhaps then, fourth, we can admit that the fullness of the truth we affirm can come into being only in God's eschatological redemption of all human history. Until then we must do our share while recognizing that we ourselves stand under God's present judgement and must leave to God what God alone can do. (pp. 67–8)

Eugene Borowitz, 'A Jewish Response: The Lure and Limits of Universalizing Our Faith', in Donald G. Dawe and John B. Carman (eds), *Christian Faith in a Religiously Plural World* (Maryknoll, NY: Orbis, 1986).

Marcus Braybrooke

Marcus Braybrooke, Chairman of the World Congress of Faiths, stresses the importance of toleration and understanding based on an acceptance of the spiritual validity of the world's major religious faiths. In 'Interfaith Prayer', he claims that interfaith worship can unite believers despite their different interpretations of the Divine.

To attend the worship of another religion as a guest or to invite guests to our own religion need not imply 'legitimizing' their religion. It may be just an educational experience, designed to increase understanding and friendly relations ... But do the hosts make any adjustments? My memory of the first Council of Christians and Jews Conference that I attended in the 1960s was that we all went to the Sabbath morning service at the Orthodox synagogue. It lasted an hour and a half and was all in Hebrew; many of us were little enlightened. One of the Jews muttered: 'It is a sin to weary the congregation.' I recall another so-called 'All Faiths Service' which turned out to be an Anglican evensong. When the officiant turned to the congregation and said, 'We shall now all say the creed', the rabbi next to me muttered, 'A bit difficult for some of us.'

So do we adjust when others are present? It would not be appropriate to 'missionize' – or is that an example of the 'watering down' that critics mention? We might, if Christian, need to look at the lections. On one such occasion I was asked to preach when Jews had been invited to the communion and the gospel was Peter's confession, 'You are the Christ...'.

And if we are guests do we adapt? Most Christians would be willing to cover their heads in a synagogue – although some Pentecostalists might object. In a Hindu temple do we greet the 'idol'?

Are we just there as observers – or does the occasion become an experience of worship for us? I recall one conference when an African was leading us in his traditional worship and we were invited to drink from the water which had been offered to the god. At the time, I was feeling rather depressed – and in taking part I had an experience of welcome and acceptance which was in tune with other deep religious experiences. It was, too, with a real sense of privilege that I shared in a Shinto rite – and felt something of the Shinto love of nature ...

To what extent can we enter into the religious experience of another community of faith? I feel we have still much to learn from Swami Abhishiktananda and other pioneers in this field. I have taken part in some weekends of shared meditation with Swami Bhavyananda. Personally, if I am with Hindus meditating, I can, as in my own meditation, sense a oneness with the Divine – but then I am at home in the mystical religious tradition which perhaps points to an underlying unity, or am I merely superimposing Christian meaning on other symbols?

I personally believe that we can share a little, at a religious and experiential level, the worship of another faith. Otherwise we have to say that religions, at their centre, are impervious to each other – and this has serious consequences for interfaith dialogue. (pp. 152–3)

Interfaith services which are prepared as a unity and in which all are invited to participate assume that beyond our differences we worship the One Eternal One – that all our religious dogma and ritual point to the Divine Mystery who can never be fully named. 'All names are given to you and yet none can comprehend you. How shall I name you then, O You, the Beyond all name?', said Gregory of Nazianzen long ago; or as Alan Paton said, our language and rituals are 'a net of holes to capture essence, a shell, to house the thunder of the ocean ... a range of words to hold One Living Word'... .

While many Christians who take part will wish to maintain the uniqueness of Jesus Christ, they will wish to balance this by belief that God the Creator has made all people in the divine image and from common parents and that the Holy Spirit is active in the whole of human history.

In services of this type the distinctiveness of the great faiths is affirmed; it does not replace the regular liturgy and prayer of a faith community. In my view, it needs to develop appropriate new symbols rather than adapt existing symbols of particular faiths. Further, differences are seen to be enriching and God-given. Some Christians insist that all prayer should be 'through Jesus Christ Our Lord'. As a Southern Baptist leader has been quoted as saying: 'God does not hear the prayer of a devout Jew.' Is there one divine reality whom all seek to address or are the gods of other faiths 'false gods and idols'? I would hope all prayer is in the spirit of Jesus Christ, who endorses all that is good and true and lovely, so that I did not feel that I must necessarily name him. (pp. 154–5)

Marcus Braybrooke, 'Interfaith Prayer' in Dan Cohn-Sherbok, *Many Mansions* (London: Bellew, 1992).

Michael von Bruck

Michael von Bruck, who has served as Professor of Religion at the University of Munich, argues that while Christians are impelled to engage in mission, this activity must be reinterpreted in a pluralistic context.

How about the whole problem of mission? Christianity is a missionary religion, but so too are Buddhism, Islam and others. Are we to discard mission? Are we to give up any search and struggle for truth that imply also arguments and conversion of ourselves and perhaps others? This is a thorny subject, but it is the touchstone for any theology of religions. Are there several truths or only one, and how can this question be decided if we are always talking on the basis of different claims of truth?

Religions with universal claims and respective experiences of life have shaped and influenced other cultures and religions during the last three millennia or so. Each religion of this type has not only the right but maybe the duty to express itself and witness its basic event and experience to other people. The Christian understanding of mission and its respective history has two aspects:

1. Mission is the legitimate expression of the witness of Christian faith in the world as an offer of salvation for all human beings.
2. The history and the notion of mission are aspects of a bloody power struggle and very much connected to the colonial history of Europe and North America. Therefore, the whole concept of mission today is unbearable, because too much historical guilt and aberration is connected with it.

Mission today actually covers and hinders precisely what is to be done in a dialogical way: to give witness to the original experience of the Christian community, a witness of the unconditional love of God expressed in the person of Jesus Christ. Should we not recognize this fact and give up our hidden or open interests of power and identity, which are so connected with the Christian understanding of truth, salvation and mission?

The universal claim of unconditional love of God in Christ has to be expressed in a totally different language in order to say theologically and in a hermeneutically reflected way precisely what it said to the early Christians – but now under the conditions of interreligious communication.... . We have to say clearly that we do not regard our truth claims as superior, although we still feel that we need to be embedded in our truth claims even if they are relative. (pp. 37–8)

In interreligious encounter pluralism and identity are sometimes experienced as contradictions. Pluralism is the equality of different claims; identity is the search for continuity in the midst of our constructed borderlines, so that identity turns often into the denigration of the other or the stranger. But at the same time all religions are syntheses of originally different traditions... .

Each tradition forms a unique identity and still can integrate others. This is precisely what happens today in the whole world. Religions are in a fundamental crisis facing secularism and the economized culture into which the world seems to be developing. This is similar in India, Japan, Europe and America. All religions, therefore, face the question of what their unique and important contribution to humankind is. They are called not just to legitimize or strengthen their religious institutions but to offer selfless service to human beings on the basis of their original impulses.

What is called fundamentalism ... today is the denial of a reflection on and relativizing of one's own knowledge in view of other claims, as well as a refusal of this assimilation or integration just spoken about. However, different forms of fundamentalism, which are always politically motivated and supported, have to be distinguished. Yet these two forms of denial and refusal of a living change probably have two basic roots.

One root is an individual point: fear. It is the fear of losing something because faith in the reconciling God is not strong enough. Clinging to traditional forms or rigid institutions or certain dogmatic formulations is an attitude of weakness... . The other root is a social point: the search for power. The ardent desire for safety and security we have just described can be and is being politically exploited. Different parties or groups use the search for identity in order to legitimize their interest in power, that is to say, they organize and proclaim fixed identities... .

My argument is that in the present partnership of religions on all levels of human expression and formation a common identity emerges that has not yet been there in our respective traditions and therefore has no model to draw on... . That Jesus reveals truly God's saving presence can be established only if this 'truly' implies that this revelation is also sufficient (*satis est*); if so, all other claims have to be interpreted again in the horizon of this sufficiency, and this is basically an inclusivistic model of understanding... . (pp. 41–3)

Michael von Bruck, 'Identifying Constructively Our Interreligious Moment' in Leonard Swidler and Paul Mojzes (eds), *The Uniqueness of Jesus: A Dialogue with Paul F. Knitter* (Maryknoll, NY: Orbis, 1997).

Emil Brunner

Emil Brunner, born in 1889, served as Professor of Theology at the University of Zurich. In 'Revelation and Reason', he argues that the Christian faith alone lives by the Word of God. Hence it is utterly different from other faiths even though non-Christian religions have a knowledge of God.

The Christian faith, faith in the God revealed by Jesus Christ, is not 'one of the religions of the world'. A religious and geographical survey of the world would, of course, include 'Christianity' under the general concept of religion. It is impossible for a non-Christian to take that which distinguishes the Christian faith from 'the other religions' so seriously that on that account he would give up his general concept of 'religion'. But the Christian faith itself cannot recognize this general conception, without losing its own identity. It cannot admit that its faith is one species of the genus 'religion', or if it does so, only in the sense in which it regards itself as the true religion in contrast to the other false religions. To the outsider this looks like narrow-minded or fanatical intolerance; actually, it is a necessary expression of sober truth. The Christian faith alone lives by the Word of God, by the revelation in which God imparts himself. We have already shown how erroneous is the idea that these 'other religions' make the same claim to revelation. This can be proved to be incorrect; not one of them dares to assert, 'The Word became flesh, and we beheld his glory, the glory of the only begotten Son of the Father, full of grace and truth.' Therefore, because the Christian faith stands on this foundation, it is something wholly different from 'the other religions'. (pp. 115–16)

There are phenomena in the religions of non-Christian peoples which 'we must refer back to stirrings of the divine Spirit in their hearts'. The most important of these 'effects' of the original revelation is the sense of God, in general. Men have always had a certain knowledge (*notitia*) of God, and this knowledge of God 'will not allow itself to be stifled. There may indeed have been people like the Epicureans, Pliny, and the like, who deny it with their mouth. But this does not help them; their conscience tells them otherwise' (Luther). Calvin teaches that this sense of God is so deeply interwoven with the nature of man that 'the knowledge (*notitia*) of God and of ourself is connected by a mutual bond'. Hence the transcendental theory of religion is both right and wrong: right, in so far as it sees the sense of God as an integral element in the nature of man; and wrong, in so far as the original revelation is different from anything that man can come to know by his own efforts. (pp. 121–2)

Only from the standpoint of the Word of God can we understand the phenomenon of human religion, with all that it contains of wonderful and terrible, sublime and gruesome elements. From that standpoint alone can we do justice to its impressive, as well as to its repellent, elements, to those which are divinely true and to those which are daemonically false. In all religion there is a recollection of the divine truth which has been lost; in all there is a longing after the divine Light and divine Love; but in all religion also there yawns an abyss of daemonic distortion of the truth, and of man's effort to escape from God. In all religion, even in the most primitive form of idolatry, there is something of reverence and gratitude toward a Power on which man knows himself to be dependent, which is different from his dependence on natural facts; but in all religion, too, even in the 'higher religions', this reverence is mingled with fear of the absolutely Terrible, which only leads to a slavish submission to overwhelming Power, while gratitude is mingled with a selfish longing for happiness, for which the Deity is 'used'. (pp. 123–4)

Jesus Christ is both the Fulfilment of all religion and the Judgement on all religion. As the Fulfiller, he is the Truth which these religions seek in vain. There is no phenomenon in the history of religion that does not point toward him: the bloody sacrifice of expiation, the sacred meal, the ecstatic element, the seeking of the Holy Spirit, the magical element, the indication of the *dynamis* of God in the reality of his revelation, prayer, the divine Father, and the divine Judge. All this the world of religions knows in a fragmentary and distorted form, as almost unrecognizable 'relics' of an 'original' revelation. From the standpoint of Jesus Christ, the non-Christian religions seem like stammering words from some half-forgotten saying. None of them is without a breath of the Holy, and yet none of them is the Holy. None is without its impressive truth, and yet none of them is the Truth; for their Truth is Jesus Christ. ... (p. 129)

Emil Brunner, 'Revelation and Reason' in Owen C. Thomas, *Attitudes Toward Other Religions* (London: SCM Press, 1969).

M. Darrol Bryant

M. Darrol Bryant, Professor at Renison College, University of Waterloo, argues in 'Interfaith Encounter and Dialogue in a Trinitarian Perspective' that Christians do not need to abandon their commitment to the central tenets of the faith to enter into dialogue with members of other religions.

The perspective that I have outlined here has implications for our future relations as Christians with men and women of other faiths. It seeks to move us beyond intransigence and fear to welcome the opportunity to enter into a new relationship with other faiths on the basis of the Christian faith itself. I have found that such a dialogue with others does not diminish my faith as a Christian, but deepens and enlarges it in the rhythm of the Word: listening and speaking, silence and inward meditation, dying and being reborn. It has led me to see more deeply the wonder of divine presence and absence both in my own life and in the lives of others. It has led me to a greater respect for the faith of others, including the faith I share with other Christians, and a need to discern the meaning of this type of meeting. That meaning must, I believe, be articulated for Christians in the horizon of our trinitarian faith – and in the horizons of the faith of others too. And that process, as I have already asserted, will only unfold over the coming generations as faith speaks to faith both within the family of Christian traditions and across traditions.

But are we not, as Christians, obliged to give up our central claims or, as some have put it, our 'title deeds' in order to enter into dialogue with other faiths? I think not. The absurdity of such a view becomes obvious if, for the moment, we look beyond Christianity and consider persons of other faiths. Would we, for example, expect the Taoist to deny the Tao as a precondition for dialogue, or expect the Caitanya Vaishnavite to deny the conviction that Krishna is the Lord, or the Muslim to forsake faith in Allah? Of course not. What we are, however, all obliged to give up is an *a priori* conviction that dialogue with other faiths is of no value or constitutes a denial of our own faith since we, whoever the 'we' is, already have the whole truth.

But will we not be obliged to compromise our faith in Christ? Again, I have not found such compromise necessary at all, at least not at the level of faith. But at the level of articulated doctrine, I think the answer is both yes and no. Christian faith is always in the process of finding adequate ways to articulate its faith in Christ; the whole history of Christianity testifies to this ongoing process. Thus it is misleading to assume that it is only the encounter and dialogue with men and women of other faiths that will have this consequence.... Such dialogue may intensify that process, but it does not, in my view, alter it in kind. At the same time, it must be acknowledged that Christians will be challenged to find adequate ways to express what I have called the mystery of the universal and particular in relation to God as Redeemer. What will be more deeply challenged will be the tendency among many Christians to hold faith in Christ apart from faith in God as Creator and Spirit. Seen in its three-articled context, our faith in Christ will be deepened and enlarged.

But what happens to the Christian call to 'conversion'? My own sense is that we need to avoid misconstruing the issue as 'dialogue versus conversion'. This misconstrues the issue because dialogue is not just polite chit-chat, nor is it the scholarly study of comparative religions. Rather, dialogue is, in a Christian perspective, the means through which the Word continues to deepen and trans-form our lives. Thus conversion is not just for the other, but a continuing process in the heart of the Christian believer. While the motivation for dialogue cannot be conversion understood as getting others to abandon their faith for mine, neither can we exclude the presence of the Spirit that will continually transform us all. The conversion, we should seek as Christians is not to an extrinsic set of propositions, but to a vital interior spirituality keyed to love as the central chord in the divine symphony... .

The first end of dialogue is meeting itself in an ethos of mutual respect and mutual willingness to be together in silence and in words... . The second end is to create the possibilities of genuine community and peace... . The third end is a shared quest for the Ultimate... . Without in any way denying what has been given to each of us as persons in traditions, but rather in sharing those ways, we can come to recognize each other as fellow pilgrims. (pp. 15–16)

M. Darrol Bryant, 'Interfaith Encounter and Dialogue in a Trinitarian Perspective', in Peter Phan (ed.), *Christianity and the Wider Ecumenism* (New York: Paragon, 1990).

Martin Buber

Martin Buber, born in 1878, grew up in Lemberg, studied at the universities of Vienna, Leipzig and Berlin, and taught at the University of Frankfurt. Later he settled in Israel and served as Professor of Social Philosophy at the Hebrew University. In I and Thou *he formulates a theology of encounter between God and man.*

Men have addressed their eternal Thou with many names. In singing of him who was thus named they always had the Thou in mind: the first myths were hymns of praise. Then the names took refuge in the language of It; men were more and more strongly moved to think of and to address their eternal Thou as an It. But all God's names are hallowed, for in them he is not merely spoken about, but also spoken to.

Many men wish to reject the word God as a legitimate usage, because it is so misused. It is indeed the most heavily laden of all the words used by men. For that reason it is the most imperishable and most indispensable. What does all mistaken talk about God's being and works (though there has been, and can be, no other talk about these) matter in comparison with the one truth that all men who have addressed god had God himself in mind? For he who speaks the word God and really has Thou in mind (whatever the illusion by which he is held), addresses the true Thou of his life, which cannot be limited by another Thou, and to which he stands in a relation that gathers up and includes all others.

But when he, too, who abhors the name, and believes himself to be godless, gives his whole being to addressing the Thou of his life, as a Thou that cannot be limited by another, he addresses God. (pp. 99–100)

In the relation with God unconditional exclusiveness and unconditional inclusiveness are one. He who enters on the absolute relation is concerned with nothing isolated any more, neither things nor beings, neither earth nor heaven; but everything is gathered up in the relation. For to step into pure relation is not to disregard everything but to see everything in the Thou, not to renounce the world but to establish it on its true basis. To look away from the world, or to stare at it, does not help a man to reach God; but he who sees the world in him stands in his presence. 'Here world, there God' is the language of It; 'God in the world' is another language of It; but to eliminate or leave behind nothing at all, to include the whole world in the Thou, to give the world its due and its truth, to include nothing beside God but everything in him – this is full and complete relation. (pp. 103–4)

Man's sense of Thou, which experiences in the relations with every particular Thou the disappointment of the change to It, strives out but not away from them all to its eternal Thou; but not as something is sought: actually there is no such thing as seeking God, for there is nothing in which he could not be found. How foolish and hopeless would be the man who turned aside from the course of his life in order to seek God; even though he won all the wisdom of solitude and all the power of concentrated being he would miss God. Rather is it as when a man goes his way and simply wishes that it might be the way: in the strength of his wish his striving is expressed. Every relational event is a stage that affords him a glimpse into the consummating event. So in each event he does not partake, but also (for he is waiting) does partake, of the one event. Waiting, not seeking, he goes his way; hence he is composed before all things, and makes contact with them which helps them. But when he has found, his heart is not turned from them, though everything now meets him in the one event. He blesses every cell that sheltered him, and every cell into which he will yet turn. For this finding is not the end, but only the eternal middle, of the way.

It is a finding without seeking, a discovering of the primal, of origin. His sense of thou, which cannot be satiated till he finds the endless Thou, had the Thou present to it from the beginning; the presence had only to become wholly real to him in the reality of the hallowed life of the world. (pp. 104–5)

Martin Buber, *I and Thou* (Edinburgh: T. and T. Clark, 1987).

John Carman

John Carman, who was born in India, served as Director of the Center for the Study of World Religions at Harvard University. In 'An Ecumenical Protestant Perspective', he argues that interreligious dialogue is a task for Christian discipleship which is distinct from evangelism.

In my opinion interreligious dialogue is a very distinct task of Christian discipleship, a task that is neither the same as nor a substitute for evangelism, any more than educational work or medical work is the same as or a substitute for evangelism. All of these tasks have a distinctively modern form; all carry more baggage than Jesus allowed his first disciples when he sent them out two by two. We need to remind ourselves of that fact, as well as of the spiritual outfitting of the disciples of which Saint Paul writes.

The expensive equipment of the modern world, such as the betatron in the cancer unit of a hospital, can be a great boon, but it has to remain a tool in our hands, as we have to remain tools in our Lord's hands. Sometimes we must do without such tools because we cannot afford them, sometimes because we cannot control them, and sometimes because they are no longer what the situation requires. It may be that the increasing cost of oil and other natural resources will force us to trim our present equipment, as well as to forge new tools for the years ahead.

I say this as a word of criticism to myself and to my fellow scholars who are trying to provide this modern equipment for the task of interreligious dialogue. We utilize and grow dependent upon expensive modern libraries and expensive modern transportation – the airplanes that fly us from one continent to another to participate in conferences like this one.

Dialogue, I would suggest, needs to begin with modest expectations and a modest definition. In our present context it is very simply a deliberately planned conversation where conversation has previously not occurred or where such conversation has reached an impasse. It is needed precisely where there is disagreement, misunderstanding and division. Undoubtedly it can have deeper and deeper levels, but it need not imply them and it should not be confused with the worship of God in the fellowship of the church.

The agreement it requires initially is whatever is necessary to get the conversation going: some agreed procedures, usually a common language, and certainly a common will to converse both in spite of and because of the differences between us. This discussion itself is such a dialogue among Christians with different backgrounds and different convictions. Here we should worship together because we are united in Christ, but we need to talk together because we are divided, and we should not expect the division to disappear by the time our discussion ends.

Some sense of shared interests or value is needed to motivate any dialogue, but I believe that common meeting point is much clearer in a meeting of Christians, however widely separated, than in interreligious dialogue. That does not mean that our discussions here are necessarily more amicable or more fruitful. The courtesy of which Kenneth Cragg writes is not always in evidence in meetings among Christians. Such courtesy is all the more necessary in interreligious dialogue where the different participants bring not only different perspectives, but also different views of the very basis for meeting, and often different expectations of the results... .

There is a genuine and sometimes profound nonscholarly dialogue in which those of different religions communicate, in which they open their hearts and minds to one another and share their convictions and their aspirations. Scholarly dialogue, or the scholarly assistance for dialogue, is not superior to nonscholarly dialogue, but it is different. It tries to take seriously the tradition that the living contemporary partner in dialogue holds sacred, which means to be in dialogue with the great voices and also the pervasive murmur of the lesser voices of that tradition. I am speaking of what can be a lifetime vocation, though it can also be a shorter-term and less-consuming endeavour. It is in any event a constant back-and-forth between one's own faith with all its intellectual and emotional expression, and at least one other religious tradition.

To what extent it can be such an inner conversation with all other religious traditions it is hard to say. There are some mental and spiritual giants who may attempt such a task. I find it hard myself to do more than keep in conversation with one strand of the Hindu tradition, the devotion to the Lord Vishnu and his divine consort Lakshmi. The negative view of the theistic tradition toward atheistic Jains and Buddhists, as well as toward the monistic Hindu school of Sankara, has certainly made it harder for me to converse at the same time with these other traditions. (pp. 193–5)

John Carman, 'An Ecumenical Protestant Perspective' in Gerald H. Anderson and Thomas F. Stransky (eds), *Christ's Lordship and Religious Pluralism* (Maryknoll, NY: Orbis, 1981).

Teilhard de Chardin

In 'The Mystical Milieu' the Catholic theologian Teilhard de Chardin argues that God's presence infuses all creation – his conception of the universe as an evolutionary process toward higher levels of consciousness offers a bridge between Christian thought and other religious faiths.

We have seen the mystical milieu gradually develop and assume a form at once divine and human. At first, we might have mistaken it for a mere projection of our emotions, their excess flowing out over the world and appearing to animate it.

Soon, however, its autonomy became as apparent as a strange and supremely desirable Omnipresence. This universal presence began by drawing into itself all consistence and all energy. Later, embodied in a great wind of purification and conquest that excites man at every stage in his history, it drew us into itself – so fully as to assimilate us to its own nature.

Sometimes, when I scrutinize the world very closely ... I [see] a shadow floating, as though it were the wraith of a universal soul seeking to be born. What name can we give to this mysterious Entity, who is in some small way our own handiwork, with whom, eminently, we can enter into communion, and who is some part of ourselves, yet who masters us, has need of us in order to exist, and at the same time, dominates us with the full force of his absolute Being?

I can feel it: He has a name and a face, but he alone can reveal his face and pronounce his name: Jesus! ...

Together with all the beings around me, I felt that I was caught up in a higher movement that was stirring together all the elements of the universe and grouping them in a new order. When it was given to me to see where the dazzling trail of particular beauties and partial harmonies was leading, I recognized that it was all coming to centre on a single point, on a Person: your Person: Jesus!...

In that superabundant unity that Person possessed the virtue of each one of the lower mystical circles. His presence impregnated and sustained all things. His power animated all energy. His mastering ate into every other life, to assimilate it to himself. Thus, Lord, I understood that it was impossible to live without ever emerging from you, without ever ceasing to be buried in You, the Ocean of Life, that life that penetrates and quickens us. Since first, Lord, you said, 'This is my body', not only the bread of the altar but (to some degree) everything in the universe that nourishes the soul for the life of Spirit and Grace has become yours and has become divine – it is divinized, divinizing and divinizable. Every presence makes me feel that you are near me; every touch is the touch of your hand; every necessity transmits to a pulsation of your will. And so true is this, that everything around me that is essential and enduring has become for me the dominance and, in some way, the substance of your heart: Jesus!

That is why it is impossible ... for any man who has acquired even the smallest understanding of you to look on your face without seeing in it the radiance of every reality and every goodness. In the mystery of your mystical body – your cosmic body – you sought to feel the echo of every joy and every feat that moves each single one of all the countless cells that make up mankind. And correspondingly, we cannot contemplate you and adhere to you without your Being, for all its supreme multiplicity, transmuting itself as we grasp into the restructured Multitude of all that you love upon earth: Jesus. ...

When I think of you, Lord, I cannot say whether it is in this place that I find you more or in that place – whether you are to me Friend or Strength or Matter – whether I am contemplating you or whether I am suffering – whether I rue my faults or find union – whether it is you I love or the whole sum of others. Every affection, every desire, every possession, every light, every depth, every harmony and every ardour glitters with equal brilliance at one and the same time in the inexpressible Relationship that is being set up between me and you: Jesus! (pp. 570–1)

Teilhard de Chardin, 'The Mystical Milieu' in *Writings in Time of War,* (San Francisco, CA: Harper & Row, 1968), republished in H. Egan, *An Anthology of Christian Mysticism* (Collegeville, MN: Pueblo, 1991).

Ellen Zubrack Charry

The Jewish scholar Ellen Zubrack Charry received a Ph.D. from Temple University and has served as Associate Program Director of the National Conference of Christians and Jews. In 'A Step Toward "Ecumenical Esperanto!"', she argues that those engaged in dialogue should search for a common anthropological foundation among the world's religions.

One possible foundation for an ecumenical theology might be developed by identifying threads of a common theological anthropology among the world's religious traditions and worldviews. The task of identifying an ecumenical theological anthropology is an awesome one: different traditions are not always sympathetic to one another's questions about, let alone answers to, the basic issues of human life and death.

For example, at the risk of oversimplification, Hindus are concerned to escape from the ceaseless cycle of rebirth and redeath, whereas Christians have been concerned to achieve eternal life. Marxists are concerned with transformation of the material world, whereas some Buddhists are concerned with transformation within themselves in order to let go of the world. Protestants maintain that humans are unable to save themselves, being wholly dependent upon God's grace, whereas Muslims believe that one earns one's salvation by obedience to divine law. Additionally, and this is particularly evident in the USA at the moment, some religious persons see religious faith as crucial to preserving stability in the world, and productivity and morality at home, whereas nonreligious persons see religious faith as a source of division and prejudice among human beings, and await the day when religion will wither away. Finally, there are those who cling to this world and press for accommodation among opponents, and those who see the world passing away in any case, and so are not as concerned with the resolution of ancient or modern religio-political conflicts.

Nevertheless, and acknowledging the inevitability of oversimplification, what follows is a proposal for beginning to identify an ecumenical anthropology by examining how several traditions might assess the human condition. The audacity of this project is at once overwhelming and unavoidable. It is an ecumenical experiment in a field known for a paucity of such attempts. I shall attempt to draw a macrosketch of some of the world's religions and ideologies to see if there might be threads of a common anthropology. The traditions included in this macrosketch are Buddhism (primarily Mahayana), Christianity (primarily Western), existentialism (primarily the modern nontheistic West European school of thought), Hinduism (primarily the nondualism of the school of Sankara), Islam (primarily the nonmystical movements in Islamic thought), feminism and black theology, Judaism, and the thought of Karl Marx and liberation theology.

A further caveat is in order before proceeding. It has often been maintained that many of the world's traditions are exclusive, so that one cannot be, say, a Christian and Muslim simultaneously, but this generalization is beginning to give way to a more complex picture. Today we have many Christian Marxists, and many existentialist Christians. There is also strong evidence of the blending of Christianity and Buddhism in both directions and even the development of Christian Judaism, a phenomenon thought to be a contradiction in terms since the middle of the second century CE. All this is to say that opening one's ears to listen to other persons' questions about and assessments of the human predicament or of ultimate reality involves genuine risk, including the risk that one will be moved to redefine one's ancestral home, or leave it altogether. (pp. 219–20)

All these traditions assess the human condition as problematic, and everyone in pain seeks relief. All these traditions provide an analysis of the problem and propose a solution that applies to every human being. Overwhelmingly the evidence of the ages is that human beings are not happy with their lot. All these traditions conclude that something is wrong that should and can be made right... .

It seems from this brief sketch that, with a few important exceptions, far from being deeply divided, the traditions examined here suggest that an ecumenical anthropology could be identified. The traditions by and large agree that human beings are in pain and that release from pain defined in multiple ways is available with sufficient trust or faith, attention, study, devotion, ritual, prayer, obedience, work, meditation, political action, or – if I might add a personal note – just plain luck. Adherents of all these traditions have, over the course of centuries and in many cases millennia, devised prescriptions for dealing with the problems. (pp. 222–3)

Ellen Zubrack Charry, 'A Step Toward "Ecumenical Esperanto"', in Leonard Swidler (ed.), *Toward a Universal Theology of Religion* (Maryknoll, NY: Orbis, 1987).

John Cobb

Professor at the School of Theology at Claremont, John Cobb argues in Beyond Dialogue *that Christian triumphalism should be superseded by a new sympathetic approach to other religions.*

An inescapable feature of Christian self-understanding is the recognition that we share the world with people of other traditions. This was very apparent indeed during the first centuries of the Christian movement, and it has forced itself upon Christian attention again in the past two centuries.

The most common Christian response to this recognition has been to assume that those who are different from us are for that reason inferior. They lack the saving truth we possess and, accordingly, it is our task to convert them.... .

We have believed that there is no name under heaven by which people can be saved other than that of Jesus Christ. Because of that conviction we have done all we could to bring others to faith in him. Now we find that our achievements have been in many ways ambiguous. Does that mean that we were wrong in our belief in the universal and exclusive salvific power of Jesus Christ? If so, what is the theological meaning and reality of Jesus Christ? Should we abandon all efforts to proclaim him to those who do not now believe? Or should we distinguish between those who have satisfactory Ways of salvation through other saviours and those who are yet in need of such a Way? If so, how?...

To hear in an authentic way the truth which the other has to teach us is to be transformed by that truth. Once we have heard the truth of Islam, our Christian witness cannot remain what it was. And in our day only those Christians who have really heard that truth can deserve a serious hearing from Muslims. Further, only those Christians who have been transformed by appropriation of the universal truth found in other religious Ways can proclaim the universal truth of Jesus Christ without a false imperialism. It will be in the process of multiple transformations through and beyond multiple dialogue that the Christian movement as a whole will gain an adequate understanding of the universal truth of Jesus Christ on a new and more faithful level... .

Prior knowledge of the religious tradition from which the other speaks is beneficial to dialogue. But it is a mistake to demand too much here. If only those Christians who are scholars in the field of Islamics take part in dialogue with Muslims, the deeper purposes of dialogue are unlikely to be realized. Too often in this country the dialogue with representatives of other traditions has been in this way handed over to historians of religion, many of whom are not committed to the Christian faith and its fresh articulation. Dialogue with Buddhism is not primarily the province of Buddhologists but rather of Christian theologians who are, for the most part, but little informed about the Buddhist traditions.

The dialogue with Buddhists will, of course, have failed if Christian theologians who take part in it are not stimulated thereby to learn from the work of Buddhologists. They must understand enough to see that no dialogue partners can possibly speak for all the segments of Buddhism any more than any Christian theologian can speak for all branches of Christianity. But the purpose of dialogue, in distinction from scholarship, is to encounter living representatives of an alien religious Way – individuals who find the Way adequate and salvific but who are also involved in the continuing process of understanding it in an ever-changing situation. In an important sense the texts studied by the scholars remain static, whereas in a successful dialogue both partners are engaged in fresh thinking... . (pp. vii–xi)

We not only need to be open to truth wherever we can find it and engage in the hard work of incorporating it into our theology, we also need to witness to the truth with which we have been entrusted through our own history. We know that too often in the past we have confused accidental cultural accretions with that truth and have idolatrously identified that truth with our own opinions. We also know that we have usually spoken without listening. For all this we must repent. But to repent of past mistakes does not entail abandoning our witness. It means learning to witness aright. And the goal of that witness is to lead the other to attend to what we believe to be truth and to be transformed by it... .

We cannot engage in true evangelism today except as we first listen and learn and transform ourselves in light of what we have learned. But when we have been attentive to the ambiguities in the situation of others, when we have been transformed by the truth they can teach us, then it is also time to try to show them how faith in Jesus Christ can creatively transform their traditions in such a way as to free them from bondage. (pp. 140–1)

John Cobb, *Beyond Dialogue* (Philadelphia: Fortress Press, 1982).

Dan Cohn-Sherbok

Professor of Judaism at the University of Wales, Dan Cohn-Sherbok argues in Judaism and Other Faiths *that Judaism must be open to the world's religious traditions. In his opinion, there is no way of determining which, if any, doctrines are true within any religious system.*

Given the largely tolerant attitude of Judaism to other faiths, should Jews move beyond such inclusivism?... The inclusivist position suffers from serious theological defects: Inclusivists appear to affirm two incompatible convictions – the belief in God's universal concern and the conviction that he has definitively revealed himself to a particular group. Arguably such a position is internally incoherent: if God is truly concerned with the fate of all humanity, he would not have disclosed himself fully and finally to a particular people allowing the rest of humanity to wallow in darkness and ignorance. Rather what is required today is an even more open approach to the world's religions. To use the model of the universe of faiths formulated by the Protestant theologian John Hick, a Copernican Revolution is now required in our understanding of religion. In the past even the most liberal Jewish thinkers retained the conviction that Judaism contains the fullest disclosure; while recognizing the inherent value of other religions – particularly Christianity – they were convinced that Judaism is humanity's future hope. These Jewish thinkers were like scientists who previously endorsed a Ptolemaic view of the universe in which the earth is at the centre.

In the modern world however where Jews continually come into contact with adherents of other religious traditions, it is difficult to sustain such a narrow vision. Instead a Copernican Revolution is currently required in our understanding of the universe of faiths. Instead of placing Judaism at the centre of the world's religions, a theocentric model should be adopted – such a transformation demands a paradigm shift from a Judeo-centric to a theo-centric conception of religious history. On this basis, the world's religions should be understood as different human responses to the one divine reality. In previous ages religions conceived of this one reality either theistically (as a personal deity) or non-theistically (as non-personal), but such differences were in essence the result of historical, cultural or psychological influences... .

On this view there is one ultimate Reality behind all religious expressions. To use kabbalistic terminology, the Godhead is the *Ayn Sof* – the Infinite beyond human comprehension. The Godhead is the eternal Reality which provides the inspiration for all religions including Judaism. This ultimate Reality is interpreted in a variety of different modes, and these different explanations of the one Reality have inevitably given rise to a variety of differing and competing conceptions... .

Such a view of the Divine in relation to the world's religions can be represented ... by the image of alternative paths ascending a single mountain – each route symbolizes a particular religion with divine Reality floating like a cloud above the mountain top.

The routes of these faith communities are all different, yet at various points they intersect: these intersections should be understood as those areas where religious conceptions within the differing traditions complement one another. Thus as pilgrims of different faiths ascend to the summit, they will encounter parallels with their own traditions. But the divine Reality they all pursue is in the end unattainable by these finite quests. As the Infinite, it is unknowable and incomprehensible. It is the cloud of unknowing.

Such a pluralistic model implies that conceptions of the Divine in the world's religions are ultimately human images – they represent the myriad ways of approaching the one indescribably divine Reality. (pp. 157–9)

The formulation of a Jewish global, interreligious theology hinges on two major preconditions. First, Jewish theologians must learn about other faiths than their own ... Jewish thinkers ... must enter into the subjectivity of other traditions and bring the resulting insights to bear on their own religious understanding: such theological reflection calls for a multi-dimensional, cross-cultural, interreligious approach in which all religions are conceived as interdependently significant. Given the quest for a global perspective, Jewish pluralists must insist that the theological endeavour occurs in a trans-religious context. This enterprise calls for a religious encounter in which Jews confront others who hold totally different truth-claims – such individuals can help Jewish thinkers to discover their own presuppositions and underlying principles. In this process the Jewish partner should be able to recognize the limitations of his own tradition, and as a result make a conscious effort to discover common ground with other faiths. Such an interchange is vital to the elaboration of a multi-dimensional theological outlook. (p. 177)

Dan Cohn-Sherbok, *Judaism and Other Faiths* (London: Macmillan, 1994).

Demetrios J. Constanteolos

Born in Greece, Demetrios Constanteolos was ordained a Greek Orthodox priest and has served as Professor at Stockton State College, Pomona, New Jersey. In 'An Orthodox Perspective', he contends that Christ is not limited by space or time, and that his spirit is present in human history.

How does one anticipate the relations of the Orthodox with other faiths in the context of religious pluralism? Is there any basis to expect institutional realignments in the coming years? In order to answer these questions, we need, once again, to see the Orthodox Church in history, within the Christian *ecumene* as well as within a religiously plural world.

The Orthodox have always emphasized the continuity of God's revealing truth before as well as after the incarnation of the Logos. The living God 'in past generations allowed all the nations to walk in their own ways; yet he did not leave himself without witness' (Acts 14:16–17), and 'what can be known about God was known to them, because God revealed it to them. Ever since the creation of the world his invisible nature, namely, his external power and deity, has been clearly perceived in the things that have been made' (Rom. 1:18–19). On the other hand, Pentecost is an ongoing event. The Holy Spirit continues to live in the church, to guide it to new interpretations and to new revelations. It is the same Spirit who created, who spoke through the prophets, who guided the apostles, and in whom we live, move, and have our existence (Acts 17:28).

Christianity's claim to be inherently exclusive of other religions was an inheritance from its Hebraic roots. But as early as the apostolic age Christianity became rooted in the Hellenic tradition as well. The tension between the Hebraic and the Hellenic elements were constant in early Christianity. There is little doubt, however, that the future of Christianity was shaped not by people like Tatian and Tertullian, who rejected what the Orthodox call natural revelation, the truth of God outside the Old Testament, but by Justin, Clement and Origen of Alexandria, Synesios of Cyrene, Basil the Great and the other Cappadocians, who achieved a synthesis between indirect, or natural, revelation, and direct – the self-disclosure of God in Christ. For the early church, Christ was the point of convergence between the Jewish Messiah and the Logos of the Greeks... .

The Hebraic and Hellenic tensions in early Christianity gave rise to two different attitudes toward the religious truths of the outside world, as evidenced by the Bible itself, as well as in early Christian literature. In his Areopagus speech, Saint Paul implied that the Athenians who worshipped the unknown God were actually crypto-Christians, Christians without knowing it. The opening words of John's Gospel, that in the beginning was the beloved Logos of the Greeks, prepared the way for the early church to take a positive attitude toward nonbiblical truth. Many acknowledge that there was more divine truth in Socrates' teachings than in some Old Testament books... .

Apologists, ecclesiastical writers and church fathers of the Christian East adopted Saint Paul's attitude toward nonbiblical truth as expressed in the seventeenth chapter of Acts as well as in his epistle to the Romans to such an extent that Orthodox Christianity developed a more positive attitude toward non-Christian religions. With very few exceptions, among them Augustine, the Christian West was more influenced by Old Testament attitudes and by people like Tertullian, and developed not only an exclusiveness like that of the Old Testament but also a militancy against dissenters and non-Christians... .

In the history of Christianity much emphasis has been placed on the partial Abrahamic covenant, whereas the universal or cosmic covenant that God made with Noah has been overlooked. It is on the basis of this covenant that a fruitful dialogue can be conducted between Christians and non-Christians. The Greek Fathers recognized that God was revealing his truth outside biblical revelation... .

The Orthodox emphasize their sense of divine presence, of individual saintliness within the world, the communion of God's people across both space and time, of *koinonia*, or community, in God's bosom. This in no way denies Christ's claim that he is 'the Way, the Truth, and the Life'. But Christ is not limited by space or time; his Spirit lives, speaks, and acts in human history everywhere, often through mysterious and humanly unintelligible ways. (pp. 184–8)

Demetrios J. Constanteolos, 'An Orthodox Perspective' in Gerald H. Anderson and Thomas F. Stransky (eds), *Christ's Lordship and Religious Pluralism* (Maryknoll, NY: Orbis, 1981).

Harvey Cox

Harvey Cox, Professor of Divinity at Harvard University, received a BA from the University of Pennsylvania, a BD from Yale Divinity School, and a Ph.D. from Harvard University. The author of numerous books, he emphasizes the need to balance the universal with the particular in dialogue between Christians and members of other faiths.

I believe that the most mettlesome dilemma hindering interreligious dialogues is the very ancient one of how to balance the universal and the particular. Every world faith has both. Each nourishes in rite and sage its own unique and highly particular vision. Maybe it is the message of the one true God delivered without blemish to the Prophet. Or it is the fathomless Brahman from which all that is and all that is not come and return. Or the faithful Son of God dying on the cross. Or the supreme moment when enlightenment comes to the patient figure seated under the Bo tree. Or the bestowal of the life-giving gift of Torah on a chosen people. Whatever it is, the particular hub defines the centre around which each world faith rotates, endowing it season after season and century after century with its characteristic ethos.

At the same time every world faith, if it is truly a world faith and not a local *cultus*, also generates a universal vision. Brahman embraces all ages, each drop of water and every saviour. The Koran names a God who created all people equal and who decrees that a unified human family should mirror his sublime unity. The dying Christ is raised to life by a God who favours the outcasts and the heartbroken and who summons all tribes and tongues into an inclusive community of service and praise. The Bodhisatva compassionately refuses to enter nirvana until every sentient being can enter with him.

Thus each world faith has both its axis and its spokes, its sharply etched focus and its ambient circumference. Further, it is the mark of a truly world faith that these two dimensions are not only held together: they strengthen and reinforce each other. Somewhere, somehow, all that now seems fragmented and contradictory, all that appears tragic or inexplicable, is gathered into a single mystery of meaning and value.

The crisis in the current state of interfaith dialogue can be stated simply: the universal and the particular poles have come unhinged. Faced with a world in which some form of encounter with other faiths can no longer be avoided, the ancient religious traditions are breaking into increasingly bitter wings. Those who glimpse the universal dimension advocate dialogue and mutuality. They search out what is common and that which unites. Those who emphasize the particular often shun dialogue and excoriate their fellow believers who engage in it more fiercely than they condemn outsiders. This ugly chasm, running through all religions, gives rise to a 'worst-possible' scenario one might envision if the current trend persists.... .

But we need both poles. I count myself as one of the universalists. Yet sometimes as I have sat in genteel – or even mildly acrimonious – gatherings of urbane representatives of different faith traditions ... my mind has strayed from the conference room out to those jagged corners of the world where other confessors of these same faiths are killing or proselytizing – or just frigidly ignoring – each other. I have wondered at such moments whether the 'dialogue' has not become a tedious exercise in preaching to the converted and I have secretly wished to bring some of those enthusiasts in.... .

At the same time I fully believe that without the large-hearted vision of the universal that the interfaith conversation incarnates, particularism can deteriorate into fanaticism. And in our present overarmed world, zealotry can easily hasten the moment when everything ends with a bang. So we are left with a paradox. Without the universal pole, there would be no dialogue at all. But without the particular, the dialogue dissipates its source of primal energy. Without the Cross or the Koran or the Bo tree, the religions that were called into being by these sacred realities would atrophy and along with them the inclusive visions they spawned would fade away too.... . It seems too formulaic simply to say that the universalists and the particularists need each other, especially since they seldom think they do. Still, I believe they do.... . (pp. 2–4)

The ... way the Jesus of the Gospels helps facilitate interreligious encounter is that he teaches us to expect to find God already present in the 'other', including the one with whom we are in dialogue, no matter how strange or unfamiliar that other's ideas or religious practices may seem. Christ meets us in and through the stranger. I have always known that this is true 'in principle', but by participating in the dialogue I have learned it is also true in reality. (pp. 16–17)

Harvey Cox, *Many Mansions: A Christian's Encounter with Other Faiths* (Boston, MA: Beacon and London: Collins, 1988).

Kenneth Cracknell

Kenneth Cracknell has served as Director of Global Studies and Research Professor in Theology at Texas Christian University. In Towards a New Relationship: Christians and People of Other Faiths, *he argues that there must be a new christological under-standing of God's working within other communities.*

The canonical Scriptures taken as a whole are not exclusivist in their under-standing of God's activity in this world. This in itself is a great step forward. But nevertheless the basic question for the Christian remains. For however telling the evidence is for biblical understanding of God's activity beyond the boundaries of historic Israel and the new Christian community, the question that confronts us has to do with the specific activity of God in Christ. For the Christian community lives from its faith that the Word has become flesh, and that in Jesus we have beheld his glory, 'glory as of the only Son from the Father' (John 1:14). In a world of religious pluralism our questions have primarily to do with the uniqueness and finality of the revelation of God in Jesus of Nazareth. We confess this man to be the Christ, the Anointed of God. Therefore the christological question is unavoidable, and why should we want to avoid it? It belongs to the heart of Christian faith. Without an assertion of once-and-for-allness and a declaration of its cosmic implications, the Christian faith must change both its name and its nature. So we must tackle the issues of faithfulness in a religiously plural world as they come to us in the word of such often-cited verses as John 14:6: 'no man comes to the Father but by me'; Acts 4:12: 'there is no salvation in anyone else, for there is no other name by which we may be saved'; John 3:18: 'he who does not believe in me is condemned already, because he has not believed in the name of the only Son of God'. We must take head on the issues that are raised by such texts. As believing Christians we have to work out our theologies of religion and interfaith dialogue against this background.

I who believe that in Jesus' teaching there is a message 'like no other man', that in his death there are cosmic significances, and that because of his resurrection there is indeed a new creation, must search for a christology that is inclusive rather than exclusive. I need a way of seeing that what I believe about Jesus opens doors rather than shuts them, pulls down barriers between people rather than builds them higher, and sets us free to enter into marvellous new relationships with just that sense of expectation and yet with just as much vulnerability as Jesus himself demonstrated when he walked the paths of Galilee and Samaria and the streets of Jerusalem. Christology must affirm both our conviction that the symbols of resurrection and ascension remain central to Christian faith and at the same time that goodness and grace, truth and sanctity are to be found in individuals and communities of other than Christian faith... .

I write as a believing Christian first of all to my fellow believers. But I know full well that men and women of other convictions will be looking over our shoulders to see what is being said or implied about them. Scores and scores of them will be my personal friends: Jews, Muslims, Hindus, Buddhists, Sikhs, Baha'is, followers of new religious movements as well as some who would not call themselves religious at all. I hope two things will come to them as they read. First of all, that they may see one Christian wrestling with an issue that confronts all people everywhere in every tradition. As I wonder how I am to remain faithful to Christ and yet make sense of the faith of other people, so, for example, a devout Hindu or Muslim must also have a conceptual framework which makes sense of the faith of those who are not Muslims or Hindus, Jews or Buddhists. They, too ... must 'aspire to a statement of God and his diverse involvements with humankind'. Secondly, I hope that they will see ... the universal implications of what I am saying though this be couched in Christian terms. (pp. 5–6)

Our whole intention in setting out the visions of a pluralist religious eschatology and especially an inclusivist christology is to make it possible for Christians to behave with a new freedom in the light of their understanding of Jesus Christ. We have argued that such an openness towards others is part of the obedience of faith in one whom we confess to be the Way, the Truth and the Life... . Our participation as Christians in interfaith encounter will depend upon an understanding of God's purposes which allows us to be both open and honest, vulnerable and yet committed, and, in the words of the fourth Gospel, 'to do the truth' in our time. (p. 110)

Kenneth Cracknell, *Towards a New Relationship: Christians and People of Other Faiths* (London: Epworth, 1986).

Kenneth Cragg

Kenneth Cragg, formerly Assistant Bishop in the Jerusalem Archbishopric, argues in
The Christian and Other Religions *for Christians to assess their beliefs in the light of religious dialogue.*

The questions deepen if we compile another list – Buddha, Christ, Krishna, Muhammad, Zoroaster. The last, perhaps, is only history. But the others are in actual catalogue with 'the prince of glory' of our devotion, with 'the Lord from heaven' of our theology. How then should faith in him relate to the pluralism of religious man? What should be our measure of these alternative figures in the history and the making of the world's religions? They are certainly alternative in the considerable sense that they are other guides than ours to life and meaning, though the faiths that cluster round them have not, for the most part, been options freely chosen out of a feasible neutrality, but rather denominators of birth and culture, of language and geography.

Our Christian co-existence with them in the contemporary world raises sharp questions both for theology and for pastoral activity. Other religions are no longer – if they ever were – remote and academic factors in a world-picture which the ordinary Christian could ignore. In the day of Asian and African nationhood they have a living, if indeterminate, role in world affairs. They belong with massive and multiplying populations of mankind. Further, their adherents are in our own midst, immigrant and other communities side by side with us in local residence, sharing our schools, needing our facilities, circulating among us. These bring the problems of interreligon – if we may so speak – right into the life and thinking of our parishes.... .

Exposition of Buddhist, Hindu, Muslim, or other doctrines is seen as contributory to exploring the dimensions of Christian obligation. The question: What do they teach? is not isolated from the kindred issue: How do we, how may we, respond?

Correspondingly, the relevant interior Christian themes of finality, authority, truth, mission and ministry, are not to be handled only from within. In every case they must be set in the active sphere of attention to the other, of mutual openness and reckoning. Abstract comparison or theological theory alone, whether dogmatic or sentimental, are no adequate relation to what is involved. The art of loyalty and the art of relationship must be understood, and practised, as complementary.... . (pp. xi–xii)

Beyond tolerance – what? Our discussion thus far has been via people, theologians, writers, with only occasional reference, as they might choose, to the New Testament. It is fair to ask what light its text should throw upon our problems. But will it be by bare citation, whether pointing, as the passages admit, in the direction of inclusive, or of exclusive conclusions. We may cite Peter, addressing the rulers of the people in Acts 4:12, and saying 'Neither is there salvation in any other', and assume that this is a verdict which answers all questions.... . Or there is the word of Jesus that 'no man cometh to the Father but by me' (John 14:6). Truly we come to the Father, in experience and in language, through the Son. But is this to say that no man, otherwise, comes to the Creator, to the Lord, as indeed did Abraham and the psalmist?

Or is the Logos of John 1:9, so beloved of the inclusivists, 'coming into the world' to enlighten every man receiving it? Or does the participle belong to every man, so that 'entering the world' means somehow the Logos light by birth? Or again, Paul at Athens – are we to argue from an unfinished speech a total philosophy of paganism as a kind of Christianity not yet knowing the name, or did the apostle go back on his words in writing soon after to the Corinthians?...

Even the scantiest review of recent theology of religions, like the foregoing, makes it plain that the task has still a long way to go. We must live with some bewilderment and maybe some aberrations. Continuity and discontinuity, the anonymous and the realized, waiting and fulfilment, nature and grace, are a few of the formulae to take us beyond tolerance into some rationale of Christ and the plural religions. Such a rationale, however, concluded – if concluded it can ever properly be – remains discursive and conceptual. What finally matters is the relationships achieved in the actual, in the personal and the social, in the Spirit. (pp. 79–81)

Kenneth Cragg, *The Christian and Other Religions* (London: Mowbray, 1977).

Don Cupitt

Formerly Lecturer in Divinity and Dean of Emmanuel College, Cambridge, the Christian theologian Don Cupitt, who adopts a non-realist interpretation of the Christian faith in which the literal truth of religious belief is denied, argues in 'Identity versus Globalization' that interfaith dialogue is dominated by traditionalists. In his view, this is unfortunate since there must now be an awareness of the global context of interfaith encounter.

Is it not curious that the people who are chosen to represent us in the ecumenical and interfaith conversations always turn out to be very cautious and conservative characters who think like lawyers? In a world in which tradition is dying, we seem to feel safest when we are represented by extreme traditionalists. We like to be represented by people who are utterly unrepresentative of us. It is as if we very much want them to go on defending, on our behalf, positions that we no longer hold ourselves.

What then has happened? In the earliest times – or so we were told – religion was monocultural and henotheistic. Each people or *ethne* had their own language, their own sacred territory and their own god. Identities were clear-cut to such an extent that if you were to live in another territory, amongst other people, those new people become your people and their god your god (see Ruth 1:15f.; 1 Samuel 26:19 etc.). The notion that religion is – or at least ideally should be – strictly ethnic and territorial has survived to this day. People still use terms like Christendom and Islam in a territorial way, and speak of lands like France and Italy as 'Roman Catholic countries'... .

Our thinking about true religion and territoriality has become oddly confused. For more than one-and-a-half millennia the Jews were in effect the principal and most obvious example of an ancient faith that had lost its own territory and now survived within Christendom, within Islam, and elsewhere in encapsulated form. People identified themselves as Jews, and were identified, in every other way except through their possession of their own holy land. Your Jewishness was conveyed to you through genealogy, your community-membership, your language, scriptures, customs and cultural tradition: but territory – no. The Jews were often regarded as a dispersed, homeless, fugitive people, living in a state of what seemed permanent diaspora, and homelessness. The state of being exiled from one's proper sacred territory seemed pitiable. Then came the Restoration, the founding of the state of Israel, and a seemingly wonderful fulfilment of prophecy. But, fifty years later, not all Jews have wished to return, and visitors to Israel are astonished to find what a secular society it is, and how little regard is paid to the Torah. Can Judaism not survive the fulfilment of its own hopes? Is the recovered possession of one's own holy land somehow a religiously bad thing? In countries like the United States there has for some time been anxiety that the Jews in diaspora may disappear within half a century by marrying out, and by complete assimilation into the host culture. But now we find that a worse danger threatens in the opposite direction: the return to Israel fulfils Judaism – and then eclipses it, as all the precious old religious values of Judaism disappear into militant nationalist politics.

Judaism then seems to be caught between Scylla and Charybdis. In America, and in 'the West' generally, it threatens to become just one more strand in the new globalized world-historical culture, like Platonism. It will become simply part of the universal syllabus, part of everybody's heritage, and will no longer be, nor need to be, embodied in a distinct visible human society. At the opposite extreme, Judaism also disappears in Israel. The ancient dream of monoethnic theocratic society cannot be realized in the modern world except by turning religious values into (rather extreme) political ones.

Islam is, of course, nowadays caught in just the same dilemma; and so is Christianity. The ideal of 'a Christian country' is fading, disappearing. In Western society at large, 'the Christian tradition' has become just one more strand in everybody's cultural heritage. What survives of 'the Church' is so drastically reduced that it no longer has any special claim to, or expertise in, the old 'great' tradition. In which case, conversations between officially nominated teams of Jewish and Christian representatives will be mainly exercises in denial. They will be conducted as if old-style distinct, homogeneous faith communities, in which traditional religious values are preserved intact, still exist – which is not the case, in the world where all of us alike are 'mediatized', immersed in the new media culture. And so long as we go on clinging to the memory of our lost closed worlds, for so long we will be failing to discuss the prospect that faces us all alike – both people who are ancestrally Jewish, and people who are ancestrally Christian – in the new globalized world-culture. At our interfaith conversations we try to reassure ourselves that we really are still different from each other and do still possess our own distinct 'identities'. But the reality is that the process of world-cultural assimilation is swallowing us both up. We are becoming more and more alike. All distinct ethnic and religious identities, of the old kind that we are so desperately nostalgic for, are rapidly vanishing. (pp. 287–90)

Don Cupitt, 'Identity versus Globalization', in Dan Cohn-Sherbok (ed.), *The Future of Jewish–Christian Dialogue* (Lewiston, NY: Edwin Mellen, 1999).

D

Dalai Lama (Tenzin Gyatso)

The Tibetan Dalai Lama, born in 1935, has lived in India since 1959. In '"Religious Harmony" and Extracts from the Bodhgaya Interviews', he states that all religions further human compassion and alleviate human suffering.

All of the different religious faiths, despite their philosophical differences, have a similar objective. Every religion emphasizes human improvement, love, respect for others, sharing other people's suffering. On these lines every religion has more or less the same viewpoint and the same goal.

Those faiths which emphasize Almighty God and faith in and love of God have as their purpose the fulfilment of God's intentions. Seeing us all as creations of and followers of one God, they teach that we should cherish and help each other. The very purpose of faithful belief in God is to accomplish his wishes, the essence of which is to cherish, respect, love and give service to our fellow humans.

Such an essential purpose of other religions is similarly to promote such beneficial feelings and actions. I strongly feel that from this viewpoint a central purpose of all the different philosophical explanations is the same. Through the various religious systems, followers are assuming a salutary attitude toward their fellow humans – our brothers and sisters – and implementing this good motivation in the service of human society. This has been demonstrated by a great many believers in Christianity through history; many have sacrificed their lives for the benefit of humankind....

Although in every religion there is an emphasis on compassion and love, from the viewpoint of philosophy, of course, there are differences, and that is all right. Philosophical teachings are not the end, not the aim, not what you serve. The aim is to help and benefit others, and philosophical teachings to support those ideas are valuable. If we go into the differences in philosophy and argue with and criticize each other, it is useless. There will be endless argument; the result will mainly be that we irritate each other – accomplishing nothing. Better to look at the purpose of the philosophies and to see what is shared – an emphasis on love, compassion and respect for a higher force.... (pp. 163–4)

If we view the world's religions from the widest possible viewpoint and examine their ultimate goal, we find that all of the major world religions, whether

Christianity or Islam, Hinduism or Buddhism, are directed to the achievement of permanent human happiness. They are all directed toward that goal. All religions emphasize the fact that the true follower must be honest and gentle, in other words, that a truly religious person must always strive to be a better human being. To this end, the different world religions teach different doctrines which will help transform the person. In this regard, all religions are the same, there is no conflict. This is something we must emphasize. We must consider the question of religious diversity from this viewpoint. And when we do, we find no conflict.

Now from the philosophical point of view, the theory that God is the creator, is almighty and permanent, is in contradiction to the Buddhist teachings. From this point of view there is disagreement. For Buddhists, the universe has no first cause and hence no creator, nor can there be such a thing as a permanent, primordially pure being. So, of course, doctrinally, there is conflict. The views are opposite to one another. But if we consider the purpose of these different philosophies, then we see that they are the same. This is my belief... .

The variety of the different world religious philosophies is a very useful and beautiful thing. For certain people, the idea of God as creator of everything depending on his will is beneficial and soothing, and so for that person such a doctrine is worthwhile. For someone else, the idea that there is no creator, that ultimately one is oneself the creator – in that everything depends on oneself – is more appropriate. For certain people, it may be a more effective method of spiritual growth, it may be more beneficial. For such persons, this idea is better and for the other type of person, the other idea is more suitable... . (pp. 167–8)

Dalai Lama, '"Religious Harmony" and Extracts from the Bodhgaya Interviews', in Paul J. Griffiths (ed.), *Christianity Through Non-Christian Eyes* (Maryknoll, NY: Orbis, 1990).

Gavin D'Costa

Reader in Theology at the University of Bristol, Gavin D'Costa, in The Meeting of Religions and the Trinity, *argues that the Trinity offers a basis for religious encounter between members of the world's religions.*

First, it is clear from our exegesis that all talk of the Spirit is only properly related to the ecclesial set of events in which the church's discernment of the Spirit actually generates new forms of practice and articulation in its non-identical repetition and reception of Christ's gift of redeeming love. This means that we must be extremely reticent about any abstract talk of the 'Spirit in other religions', for this bears little Johannine rhetorical sense. If it is to bear any Johannine sense, then it can only be generated in the context of specific Christian engagements with non-Christian cultures and practices, for the claim that the Spirit is at work in the world can only be part of the church's discernment (not ownership) of the hidden depths of God's trinitarian action of love, struggling to be born into creation and culture... .

Second, John helps us to make clear from the outset that a bogus question has haunted much of the contemporary discussion on other religions regarding whether 'revelation' takes place within the religions of the world. For John, the resurrection means that the question of new, different, and alternative 'revelations' is a non-question, for it posits a false understanding of time and history. All creation, all time and history, all the irreducible particularities of each person, are now taken up into the new creation inaugurated by Jesus... .

Third, this 'observing' the likeness of Jesus in others is precisely part of what it also means to say that the Holy Spirit is present in the world, in the 'Other', and requires an ecclesial act of discernment, as it is here that the possible use of 'Christ' language takes shape. The Spirit in the church allows for the possible (and extremely complex and difficult) discernment of Christ-like practice in the Other, and in so much as Christ-like activity takes place, then this can also only be through the enabling power of the Spirit. It must be clear from this that other religions, in keeping with their own self-understanding, may generate profoundly Christ-like behaviour. It may also be that such Christ-likeness is in resistance to elements within their own tradition... .

Fourth, this brings out the dynamic of John's theology, for it properly means that in so much as the Spirit is present in the world, then the world can be challenged on account of the elements of truth it might already hold, and these elements, when incorporated into Christian articulations and practice, serve to once more give praise to the triune God – even though such incorporation may rightly involve radical discontinuity. This understanding certainly precludes any triumphalist understanding of the Spirit's presence, for it does not elevate to an Archimedian point either the practices or articulations of the church, but shows the constant need to re-engage and re-present the gospel under the guidance of the Spirit.

Fifth, in the light of the saying of John, saying that the Spirit is present in the lives of non-Christians as do the Conciliar and post-Conciliar documents, is both a judgement upon the church and a sign of promise to the church. It is a judgement, for John has told us that the Spirit presence in bringing to form a new Christ-like creation is always a condemnation on the powers of darkness, 'the rule of the world is judged' (John 16:11). For the church, it may be that through the actions of non-Christians it comes to recognize how it is itself ensnared by the powers of darkness... .

Sixth, despite the above, one should certainly not say that every event that prompts new practices of non-identical repetition is of the Spirit, for this would simply be an uncritical baptism with the Spirit of all creation and culture. Rather it is to say that when the church's encounter with religions generates this type of Spirit language from the Christian (since it is a language that belongs within the Christian context), then we must remain radically open to its implications which are deeply ecclesiological and trinitarian.

Seventh, John's theology of the Spirit drives us even further to explore any such affirmation of the Spirit's presence in other religions, for the new practice enjoined of the church in the making of such statements requires also the issues of indigenization and mission to be further clarified and developed for they are intrinsically interrelated.... .

Finally, it is right and fitting that we end where Christ began, and from where John's theology of the resurrection unfolds: mission. The Holy Spirit given to the church is always a call to follow the commandment of love, as Jesus has loved us, with the love of the Father, through the power of the Spirit. And this is an invitation to respond to a gift which is so freely given that nothing can contain it, neither the heavens nor the earth.... . It is inconceivable that witnessing to the gospel can ever be less than the meaning of living this new creation, so that John reminds us that in effect there can be no real dialogue (as it is often called today) between religions, without mission, for Christians have nothing to share with others, other than what has been given so bountifully to them. (pp. 128–32)

Gavin D'Costa, *The Meeting of Religions and the Trinity* (Maryknoll, NY: Orbis, 2000).

Gunapala Dharmasiri

Educated in Sri Lanka, Gunapala Dharmasiri has taught at the Peradeniya campus of the University of Sri Lanka. In extracts from 'A Buddhist Critique of the Christian Concept of God', he argues on Buddhist grounds that Christian views of the soul are misguided.

In traditional Christianity, the reality of the soul is somehow dependent on God, in terms of the Spirit. It is in this sense that Maritain speaks of the soul as a permanent principle in man. 'The person is a substance whose substantial form is a spiritual soul. A soul which is spiritual itself, intrinsically independent of matter in its nature and existence, cannot cease existing.' It is here when they talk of the soul as a permanent principle within the personality that it becomes really vulnerable to empirical verification. Here, it is important to notice, one of the central Christian dogmas becomes exposed to empirical investigation.

The soul as a permanent principle was a favourite idea of the Upanishads too, and the Buddha was therefore very familiar with this conception. The Buddhist critique starts by inquiring into the possibility of finding such a permanent soul in man's personality. The Buddha takes the basic constituents of personality and looks into them, viz., (i) body, (ii) feelings, (iii) sensations, (iv) dispositions, (v) consciousness. The Buddha questions his disciples:

> 'Is body [consciousness, etc.] permanent or impermanent?'
> 'Impermanent, revered sir.'
> 'But is what is impermanent non-satisfying, or is it satisfying?'
> 'Non-satisfying, revered sir.'
> 'And is it right to regard that which is impermanent, non-satisfying, liable to change, as "This is mine, this am I, this is my self"?'
> 'No, revered sir.'

The Buddha emphasizes that the selflessness of the body, consciousness, etc., are seen when they are seen as they really are (*yathabhuta*). If one cannot see any such soul, the burden of proof falls on the soul theorist.

If there is no reason to believe in a soul theory, why do some people have such a view? The Buddha maintained that if a rational explanation cannot be given to a belief then its origin should be traced to an emotional bias. Therefore he called the ideas about 'I' and 'self' to be the 'thoughts haunted by craving concerning the inner self'. For example, the desire for an immortal life ... might prompt one to believe and find security in the idea of an eternal soul. Also, the Buddha points out that there is another form of desire at work here. It is the desire and attachment, for the consciousness and its types. 'Whatever is desire, whatever is attachment, whatever is delight, whatever is craving, for all types of consciousness as eye-consciousness and for the mind, mental states, mental consciousness with mental states cognizable through mental consciousness ... (these are called to be) dogmas, emotional biases, tendencies.' Therefore the idea of the soul is essentially an emotional bias.... .

The Buddhist, of course, has to clear up certain problems before he formulates the no-soul theory. A soul theorist can point out that without accepting the existence of a soul there would be no way of explaining the facts of personal identity and moral responsibility. The Buddhist can give two answers. One is to show the defective nature of the soul theorist's contention. He is presupposing the meaningfulness of the concept of soul in advancing his argument. But we have tried to show how the concept of the soul becomes absolutely meaningless when it is subjected to a proper and detailed analysis. Therefore, the soul theorist, before he advances his argument, has to show that the idea of soul is a meaningful concept. Thus his contention becomes meaningless because his essential presupposition is meaningless. (pp. 155–6)

It is instructive to see the Buddhist and Christian attitudes to the pragmatic value of the idea of the soul. The Christian believes that the idea of the soul is spiritually and morally satisfying and is positively conducive to moral and spiritual progress, the Buddhist reaction follows partly from the epistemological and onto-logical arguments discussed earlier, e.g., a fiction cannot lead to any real and enlightening moral and spiritual progress. But the Buddha opposed the idea of the soul on moral and spiritual grounds, too. (pp. 159–60)

Gunapala Dharmasiri, 'A Buddhist Critique of the Christian Concept of God', in Paul J. Griffiths (ed.), *Christianity Through Non-Christian Eyes* (Maryknoll, NY: Orbis, 1990).

Tom Driver

Tom Driver, Paul J. Tillich Professor of Theology and Culture at Union Theological Seminary, argues that in the modern world pluralism is on ethical grounds the only plausible approach to the religious experience of humanity.

Espousing pluralism, I take a stand not as proposing something 'universal', or as having discovered a new norm of truth for all the world to follow, but rather as proposing a step that is ethically, and therefore theologically, necessary for Western Christianity now to take. At stake is Christianity's self-understanding, its view of its own place in history, and its understanding of God. Pluralism is a demand laid now upon us Christians, brought upon us by our own history, which has largely been one of 'universal colonialism'.

Born within an empire, in one of Rome's minor but troublesome colonies, Christianity soon proved upwardly mobile and found itself, in about three centuries, established as the official religion of the colonizing state. 'Christendom', the 'rule of Christ', came to be. From that time, most of Christianity's expansion in the world has accompanied and often rationalized the colonizing adventures of nations. Moreover, its attitude to other religions has been shaped by the colonial mentality: the 'other' religions that Christianity encountered in its expansions were to be subdued and brought into conformity with Christian ideas and prac-tice, the pattern most evident in the christianizing of Europe. Local divinities frequently became Christian saints. Local feasts found their way into the Christian calendar. Syncretism was strongly opposed only when it threatened the hegemony of the Christian church, just as colonialist nations tolerated local customs as long as it remained clear who was in charge. When local religions could not be brought under the Christian banner, and if there was sufficient power, these religions were eradicated, not infrequently by the burning of books, destruction of symbols, and the torture and slaughter of 'infidels'. Practices contrary to the mores of the missionaries' home country were usually discouraged or forbidden, with little or no attempt to understand their meaning locally.

In all this, there was precious little attempt to listen or to learn. Even when Christian mission has been informed by sophisticated political and anthropological thought, this knowledge has mostly been used in the service of communicating to others, not to learn from non-Christians, particularly not in the weighty matters of theology, ethics and spiritual life... .

The history of Christianity is, by and large, one of not listening to followers of other spiritual roads. On the contrary it has largely been a history of combating, to the death if necessary, those who worship 'other gods'. To do so is enjoined in Christian scriptures, a duty as convenient now as it was in Old Testament times for those who would employ religious prejudice in the conquest of territory... . (pp. 207–8)

Pluralism discerns that creation comes about by collaboration, encounter, exchange. Creation is the product not of one alone but of at least two in interaction. Pluralism is attuned to the mix that makes life. Hence, the pluralist is out to remind Christian theology how important it is not to regard God as basically remote from humanity, lest when theology comes to emphasize, as now it must, the historicality of the human condition, it would sound as if it had ceased to speak about God. On the contrary, one should recognize that within the purview of a Christian incarnational theology the more radically one addresses the human condition, the more one speaks of God. This way of thinking, however, requires a theological move enabling one to affirm not only that human beings have histories but that God does also. Just as, from a historicistic point of view, having a history and existing in history are constitutive of human beings, so also does history belong to the being and the becoming of God. It is something that process theology, in its own way, has taught... .

Christianity, Judaism and Islam have almost always taught that God is active in history, but they have tended to combine this teaching with an unfortunate concept of divine transcendence that suggests (and sometimes insists) that God's essence is outside time and space. When applied to Jesus as the Christ, such ideas have long been regarded as docetic, as if the essence of Christ were beyond history, and its instantiation in Jesus of Nazareth was more apparent than real. Today I think we are being led to see that there may be a docetism in the doctrines of God as well as in christology, and that this will occur whenever divine transcendence is permitted to diminish the divine immanence... . (pp. 211–12)

For Christians at the present time, the imperative is to ponder the integrity and destiny of religions not our own. We have too long supposed that their destiny was to give way to the rule of Christ.

Neither individuals, religious traditions, nor theological images can jump out of their historical skins. Pluralism is the recognition of this as real, more or less necesssary and good. That is to say, although human history is pervaded with evil and injustice, there would be more if this history had been unitary rather than multiple. In diversity there is truth. Nothing but the truth? Certainly not. But truth there is nonetheless.... (p. 213)

Tom Driver, 'The Case for Pluralism', in John Hick and Paul F. Knitter (eds), *The Myth of Christian Uniqueness* (London: SCM Press, 1987).

Francis Xavier D'Sa

Professor at the Snehasadan Institute for the Study of Religion, Pune, India, Francis Xavier D'Sa argues in 'Ecumenism and the Problem of Religious Language' that religious absolutism is a fundamental hurdle in religious dialogue.

A major hurdle in the path of the Christian as well as the wider ecumenical enterprise is the fact that every tradition tends to make absolutistic and exclusivistic claims, without taking into serious consideration the unique nature of the other traditions. Because they neglect to reflect on the nature of human understanding and language, they are prone to interpret their Scriptures and traditions as if they were informative-descriptive statements.

By now it should be obvious that no absolutistic claims can be upheld in the human realm. Even when linguistic expressions tend to appear absolutistic there remains the further task of interpreting them, first from the context – which is usually proclamatory – and second, from the standpoint of the nature of language and understanding. Interpretation that is based on blind loyalty to one's tradition is of course suspect from the start. It has to be undertaken in a context where the claims of all the religious traditions are taken seriously and the characteristics of human understanding and language are not ignored. If this is done, then it will be seen that the concept of relative uniqueness will fit in here very appropriately. (pp. 125–6)

It might appear that I have given undue importance to the role of language and have overestimated its contribution to the field of ecumenism. As I see it, language plays a far more important role in our lives than is commonly realized. It is so pervasive that we are hardly aware of its unique mode of being. The general tendency is to consider language as a mere tool. As a matter of fact the tool-aspect of language is only one aspect which is more often than not misunderstood. For language is not like any other tool which after use we can set aside. Rather it is such that all understanding expresses itself only in and through language. Without language, understanding cannot express itself. No understanding can take place without language, and without understanding there is no language. Language is the expression of what we understand.... .

However, language and understanding are different, and that difference is fundamental, as fundamental as the symbolic difference between symbol and symbolized reality. The symbols are the expression and the symbolized reality is the expressed. The main function of the symbol is to lead to and express the symbolized reality.

Applying this to symbol-language and the symbolized reality of Meaningfulness, it should be clear that the symbol-language of religion purports to lead to Meaningfulness; and that doctrines about uniqueness and absoluteness cannot be part of such symbol language, and that therefore they cannot really belong to divine revelation.

Given the nature and function of religious language, I am suggesting that an ecumenical attitude is the only sensible way of looking at religious pluralism, and this is not from any strategic considerations. The one-sided view of the mountain of Meaningfulness that each tradition (rightly) proclaims has to be (equally rightly) complemented by the other views of the mountain as proclaimed by the other traditions. Such complementarity will necessarily correct exaggerated claims made by the religious traditions. More importantly, traditions will realize not only what they do not have and where they need to be complemented, but also what they have always had in their tradition but have for one reason or another consistently overlooked. (p. 127)

Francis Xavier D'Sa, 'Ecumenism and the Problem of Religious Language', in Peter Phan (ed.), *Christianity and the Wider Ecumenism* (New York: Paragon, 1990).

Randall Falk

Randall Falk, who served as a rabbi in Nashville, Tennessee, argues in Jews and Christians *that the Jewish people is bound by its covenant with God to bring about God's kingdom. In this process, Jewry is obliged to witness to God's truth to all people.*

It is in this sense of having been chosen by God for a special relationship as well as for a special mission that has sustained the people Israel through the centuries. It has provided a purpose for existence and for enduring the trials and persecutions of the ages. Never was there the concept within Judaism that the special relationship came about because of special merit. Nor have Jews felt that we were chosen to be blessed above other peoples. Rather were we chosen for a mission that began with glorifying the name of God throughout the world, bringing God's presence, God's omnipotence, and God's omniscience to all the nations on the earth. The ultimate goal of the Jews' mission was acknowledgement by all humankind of the universality of the One God. This was summarized best by the prophet Isaiah when he proclaimed: 'Turn to me and gain success, All the ends of the earth! For I am God and there is none else' (Isaiah 45:22). This is the same message that we read in the teachings of Jeremiah and Ezekiel and of most of the other post-exilic prophets. (p. 176)

Continuing through the Jewish historical development, we find that mission as understood by the Pharisees in the rabbinic period becomes an important focus in their teachings. The Pharisees were particularistic in their mission in the sense that they were primarily concerned with bringing about a change in mind and heart that would enable the Judaeans to enter the messianic age. At the same time we see in Matthew 23:15 that the Pharisees were proselytizers whose mission was 'to traverse sea and land to make a single proselyte'. The eventual hope of the Pharisees was to convert the entire Roman empire to Judaism. Though it appears that this hope was thwarted very quickly, we should realize that at one point in time approximately twenty per cent of the population of the Roman empire was Jewish, and Jewish missionaries were zealous in seeking to convert the entire populace. Ultimately it was Christianity that succeeded in converting the Roman empire from its paganism to the worship of the one God. This competition between Jews and Christians in the missionary field was certainly one of the areas of sharp conflict between the two faiths.

As it became obvious by the first Nicean Council, already in the early fourth century of the common era, when Constantine proclaimed Christianity a recognized religion of the Roman empire, that Judaism would not become the religion of the empire, the missionary focus of the Jews changed. The mission was to take both the written and the oral Torah to all peoples as the source of God's word which would guide them to pursue God's paths of justice and compassion. This mission is expressed beautifully in one of the oldest prayers in Jewish liturgy. (pp. 178–9)

Israel's mission, though, is not only as teachers of Torah but as witnesses to its teachings. There is a striking illustration of the concept of Israel's witness to the one God in a rabbinic interpretation of verse four of the sixth chapter of Deuteronomy... . The witness does not end there, however. Equally important to the prophets is that the witness is to God's moral law by which God's children shall live and bring freedom and peace to all peoples... .

Jews have always considered our witness to the universal sovereignty of one God and to the supremacy of God's law as enabling us to be God's co-workers in the establishment of God's kingdom on earth. We have not, however, been missionaries from the early fourth century CE to the latter half of the twentieth century. In recent times both Reform and Conservative Judaism have established educational centres in major metropolitan areas of the United States to encourage interested non-Jews to study Judaism with the possibility of their seeking conversion. Reform Judaism has also launched a national programme of outreach to encourage non-Jewish spouses of Jews and other interested individuals to become active participants in Jewish congregational life. We welcome Jews by choice into our midst, though we do not pursue an aggressive missionary programme such as that found in many Christian denominations. (pp. 179–80)

Walter Harrelson and Randall Falk, *Jews and Christians: A Troubled Family* (Nashville, TN: Abingdon Press, 1990).

Ze'ev Falk

Ze'ev Falk is a Jewish scholar and has served as Berman Professor of Law at the Hebrew University in Jerusalem. In 'From East to West My Name is Lauded among the Nations', he argues that although Scripture is critical of religious diversity, there is an alternative tradition within the Jewish religion which recognizes unity beyond diversity.

Judaism reflects, mainly by way of negation, the continuous experience of religious diversity. Both from outside and from inside, such diversity is perceived as a threat to the very existence of the people of Israel in their covenantal relationship to God. The emergence of Judaism indeed can be understood as an antithesis to the common form of religious diversity – polytheism. Monotheism, as well as the uniform lifestyle, represent an alternative to the diversity in the rest of the world. The patriarchs are shown in their loyalty to the one God, while their contemporaries were split by their worship of many gods. Nationhood of the people of Israel developed out of the rejection of the religious traditions of Mesopotamia, Egypt and Canaan into loyalty to the special concept of the God of Israel. Diversity among other nations thus could only be taken as a challenge.

Likewise, Jewish religious tradition emerged against the background of centralization and unification. History shows a constant tension between the centrifugal forces of particular religious experience and the leadership calling for uniformity of faith and action. When the family of Jacob, for instance, prepared for the pilgrimage, worshipping the God of their fathers, they first eliminated diverse cultic objects (Gen. 35:2). A similar rejection of religious diversity was a prerequisite for the conclusion of the covenant between God and the people (cf. Jos. 24:14). For God was perceived to have redeemed the people of Israel from the yoke of Egypt to become their only God and King (Ex. 20:2). The condition was total obedience and unity of direction, and any deviation or diversity was fatal to the relationship. There was an ark of God, a tent of meeting and a temple to attract the different parts of the people to the centre, and prevent them from developing their own separate experience and tradition.

The concrete struggle for and against religious diversity related to the 'high places' which persisted beside the central sanctuary of Jerusalem. Gradually, however, the cult of this temple, the activities of its priests, the pilgrimages of the people and the study of the law led to centralization and to the elimination of deviant practices. The victory of the 'true' over 'false' prophecy was another factor leading towards religious unity among the people of Israel. This process of centralization reached its peak in the religious reform of King Josiah. The High Priest eliminated the foreign objects of worship and their priests (2 Kings 23:4ff.), replacing thereby the comparatively large variety by a uniform ritual. The abolition of the 'high places' likewise prevented deviations from the central cult (ibid. v. 13ff). Again, the challenge of religious diversity of the Mesopotamian and Canaanite Phoenician traditions was the main challenge to Jewish religious integrity during the Babylonian exile. It was perhaps this challenge which changed the hearts of those Judeans who eventually established post-exilic religion.

Jewish history and existence thus presents many reasons against religious diversity, whether introduced from outside or developing inside. It is against this background that we must consider the famous verses of Malachi 1:10–12 which seem to contradict everything said above:

> I have no pleasure in you
> says the Lord of hosts,
> and I will not accept an offering from your hand.
> For from the rising of the sun to its setting
> my name is great among the nations,
> and in every place incense is offered to my name
> and a pure offering:
> for my name is great among the nations
> says the Lord of hosts.
> But you profane it
> when you say that God's table is polluted.

This rebuke to the priests of Jerusalem makes sense only if we assume that the one God of the world, known among the Jews as their God, is the same God revered by other nations under different names. Every offering, therefore, which is sacrificed by heathens is actually an offering to the true and only God and accepted by him. In this sense the phrase expressed a positive attitude towards religious diversity, or at least an attitude appreciating the unity which exists behind the apparent diversity. There must therefore be a tradition within the history of Judaism tolerating a universalist interpretation of religious diversity.... (pp. 24–6)

Ze'ev Falk, 'From East to West My Name is Lauded among the Nations', in John Hick and Hasan Askari (eds), *The Experience of Religious Diversity* (Aldershot, Hants.: Gower, 1985).

Anthony Fernando

Anthony Fernando, who has taught at Kelaniya University in Sri Lanka, argues in 'An Asian's View of Jesus' Uniqueness', that Christian mission needs to be reformulated in contemporary society.

In spite of my academic interest in all the religions, I have never for a moment felt inclined to give up my affiliation to Christianity, the religion I inherited from my parents. And because I consider myself Christian not only by birth but also by conviction, Jesus is for me unique. He has been a source of untold healing for me. His life and teachings have given me great strength and the courage to cope with my problems in life and to live that life in an increasingly liberated way. I therefore subscribe wholeheartedly and without reservation to what Jesus, according to St John's Gospel, is supposed to have said of himself: 'I am the way, the truth and the life. No one can come to the Father except through me' (John 14:6). But, of course, I take that verse in the context of the whole sermon of Jesus – that lengthy Last Supper sermon – of which it is only a part. In that sermon he also said:

> A new commandment I give you: Love one another... . By this all men will know that you are my disciples... . If you obey my commands, you will remain in my love, just as I have obeyed my Father's commands and remain in his love. I have told you this so that my joy may be in you, and your joy may be complete. My command is this: Love each other as I have loved you. Greater love has no man that this that he lay down his life for his friends. (John 13:34–35; 15:10–13)

When we take both these assertions together, we see better what Jesus meant when he introduced himself as 'the Way'. By his example and his teaching, Jesus was an authentic expression of the only Way by which a human being can be human to the fullest degree ordained by nature. The main element of that Way is love to the extent of self-sacrifice.

That Way of selfless love is the eternal Way for human beings to achieve in its fullness the divine 'joy' of being human. That is the Way after the birth of Christ. That had been the Way for innumerable centuries before the birth of Christ. That is the Way for people who are born into a Christian family and for people who are not born into a Christian family. Christians know of that unique Way only because of their contact with Jesus. He is for them the best life-symbol of that unique universal Way. And so by them Jesus has necessarily to be taken as unique. Thus when I profess that Jesus is unique, it is in the sense of the 'supreme Way' that I take the word Jesus. (pp. 69–70)

The distinction made above between clan-solidarity religion and life-vision religion is new, a very recent topic among scholars of world religions. But without taking that perspective into account, the uniqueness of Jesus cannot be professed by a Christian in an authentic way. The uniqueness of Jesus, further, is not a belief that Christians have to affirm just among themselves; it is also what they have to proclaim to the rest of the world. In other words, it is only to the extent that this affirmation is correctly understood and subscribed to that missionary work itself becomes meaningful.

If missionary work has fallen into confusion today, it is because the distinction has not been made about the mentality with which it has to be conducted. Though more unconsciously than consciously, most Christians so far have engaged in missionary work with a clan solidarity mentality. They have tried to diffuse and enlarge Christendom rather than the Reign of God of Jesus' expectation, which actually stands for the reign of right life-ideals in the hearts of people.

True missionary work liberates people from their inner misery and restlessness by awakening them to the life-ideals that make them mentally adult. The great weakness of contemporary humanity is the immaturity of the vast majority. The root cause for the frightful rifts and the growing tension in the modern world is exactly there. Given that background, missionary work is not something to be shunned. Mission is really needed. But it must be missionary work of the right form.

Missionaries motivated by a right life-vision mentality do not feel threatened by preachers of other religions, as long as what they preach is also life-vision religion. Christian missionaries would even join hands with them and collaborate with them. When taken as preachers of sublime life-ideals, the founders of other religions, such as the Buddha and Muhammad, are not opponents of Jesus. The healing ministry exercised by them in other cultures is implicitly affirmed when a missionary proclaims aloud that Jesus is unique.

All that goes to say how important it is for Christians in general, and theologians in particular, to take seriously the distinction made above about the two forms of Christianity as life-vision; it becomes not only an unassailable tenet of Christians but also an affirmation admired and respected by non-Christians. (pp. 72–3)

Anthony Fernando, 'An Asian's View of Jesus' Uniqueness', in Leonard Swidler and Paul Mojzes (eds), *The Uniqueness of Jesus: A Dialogue with Paul F. Knitter* (Maryknoll, NY: Orbis, 1997).

Joseph H. Fichter

Joseph H. Fichter, formerly Professor at Loyola University, points out in 'Christianity as a World Minority' that Christians now live in a religiously plural world in which other religions have increasingly gained strength and influence. As a consequence, Christians should eschew any form of ethnocentrism.

It is not my intention to speak of the decline and downfall of the Christian religion. The world of religion is changing rapidly, but we must try to maintain a balanced perspective. The 'scientific' predictions of Marxists and atheists about the disappearance of religion have been proven false. Christianity is moving unevenly – slowly in its formal hierarchic structures, but flourishing in its Pentecostal and fundamentalist manifestations. There appears also to be a revitalization of Islam after the revolution in Iran.

The social scientist who talks about minorities is usually not talking about numbers, or quantity, but about a social category of people of low status and prestige. In this sense Catholicism was a social minority in New England a century ago, as well as now in Northern Ireland and other heavily Protestant regions. Differential social status is relative to the power and prestige of other social collectivities in the population. Espiscopalians are a numerical American minority but are generally people of high social status and prestige. The social status of Baptists may be high in rural Georgia and low in urban Massachusetts.... .

It must be understood that the social status of a religion does not emerge from its inherent qualities, or from the validity of its beliefs and practices. Religion must be seen as one of several major institutions in the culture. The true believer, whether Muslim or Christian or Jew, would like to think that multitudes are won over because their religion is the revealed truth of God. The historical fact is that European Christianity spread all over the world in company with the military and commercial might of the colonial nations. The European explorers and conquerors everywhere ascribed minority status to the native peoples and their religion. The status of a religion rises or falls with the status of its adherents.

One may then hypothesize that the status of Christianity declines with the declining status of the Western nations, while simultaneously the non-Christian nations of the world are growing in prestige. The religious superiority of Christianity was closely allied with the secular superiority of Western civilization. The end of the colonial era in India, Africa and Asia has accompanied the decline of Western missionary activities. The significance of both the culture and the religion of the West has been lowered at the same time that a resurgence of native religion has brought competition to Christian missionaries who are no longer welcomed. The importance of Christianity has declined with the decreasing power and influence of the Christian nations. (pp. 61–2)

Repentance and contrition imply a willingness to make reparation, but basic to all this is the repudiation of ethnocentrism, especially the kind that has set up an idolatrous self-image of Western Christianity.

> We are always relapsing from the worship of God into the worship of our tribe or of ourselves; and therefore we Christians, whether we are Western Christians or Eastern Christians, tend to treat Christianity as if it were the tribal religion of our particular civilization. In the West we tend to treat it as something that is inseparable from the West, and even as something that derives its virtue not so much from being Christian as from being Western. (p. 65)

What is going on in much of the Third World today is the gigantic shift from colonial to national status. At the very time when transportation and communication are drawing us together, when the possibility of economic and political co-operation seems within our grasp, when representatives of the world religions are moving in an ecumenical direction – at this time the former colonial peoples are setting up independent nations. Nevertheless, it seems that the process of so-called 'Westernization' is taking place more rapidly than it did under colonization.

When cross-cultural borrowing becomes voluntary it becomes selective. It is now quite clear that westernization, or Europeanization, does not necessarily mean Christianization. If it is true that the Third World, and to some extent the Second World, are avid for westernization but indifferent to Christianization, we must acknowledge the probability that Christianity will never be the universal world religion. (p. 71)

Joseph H. Fichter, 'Christianity as a World Minority' in Peter Phan (ed.), *Christianity and the Wider Ecumenism* (New York: Paragon, 1990).

Durwood Foster

Professor at the Pacific School of Religion and the Graduate Theological Union, Durwood Foster stresses in 'Christian Motives for Interfaith Dialogue' that the encounter with other religions is a Christian imperative.

Interreligious dialogue poses for Christian faith today some momentous issues. On the one hand it is an immensely significant challenge to overcome existing parochial bigotry in response to the universalizing love, faith and hope of Jesus Christ. There is no denying that a disheartening burden of doctrinaire exclusivism does distort Christian history and continues today not only to fulminate in the shrill triumphalism of much current evangelism but also to vegetate smugly in the indifference of mainline pastors to questions posed by other faiths. The actual good news of the gospel, we shall argue, has always harboured a leaven of self-transcending outreach and now increasingly invites our threatened and aspiring pluralistic planet to a mutual commitment of creative openness. In concern herewith, moreover, there is a rising tide of impatience and disgust with bigotry all over the earth, and also the spreading insight that religious chauvinism is at the heart of all bigotry. But on the other hand present trends toward reciprocal respect and free exchange among religions have also called forth formidable resistance in the name of fidelity to the concrete truth each faith embodies. It is imperative that the authentic depth of traditions be preserved against a shallow syncretism that lacks all specific commitment. Accordingly, the present situation has become a decisive watershed, one slope of which leads outward to further affirmative association and common search among traditions, with the danger of superficialization and loss of substance, while the other slope inclines toward a guarding of known truth and value at the risk of exacerbating the rivalry of self-enclosed absolutisms. (pp. 21–2)

In the order of being as distinct from the order of knowing, the most basic Christian motive for dialogue with other faiths is that the God Christians worship is the One who creates, upholds and lovingly wills to redeem all that is... . Ultimately there is no other source or ground of truth, value, or meaning in the entire universe that this One God whom to know, serve, and in communion subjoin is the paramount concern and quest of Christian existence. Accordingly, whatever manifests, registers, reflects, or illuminates the reality, purpose and creative activity of this unique and universal God is of categorical interest and significance for Christian faith and life. (p. 22)

Not only is the God whom Christians worship the One who brings forth, undergirds and directs to its end the whole concourse of being and becoming, but biblical–Christian faith also explicitly and emphatically affirms the universal knowability of God.... This ringing assertion of God's unbounded knowability is a powerful invitation to theological dialogue in all directions. (pp. 22–3)

While according to Christian understanding the universal knowability of God is severely thwarted by sin, this situation, so far from precluding, rather accentuates the value of interreligious dialogue. Sin would destroy the possibility of meaningful dialogue only were it total, but the very idea of a total sinfulness is a contradiction in terms. Sin presupposes wholesome insight as sickness does health in the body it assails. On the other hand, were Christians themselves entirely free of sin, the latter's existence within the rest of humanity would, it is true, only enhance the value of interfaith dialogue to the extent of showing the needs of others. (pp. 23–4)

Although an attitude of self-centredness and exclusive superiority does appear ever and again in the biblical literature, and even more egregiously within church history, it is remarkable how luminously biblical–Christian faith has nevertheless expressed the opposite attitude of God-centredness and humble openness toward external sources of religious worth. (p. 24)

While he stands within a long and variegated tradition, which integrally participates in his manifestation by preparing, receiving and interpreting it, Jesus as the Christ is the normative centre of this whole tradition; so that Christian motivation for interreligious dialogue is and must be chiefly inspired and shaped by him. It is in and through him that the Christian envisagement of God, world and humanity achieves climactic concretion, and it is commitment to his humble openness of inclusive love that is the inmost wellspring of Christian wider ecumenism. (p. 25)

Durwood Foster, 'Christian Motives for Interfaith Dialogue', in Peter Phan (ed.), *Christianity and the Wider Ecumenism* (New York: Paragon, 1990).

Helen Fry

In Christian–Jewish Dialogue, *the Christian theologian Helen Fry asserts that salvation is possible outside the Church; in her view Jews can be saved if they are faithful to the Jewish tradition.*

The main challenge ... is how Christianity can make theological space for Judaism – something which it has rarely done over the last two thousand years. If Christianity is to be made credible in the dialogue it must come clean on the issue of mission. Is there, or is there not, an ultimate aim to convert Jews? Theologically, can the Church provide theological space for Judaism, particularly vis-à-vis mission and salvation?

As we have seen, the major Church statements have clearly rejected any coercive proselytism and the setting up of organizations which have the sole aim of converting Jews. The Churches have affirmed the validity of God's covenant with the Jews but the logical conclusion of their statements need to be worked out fully. If the covenant is still valid, surely it has within it the means for Jewish redemption?

For many Christians the belief that Christianity contains the fullest and definitive revelation of God in Jesus Christ necessitates a mission to the world. In addressing this issue today, Christians need to be reminded that the mission of the historical Jesus was confined to Israel during his lifetime (Matt. 10:5). Taking seriously the utter Jewishness of Jesus necessitates some reflection on this. Christians need to ask what was the nature of his mission to the Jews of his day. As many New Testament scholars have highlighted, that mission was based on a call to repentance and a turning back to the ways of Torah. It was a kingdom-centred message. Jesus pointed away from himself to God. He did not proclaim salvation through his own person – that belief was part of the developing post-resurrection affirmation of Christ. Salvation for Jews was always seen by Jesus as faithfulness to

Torah.... Much of what he said had parallels in the Rabbinic Judaism of his day. If Jews and Christians are to take seriously that message, then salvation for Jews comes through faithfulness to Torah. I do believe that the historical Jesus had a profound relevance for contemporary systematic theology – after all, Christianity has always understood itself as rooted in history. God is seen as acting in history through the incarnation. I believe that the Jewish Jesus challenges previous understandings of mission and for that matter, salvation.....

What then are the implications for the traditional mission to Jews? It means that Christians should enable Jews to be better Jews rather than converting them to Christianity. That would then be in line with the teaching of Christianity's central figure, Jesus. But there is a further dimension. Converting 'the other' has constituted the traditional Christian approach because it is usually linked to a particular understanding of salvation.... . If you believe that your tradition has the sole means of salvation then you are obliged to share the truth with others. I suggest that it is unreasonable to link a person's place in the after-life to a particular set of beliefs. First, it is elitist because it requires a correct understanding of complex doctrines; and second, all beliefs are culturally and historically conditioned and those born into the right culture would have a head start.

It is still possible for Christians to hold that Christ is central to Christian faith and yet to allow space for Judaism as a living and salvific tradition. The role of Christ is revelatory rather than soteriological. Christ can be seen as the fullest revelation of God but acknowledgement of that is not essential to salvation. Rather salvation comes, as John Hick writes in *Disputed Questions and Interpretation of Religion*, through the turning from self-centredness to God-centredness. Was this not the essence of Jesus' teaching for the Jews of his day? Mission in terms of converting someone to your tradition is no longer applicable. The witness to 'the other' comes through enabling them to turn from self-centredness to God-centredness through their own distinctive symbols and traditions. This does not mean giving up the quest for truth. Dialogue is about understanding the other, yes; but also seeking a deeper understanding of the truth. This does not imply that we cannot speak of anything meaningful in dialogue. On the contrary Christians, for example, can talk about the importance of Jesus whilst Jews accept this as a valid experience for Christians. But, such openness and trust is undermined if there is a hidden missionary agenda. (pp. 289–91)

Helen Fry (ed.), *Christian–Jewish Dialogue: A Reader* (Exeter: University of Exeter Press, 1996).

Charles Wei-Hsun Fu

The Taoist and Buddhist scholar Charles Wei-Hsun Fu studied at the National Taiwan University and the universities of Hawaii, California and Illinois. He has served as Professor of Religion at Temple University and Associate Editor of the Journal of Ecumenical Studies. *In 'A Universal Theory or a Cosmic Confidence in Reality? A Taoist/Zen Response', he proposes a functional conception of truth based on Chinese thought.*

Taoism and Zen are often misunderstood to put forward, just like any other system of thought, their own special truth claim in competition with other truth claims made by Christianity, Islam and so on. But, has not Lao Tzu made his point abundantly clear in his opening words, 'The tao that can be taoed is not the invariable Tao; the name that can be named is not the invariable Name'? Has not Chuang Tzu clarified Lao Tzu's point, saying, for instance, that 'Tao cannot be thought of as being (*yu*), nor can it be thought of as nonbeing (*wu*). In naming it "Tao", we are only adopting a provisional expression'? Has not Master Chao-chou recommended a Zen way of transcending the duality of truth and untruth in his one-word reply, *Wu* (nothingness), to the question, 'Does the dog have Buddha nature or not?' And, to those who are still struggling hard with the problem of conflicting truth claims concerning the so-called Really Real Reality, I strongly recommend as a good *koan* exercise the following poem, which Master Wu-men ('No-gate') composed at a moment of great enlightenment, after six years of his Zen inquiry into the trans-metaphysical meaning of Chao-chou's one word puzzle:

> *Wu wu wu wu wu, wu wu wu wu wu;*
> *Wu wu wu wu wu, wu wu wu wu wu.*

In 'poetizing' *wu* or 'nothingness' twenty times, does Master No-gate look like a linguistic idiot talking nonsense, or like a great liberator to all universal theory concocters and truth-claimers? ...

The most crucial question is how to resolve the problem of conflicting truth claims – claims that arise in nearly all cases as a result of overzealous attempts at an unexamined and unwarranted universalization of a particular theory, dogma, thought, faith, or experience. Prof. Panikkar has made a very thoughtful suggestion – that the meaning of 'truth' be reoriented as a matter of 'perspectivism and relativity'. I think this suggestion is very sound and should be well taken. Coincidentally, I have, for about ten years, also tried to tackle this very crucial question and have reached a tentative conclusion in terms of what I have called 'holistic multiperspectivism in functional form'. That is to say, all human truths linguistically formulated in religion and philosophy are none other than multiperspectively functional (nonsubstantive) ways of divulging, on higher or lower levels of the human mind, the holistically inexhaustible meanings of the so-called Really Real Reality, whatever that may be. (pp. 155–7)

My proposal is that the substantive (or, what-to-see) approach be completely replaced by the functional (or, how-to-see) approach, that all substantive languages (*Substanzsprachen*) be radically transformed into functional languages (*Funktionssprachen*), that all (onto-theological) truths claimed to be objective or universally valid be undisguisedly redisclosed as no more than 'human, all too human' ... perspectives on higher or lower levels, and that the multidimensionality (in appearance) and inexhaustibility (in meaning) of the Really Real Reality, be it called 'Being', 'Substance', 'God', 'Brahman', 'Tao', 'Nothingness', or the like, be modestly reunderstood as reflecting the multiperspectival projections of the mind (experience, faith, religious sentiment, viewpoint, the spiritual impulse) on higher or lower levels.

Nothing is really changed in my proposal; what is changed is our new (Copernican) way of seeing the essential nature of the languages we use, the truths we present and the reality we speak of. In short, substantive languages are to be reoriented as functional languages; truth in the objective sense is to be reinterpreted as (what is called in Chinese philosophy) – *tao-li* (literally 'the principle or reason of the way'), which means 'human reasons or truths' and which can claim only intersubjective truthfulness or acceptability, having nothing to do with objective or absolute truth. (p. 158)

Charles Wei-Hsun Fu, 'A Universal Theory or a Cosmic Confidence in Reality? A Taoist/Zen Response', in Leonard Swidler (ed.), *Toward a Universal Theology of Religion* (Maryknoll, NY: Orbis, 1987).

G

Mahatma Gandhi

Mahatma Gandhi, born in 1869, was educated in England, and was instrumental in forcing the British to leave India. In 'The Story of My Experiments with Truth', he explains how he was drawn to various religions.

I began reading the *Gita* with them. The verses in the second chapter:

> If one
> Ponders on objects of sense, there springs
> Attraction; from attraction grows desire,
> Desire flames to fierce passion,
> passion breeds recklessness;
> then the memory – all betrayed –
> Lets noble purpose go, and saps the mind,
> Till purpose, mind, and man are all undone

made a deep impression on my mind, and they still ring in my ears. The book struck me as one of priceless worth. The impression has ever since been growing on me with the result that I regard it today as the book par excellence for the knowledge of Truth... .

The New Testament ... especially the Sermon on the Mount ... went straight to my heart. I compared it with the *Gita*. The verses, 'But I say unto you, that ye resist not evil: but whosoever shall smite thee on thy right cheek, turn to him the other also. And if any man ... take away thy coat let him have thy cloak too', delighted me beyond measure ... My young mind tried to unify the teaching of the *Gita*, the Light of Asia, and the Sermon on the Mount. That renunciation was the highest form of religion appealed to me greatly. (pp. 219–20)

If I found myself entirely absorbed in the service of the community, the reason behind it was my desire for self-realization. I had made the religion of service my own, as I felt that God could be realized only through service. And service for me was the service of India, because it came to me without my seeking, because I had an aptitude for it. I had gone to South Africa for travel, for finding an escape from

Kathiawad intrigues and for gaining my own livelihood. But as I have said, I found myself in search of God and striving for self-realization.

Christian friends had whetted my appetite for knowledge, which had become almost insatiable, and they would not leave me in peace, even if I desired to be indifferent. In Durban, Mr Spencer Walton, the head of the South African General Mission, found me out. I became almost a member of his family. At the back of this acquaintance was of course my contact with Christians in Pretoria. Mr Walton had a manner all his own. I do not recollect his ever having invited me to embrace Christianity. But he placed his life as an open book before me, and let me watch all his movements. Mrs Walton was a very gentle and talented woman. I liked the attitude of this couple. We knew the fundamental differences between us. Any amount of discussion could not efface them. Yet even differences prove helpful, where there are tolerance, charity and truth. I liked Mr and Mrs Walton's humility, perseverance and devotion to work, and we met very frequently.

This friendship kept alive my interest in religion. It was impossible to get the leisure that I used to have in Pretoria for my religious studies. But what little time I could spare I turned to good account. My religious correspondence continued. Raychandbhai was guiding me. Some friend sent me Narmadashanker's book *Dharma Vichar*. Its preface proved very helpful. I had heard about the Bohemian way in which the poet had lived, and a description in the preface of the revolution effected in his life from his religious studies captivated me. I came to like the book, and read it from cover to cover with attention. I read with interest Max Muller's book *India – What Can it Teach Us?* and the translation of the *Upanishads* published by the Theosophical Society. All this enhanced my regard for Hinduism, and its beauties began to grow upon me. I read Washington Irving's *Life of Mahomet and His Successors* and Carlyle's panegyric on the Prophet. These books raised Muhammad in my estimation. I also read a book called *The Sayings of Zarathustra*.

Thus I gained more knowledge of the different religions. The study stimulated my self-introspection and fostered in me the habit of putting into practice whatever appealed to me in my studies. Thus I began some of the Yogic practices, as well as I could understand them from a reading of the Hindu books. But I could not get on very far, and decided to follow them with the help of some experts when I returned to India. The desire has never been fulfilled.

I made too an intensive study of Tolstoy's books. *The Gospels in Brief, What to Do?* and other books made a deep impression on me. I began to realize more and more the infinite possibilities of universal love. (pp. 225–6)

Mahatma Gandhi, 'The Story of My Experiments with Truth', in Paul J. Griffiths (ed.), *Christianity Through Non-Christian Eyes* (Maryknoll, NY: Orbis, 1990).

Ramchandra Gandhi

Ramchandra Gandhi served as Professor at Visra-Bharati University in India. In 'Notes Towards a Coherent Iconography of Christ, Buddha and Krishna', he illustrates the connections between Christian and Hindu thought.

One of the most fundamental Hindu, Vedic, beliefs, is that the One in a supreme joyous holocaust of himself created the infinitely varied Many of manifestation, forms of creation, the universe in its essential character of a bewildering and marvellous plurality: the fruit of an original sacrifice. In the sacrifice of Christ, in all remainderless sacrifice of ego, there is a repetition, a reenactment, of that original sacrifice of creation. In the doctrines and realities of the crucifixion, resurrection and ascension of Christ, Vedic teaching reveals and renews itself, as it does elsewhere too, again and again. No Vedic scholar, no Hindu acquainted with the centrality of sacrifice in the *Vedas*, need suffer the slightest anxiety in accepting Christ as a sacrifice and symbol, a progeny and prototype of the original *Purusa sukta*, sundering of Being, which is the Vedic image of creation, the sacrifice of the One in essence in the becoming of the Many in appearance... .

There is in Christ's passion the drama, theatre, the consummation of things which is of the essence of *avatric lila*, narrative of divinity. There is also in Christ's resurrection the sense of newness, renewal, without which even immortality would be uninspiring and incomplete, in the way in which mere repetitive reincarnation even in higher and higher forms of life in any world or heaven would be uninspiring and incomplete without liberation from self-centred separativeness... .

At this point the Buddhism of my Hinduism whispers the following thought: 'Drama, consumating theatre and achieving history, essential though they are in understanding human life and even cosmic reality, would be vanity and noise if they were not supplemented and corrected by humility and silence, by the silent eternal working of *Dharma*.' Self-sacrificial Vedic dying, certainly, e.g. Christ-like; but now without self-forgetful living, the living of self-forgetfulness, Buddha-like.

Hindu religion is *Sanatana Dharma*, eternal order, foundation, law, dispensation, cohesion. Central to such a conception of religion would be the idea of an entire self-abnegation, self-concealment, even on the part of God. God must subordinate himself to his Order, Law, *Dharma*. The cataclysmic overtones of the original *Purusa*, sacrifice of the *Veda*, or the repetition and the renewal of this sacrifice in Christ, can also in another idiom of language and mind and soul, another *raga* of conception, be regarded as the apparently *anadi* character of the universe, its beginninglessness, its effective autonomy. If it were not possible so to regard God's creation, *Purusottama* and *Christovatara* would be capable of being regarded as lacking in self-effacement. The Buddha is the incarnation of God's self-forgetfulness, self-abnegation, self-effacement. The Buddha not only does not talk of God, he does not talk of Self either, he talks only of *Dharma, Dhamma,* even the Sanskrit is self-effaced in the Pali idiom and softer sound.

Sanatana Dharma is revealed in translation, both in Buddha and in Christ, not denied. Revelation cannot be neglectful of the multilingual demands of the surrendered, infinitely expectant, human heart. Calvary and *Sarnath,* the raising of Man and the turning of the Wheel of *Dhamma,* are both needed, and are in that sense the same. Christ loses all his first disciples on the way to Calvary, the Buddha walks all the way to *Sarnath* to reclaim all his first disciples... . The suffering of extreme agony, and the discovery of the Middle Way, require each other, complete each other. We are moved to unbearable sorrow and lamentation by the Cross of Christ, and stilled to the depths of our being by the Buddha's hand raised in benediction. *Sanatana Dharma* achieves a dynamic image of itself in these two forms of blessedness. (pp. 111–13)

There can be no more powerful image of sacred literalness in *kaliyuga,* distinctive yet recurrent reality, than Christ on the Cross. All wakefulness and actuality and historicity in their uncompromised unself-deceiving essence and human truth point to the Cross, the murder of God. And *Maruti, Hanuman,* incomparable monkey-devotee of Sri *Rama,* defier of gravity and all obstacles of materiality, perfectly symbolizes sacred fantasticality, illuminating in this way also the resurrection and ascension of Christ. Man is *Hanuman.* And the recumbent Buddha symbolizes in powerful and poignant image the silent compassionate causal power of *Dhamma.* God–Man murdered, monkey-devotee liberated from the constraint of Natural Law, all power vested in unconscious impersonal *Dhamma,* only such a surreal juxtaposition of images can do justice to the theme of coherent variety in the realm of religion. (p. 117)

Ramchandra Gandhi, 'Notes Towards a Coherent Iconography of Christ, Buddha and Krishna', in John Hick and Hasan Askari (eds), *The Experience of Religious Diversity* (Brookfield, Vermont: Gower Press, 1985).

Langdon Gilkey

Langdon Gilkey lived in China, was a Visiting Professor at Kyoto University and has served as a Professor of Theology at the Divinity School of the University of Chicago. In 'Plurality and Its Theological Implications' he raises a number of serious theological implications of the pluralist stance.

My subject is the impingement of the plurality of religions on theology; or, more accurately stated, the effect of the present sense or understanding of plurality on theology. For the Christian churches have always known that religions were plural, that there were other religions than our own. This consciousness of plurality raised few theological problems, because the church was convinced on a number of grounds that Christianity was the only truly valid religion, the only effective 'way'. That we now speak of theological implications of plurality, and clearly intend serious implications, thus bespeaks a new sense of understanding of plurality, a new assessment of its meaning. (p. 37)

Plurality as parity has devastating theological effects – or at least, I believe it should have... . To recognize, as one does or must in dialogues, the presence of truth and of grace, validity of symbol and efficacy of practice, in another faith is radically to relativize not only one's own religious faith but the referent of that faith, the revelation on which it is dependent. Thus to be in dialogue is also to be driven on a new theological quest – namely, the effort so to interpret one's symbols as neither to exclude nor offend this other. That is to say, some mode of new theological self-understanding is necessary, an understanding that includes and supplements what the other offers instead of rejecting it as false or incorporating it as merely one vista in the panorama shaped by one's own viewpoint. The liberal effort to include and so to incorporate – for the two go together – thus begins to seem to be the imperial effort to take over, absorb, and dominate... .

Note that this quest – at present the central one of theology, I think – is more radical than just that of 'modernizing', 'demythologizing', or even 'representing' or 'revising'. The latter relativized only past expressions of traditional symbols in favour of modern expressions. Far more radical – painful and yet exciting – is to relativize the symbols themselves – and that is our situation, the newness of our situation... . (pp. 40–1)

Plurality ... drives in the direction of ecumenical tolerance. Plurality, however, has another face than this, a face fully as terrifying as is the relativity just described. For within the plurality of religions that surround us are forms of the religious that are intolerable, and intolerable because they are demonic. Toleration is here checked by the intolerable; and plurality means both.

This aspect of diversity we have always seen out of the corner of the eye. We know there were religious cannibals, religious sacrifices of human victims, religious wars of aggression, religious murders, religious caste – and so on. Most of these have been pushed aside in our consciousness through the need, and it is a real need, to be tolerant and to free religion from its baleful faults of intolerance, fanaticism, and unbridled cruelty. But this too was dialectical – and twentieth-century experience has also illustrated this point extravagantly. For in our century intolerable forms of religion and the religious have appeared... .

Now the point is that in order to resist – and we must, paradoxically on ecumenical grounds, if for no other reasons – we must ourselves stand somewhere. That is, we must assert some sort of ultimate values – in the face of heaven knows what social, intellectual, moral and religious pressures – in this case the values of persons and of their rights, and correspondingly, the value of the free, just and equal community so deeply threatened by this theocratic tyranny. And to assert our ultimate value or values is to assert a 'world', a view of all of reality. For each affirmed political, moral or religious value presupposes certain understanding of humankind, society and history, and so a certain understanding of the whole in which they exist. Our view of existence as a whole gives locus in reality to the values we defend. Consequently any practical political action, in resistance to tyranny or in liberation from it, presupposes ultimate values and an ultimate vision of things, an ethic and so a theology. And it presupposes an absolute commitment to this understanding of things. The union of resistance, commitment and 'world' was made crystal clear by the Barman confession: to confess our adherence to one Lord is at once to resist the Nazi claim on our allegiance; conversely to resist Nazi ideology, allegiance alone to one Lord and to one Word was required. The necessity of action, liberating action, calls first for the relinquishment of all relativity and second for the assertion of some alternative absolute standpoint. Paradoxically, plurality, precisely by its own ambiguity, implies both relativity and absoluteness, a juxtaposition or synthesis of the relative and the absolute that is frustrating intellectually and yet necessary practically. (pp. 44–6)

Langdon Gilkey, 'Plurality and Its Theological Implications', in John Hick and Paul Knitter (eds), *The Myth of Christian Uniqueness* (London: SCM Press, 1987).

Arthur Glasser

The Christian missionary, Arthur Glasser, has served as Professor of Mission Theology and East Asian Studies at Fuller Theological Seminary, School of World Mission, Pasadena, California. Here he addresses the question how Jesus would have viewed the issue of religious pluralism.

If we accept the witness of the Gospels that Jesus Christ is God incarnate, there can surely be no fuller disclosure of God in terms of manhood than is given in his person and teaching. It is the task of the church to treasure this deposit of disclosure and proclaim its mysteries.... .

'What did Jesus command his disciples to do about religious pluralism of his day? Has he given us any guidelines to follow?' True, we find no evidence in the Gospels that Jesus ever expressed a judgement about non-Jewish religions as such, only about their futile patterns of repetitious prayer (Matt. 6:7). All we know is that he gave unquestioned allegiance to the Old Testament and did not challenge its witness against gods other than Yahweh. He saw no possibility of other gods besides the One he knew as his Father in heaven (Mark 12:32–34). It seems impossible to contend that his attitude to other religious systems would have been at variance with the commandment: 'You shall have no other gods before Me' (Exod. 20:3). His Father was supreme and unique; the service of other gods was totally forbidden (Deut. 4:39; Isa. 44:6–20; Jer. 10:11; etc.).

And yet, Jesus used the Old Testament in a selective and original fashion to attack certain practices of the Judaism of his day. He exposed and rebuked the Pharisees' self-righteousness, religious externalism and exclusive nationalism. He made constant effort to make sharp distinctions between the infallible truth of Scripture and the flawed practice of that truth by his people. And he commended faith wherever he found it.

But what of Jesus' regard for Gentile religious pluralism? Had he approached the non-Jewish religions of his day we would have expected him to be serious, thoughtful and free from prejudice. We would have expected him to commend every human expression of love and every human readiness to forgive... .

Jesus would also have raised the issue of truth. Did he not say, 'All things have been delivered to me by my Father; and no one knows the Son except the Father, and no one knows the Father except the Son and anyone to whom the Son chooses to reveal him' (Matt. 11:27)? Here we are face to face with the indisputable right of God to be God, and to be free to make distinctions and choices. In the light of his perception of truth, Jesus regarded even the Samaritan offshoot of Judaism to be inferior (John 4:22), and said so. Because of this it seems difficult to argue that in the midst of the religious pluralism of our day, we should confine our witness to endorsing all religious systems as relative and deepening mutual understanding between them. And is our focus of positive attention only to commend expressions of outgoing love and social concern?

Is this the sum total of the response Christ would have us make to the issue of religious pluralism? Of course, Jesus Christ was concerned that all peoples in their interaction with one another attain the proximate goals of social harmony, civil justice and the alleviation of poverty. But his constant stress on the ultimate goal of the kingdom of God led him to conclude and in a very real sense climax his ministry with a mandate that his people 'make disciples' of the peoples of every tribe and tongue and nation. This was his response to the issue of religious pluralism. (pp. 42–4)

Arthur Glasser, 'Response' in Gerald H. Anderson and Thomas F. Stransky (eds), *Christ's Lordship and Religious Pluralism* (Maryknoll, NY: Orbis, 1981).

Paul J. Griffiths

Paul J. Griffiths, born in London, studied at Oxford University and later at the University of Wisconsin. He served as a Professor at the University of Chicago Divinity School. In 'The Uniqueness of Christian Doctrine Defended', he criticizes the pluralist stance and argues for an acceptance of the uniqueness of Christian doctrine as a prerequisite for Christian engagement with other religions.

There is a trivial sense in which Christian doctrine is unique and an equally trivial sense in which it is not. Its trivial uniqueness lies simply in its historical particularity, a particularity shared by no other doctrinal system; but every doctrinal system is, by definition, unique in just this formal sense. Hence also the trivial sense in which Christian doctrine is not unique: it shared the formal characteristic of being unique in its historical particularity with every doctrinal system. Any interesting uniqueness that Christian doctrine must have, then, must lie not at the formal level but at the substantive level. And any attempt to delineate and to flesh out in what this substantive uniqueness consists must in turn rest upon some particular attempt to construct a referent for the term Christian doctrine. But since all such attempts are partial and tendentious, because they are all themselves undertaken in unique historical circumstances by individuals or communities with a particular interest and a particular *Tendenz*, no single attempt to do this will meet with universal approval... .

I am writing these words a few days after the feast of Christ the King, a feast at which Christ's kingship and his crucifixion are celebrated together by the church. Part of the liturgical celebration of that feast is (in the Anglican communion) the reading of the christological hymn in Colossians 1:11–20, a hymn which concludes with these words:

> For in him the complete being of God, by God's own choice, came to dwell. Through him God chose to reconcile the whole universe to himself, making peace through the shedding of his blood, upon the cross – to reconcile all things, whether on earth or in heaven, through him alone.

A strong and interesting doctrinal claim is being made here, a claim as to the singularity and salvific centrality of a particular historical event. It is a claim that functions in almost all the ways distinguished in the analysis of religious doctrine given above. It is a rule governing what may properly be said by the communities for which this text is authoritative; it excludes, if taken seriously, other less daring and universalistic conceptual alternatives for understanding the work of Jesus Christ that the community has found and still finds largely unacceptable; and it is used catechetically, as well as dramatized and reinforced liturgically, in ways which make it enter the very heart of Christian spirituality. It, and its like, have deep roots and a strong grip upon the spirit, intellect and imagination of Christian communities, and it is here, in the linked doctrines of the universal significance of the incarnation and the atonement, that I would begin my construction of the referent of the term Christian doctrine. It is also from here that I would begin my engagement, serious and deep-going as I hope it is and intend it to be, with Buddhists and their equally (though very different) universalistic and exclusivistic doctrinal claims. These matters must be on the agenda, and openly so, of interreligious dialogue if it is to be anything other than a futile exercise in the exchange of ethical platitudes for all concerned. As Rowan Williams has put it:

> The problem was, is, and always will be the Christian attitude to the historical order, the human past. By affirming that all 'meaning', every assertion about the significance of life and reality, must be judged by reference to a brief succession of contingent events in Palestine, Christianity – almost without realizing it – closed off the path to 'timeless truth'.

Here lies the uniqueness of Christian doctrine, and here lies also the 'problem' that pluralists are trying to dissolve. The universalistic and apparently exclusivistic claims made here and throughout the tradition may of course turn out to be false, to have been misconceived and to be in need of abandonment; but such a judgement needs to be made in full awareness of what it entails and of how such claims function for Christians and are rooted in and definitive of their communities. Pluralists show no such awareness. My attempt to sketch the lineaments of such an awareness in this study has been intended to suggest that a certain kind of uniqueness, a uniqueness that includes both universalism and exclusivism, is integral to both the syntax and the semantics of the Christian life. I also want to suggest that this syntax and semantics are worth preserving in default of pressing and detailed reasons to abandon them, and that pluralists have offered no such reasons. Their preservation will mean that the Christian life will continue to be structured around and given meaning by a certain kind of universalism and exclusivism, and this must therefore also be a constitutive factor in the Christian engagement with religiously committed non-Christians. That the preservation of this universalism and exclusivism need not lead to the military or economic oppression by Christians of non-Christians is obvious; and that a frank acknowledgement of the universalistic and exclusivistic dimension of Christian syntax and semantics by Christians committed to interreligious dialogue will lead to the crossing of new frontiers in interreligious dialogue…. (pp. 168–70)

Paul J. Griffiths, 'The Uniqueness of Christian Doctrine Defended', in Gavin D'Costa (ed.), *Christian Uniqueness Reconsidered* (Maryknoll, NY: Orbis, 1990).

Stanley Harakas

Stanley Harakas obtained a BD from Holy Cross Greek Orthodox School and a Th.D. from Boston University, and has served as Professor at Holy Cross Greek Orthodox School of Theology. In 'Orthodox Christianity and Theologizing', he asserts that Orthodox Christians can be enriched through dialogue even though they hold to the central tenets of the the faith.

I speak consciously and deliberately as an Eastern Orthodox Christian who, although ecumenically committed, holds to the fundamental premise that Jesus Christ is the Son of God, the second person of the Holy Trinity, who in time assumed human nature, dwelt among us, taught and healed, proclaimed and manifested the reign of God, was crucified for the salvation of the human race, was resurrected from the dead, thereby conquering the enemies of authentic human life – sin, evil and death. As an Eastern Orthodox Christian it is my prayer, my earnest desire, for the well-being of every person who is living or has ever lived or who shall live, that Jesus Christ and his saving work be acknowledged, accepted, proclaimed and lived. As an Orthodox Christian St Paul's words in his Letter to the Philippians resonate truth to me: 'Therefore God has highly exalted him and bestowed on him the name which is above any name, that at the name of Jesus every knee should bow, in heaven and on earth and under the earth, and every tongue confess that Jesus Christ is Lord to the glory of God the Father' (Phil. 2:9–11).

I know that such an affirmation can be, and has been, and for some continues to be, the root of a highly intolerant and denigrating attitude toward persons who belong to different Christian churches and toward persons belonging to other religions. It is my contention, based on the sources of Eastern Orthodox teaching, that this need not be the case, and that in fact it ought not to be the case. This is not the place to develop this teaching, but suffice it to say that the ancient Logos theology of the early church is one grounding for the view, and the respect for the self-determining image of God in every human being is another.

At our worst, in our history, we Eastern Orthodox have ignored those truths and spoken in vituperation toward others and their beliefs, and have violated their integrity as peoples and as human beings. Our own sufferings over the centuries under alien religious and antireligious forces, certainly as much and perhaps more than Catholics and Protestants to this very day, have made us sensitive to our failings in this area. Rather, the road of dialogue, co-operation, the peaceful co-existence of religions and the avoidance of overt proselytizing have become hallmarks of Eastern Orthodox attitudes toward other churches and religions in this ecumenical age.

If, by God's grace, the Orthodox lifestyle, doctrines, worship and integration of many varied and rich cultural and ethnic traditions into the life of the church, provoke interest and desire to learn of the Orthodox Christian faith, we most heartily oblige. If not, we are able to look at every religious expression and find there much that we acknowledge to be true and beautiful, along with some things we find contradictory to the Christian faith and the affirmations that we hold. Because we recognize that we often misinterpret and misunderstand others in their practices and beliefs, we hold it a truly Christian thing to enter into dialogue with those with whom we differ. We often find much more to appreciate. Sometimes the constraints of our own history have caused us to de-emphasize authentic aspects of our own tradition, and dialogue with others serves to uncover these areas, and we are enriched because of the dialogue. In the process, even though our differences may never be fully overcome, we are better off for having shared: we ourselves have grown, and we hope we have communicated the vision of truth that we hold. (pp. 74–5)

Stanley Harakas, 'Orthodox Christianity and Theologizing' in Leonard Swidler (ed.), *Toward a Universal Theology of Religion* (Maryknoll, NY: Orbis, 1987).

David Hart

Senior Lecturer at the University of Derby, David Hart, who like Don Cupitt adopts a non-realist interpretation of Christianity, argues in One Faith? *that in the world's religions there is a radical element which transcends the traditional understanding of God and allows for a sharing of experience between adherents of different faiths.*

The advent of an understanding of the world faiths as global area-stories about God ironically re-introduces the question of God to the forefront of the post-modern theological agenda. Whereas the modernist project analysed the contents of the faiths in the detail of their stories and structures, and gave the liberal theologian a chance to 'compare and contrast' the different religions on the cosmic menu, the postmodern reality is a collection of *petites histoires* of the tribal deities that tell us little of the deities themselves and rather more of the cultures that formed them. Underneath a collection of stories, or perhaps more accurately alongside them, we can glimpse a patterning of meanings, and elements in the different stories contribute to what we can only take to be similar elements in the structure of the stories themselves.... .

In this work, I shall attempt to argue that across the spectrum of the world religions there exist parallel structures of stories. And although we may not attempt, in the light of postmodern consensus, to analyse that 'some thing' that Wordsworth called 'more deeply interfused', we can at least gather together stories from different traditions and highlight the common features in the human adventure and endeavour, to which they may be bearing a common witness. The only sense in which it can be called a common story is that in which it is a story of our common humanity – but in that sense it can indeed be read as a shared story or one of harking after rival deities.

My argument is that a non-realist understanding and appreciation of faith will increasingly enable believers to appreciate other traditions and take more time and trouble to 'cross over' into them, once they understand that faiths are not finished and closed revelations but collections of diverse insights, teachings and practices which have all been created as human responses to the ineffable; and that therefore the particular cultural conditioning of one is neither more nor less than that of another.... .

The exercise I propose is not meant to be a static one. Sometimes interreligious dialogue can be viewed, I believe, under a rather unhelpful image of negotiations which seek a clear but compromised position somewhere between the participants. An exercise in passing into different traditions from one's own and adding insights from them into one's own spiritual treasury is by no means an exercise of simple logic or dialogue like that. It is a challenge to be daring with one's beliefs and to risk cherished convictions, and there must be a willing attempt to allow valued shibboleths to make their way into the cultural melting-pot. But such a game may be genuinely celebrated as an art that can provide increasing pleasure and knowledge for all those who are prepared to risk playing. The stakes are high but those who are concerned for the issues of faith are usually those who have been prepared to take some risks and make some sacrifices, albeit hitherto, usually, within their own tradition, for the sake of a higher or more spiritual vocation than many are prepared to take. Their gods have prepared them well, and it is now time for them to step out boldly into other sanctuaries and experience what is holy about those other places and people.

If the non-realist theory is correct in what it claims, then the new truth that will become apparent as this postmodern pilgrimage takes place will not be simply an amalgam of previous religious truths but will be a new and fuller truth jointly created and brought into shape by those who have valued and grasped the opportunity to do so. The places and people which I suggest may be helpful to those disposed to take this route are clearly only some of many people and places. (pp. 1–8)

David Hart, *One Faith?* (London: Mowbray, 1995).

Monika K. Hellwig

Professor of Theology at Georgetown University, Monika Hellwig argues in 'The Wider Ecumenism: Some Theological Questions' that Christians should look to other faiths for religious truth.

The close interaction of peoples and nations in our times makes the call to a wider ecumenism both important and urgent in an entirely new way. Yet the possibilities and limitations of Christian participation in this wider ecumenism are deeply rooted in our Christian history.... .

It seems to me that the questions we must consider in relation to the wider ecumenism from a theological point of view come to focus around the following:

1. What is the Good News of Jesus Christ for the world?
2. How does it relate to anyone else's good news?
3. How are we as Christians called upon to share and bring the Good News of Jesus Christ?
4. Does God speak to us in other ways, as well as through Jesus of Nazareth?
5. Does our faith require us to listen to other voices or to exclude them? What can we expect to learn from others, and in what way? (pp. 75–6)

From the above it certainly follows that there is honest reason and purpose for dialogue with the other religious traditions, and indeed with all other traditions offering hope for the human situation and the human race. But there remains the question of what it is that we hope to accomplish by such dialogue, what we expect to learn.

All religious language is necessarily analogical. We speak of matters that can be observed, so to speak, from one end while they are inscrutable at the other end. No human language or expression, therefore, can contain the whole truth simply and absolutely. There are many ways of approaching the truth, many analogies that might be used in trying to express it. Moreover, because we as Christians believe in the universal salvific will of God, we must assume that God is self-revealing to all that search in good faith, and is self-revealing to them in a linguistic, cultural and historical mode that they can understand.

But if this is true then each of the other religions represents such a mode of the divine self-revelation. These traditions must then be seen not only as the truth of searching human reason but also quite appropriately as the truth of a gracious God coming to meet, and even anticipating, that searching human reason in those other traditions as in our own. Moreover, if the self-revelation of God is first and foremost in our very being and in the totality of our experience, then the verbal formulation is a human undertaking for us Christians as well as for all others. This means that to some extent we are all fumbling and struggling to give utterance to something that is greater than our speech and our intellectual concepts, to which our imagination leaps expectantly by analogies.

If all this is true, then what we expect in conversation with those of the other religious traditions is growth in our own understanding and growth in our own faith wherever that may lead us. We expect new insights, knowing that these are not a threat but rather a promise of ultimate convergence beyond anything we can predict or anticipate. We expect to find complementarity of approach, of vision, of expectation, and of redemptive action. Jesus himself spoke of strangers coming from the east and from the west to sit down with Abraham in the kingdom. He reacted with a kind of startled delight to the approach and deeper awareness of the Samaritan woman at the well, the Canaanite woman seeking healing for her daughter, and the centurion in quest of compassion for his servant. Jesus said about strangers that if they were not against us they were with us in their efforts towards driving out the evil spirits of hatred and fear and enslavement.

The wider ecumenism would appear, then, to be authentically in the footsteps of Jesus. It is he who draws our attention to the realization that in God's eyes the Sabbath and all religious observances are for the benefit of human persons. Religious traditions do not exist in their own right, to subordinate human persons to ritual formality and correctness. (pp. 85–6)

Monika Hellwig, 'The Wider Ecumenism: Some Theological Questions', in Peter Phan (ed.), *Christianity and the Wider Ecumenism* (New York: Paragon, 1990).

John Hick

Born in 1922, John Hick was H. D. Wood Professor of Theology at the University of Birmingham and Danforth Professor of the Philosophy of Religion at Claremont Graduate School. Writing as a philosopher of religion, he is the author of numerous studies of philosophical theology, and has been a leading figure in the debate about religious pluralism. In The Rainbow of Faiths *he calls for a revolution in Christian thought. In his view, what is needed is a radical transformation in the concept of the universe of faiths. Christians, he believes, must now shift from a Christianity-centred to a Reality-centred model of the universe of faiths.*

Our traditional theology tells us that Jesus of Nazareth was God – more precisely, God the Son, the second person of the Holy Trinity – incarnate, that he died on the cross to atone for the sins of the world, thus making salvation possible, that he founded the Christian church to proclaim this to the ends of the earth, and that Christians, as members of the Body of Christ, are indwelt by the Holy Spirit and spiritually fed week by week by divine grace in the eucharist. One implication of this is that Christianity, alone among the religions, was founded by God in person. It is thus God's own religion in a sense in which no other can be. Must God not then wish all human beings to enter the religion that God has come down from heaven to earth to provide? A second implication is that those of us who are part of it, a part of the Body of Christ, live in a closer relationship with God than those outside it. Ought there not then to be more evidence in Christian lives than in the lives of others of those fruits of the Spirit which St Paul listed as 'love, joy, peace, patience, kindness, goodness, faithfulness, gentleness, self-control' (Gal. 5:22–23)? If our traditional Christian theology is true, surely we should expect these fruits to be present more fully in Christians generally than in non-Christians generally... . But I have been suggesting that, so far as we can tell, these visible fruits do not occur more abundantly among Christians than among Jews, Muslims, Hindus, Buddhists, Sikhs, Taoists, Baha'is and so on. And yet surely they ought to if the situation were as it is pictured in our traditional Christian theology. I am thus led to conclude that this theology is in need of revision... . (pp. 15–16)

In order to make sense of the idea of Christ at work within the world religions, including those that precede Christianity, it will be necessary to leave aside the historical figure of Jesus of Nazareth, and his death on the cross, and to speak instead of a non-historical, or supra-historical, Christ figure or Logos (i.e. the second person of the Trinity) who secretly inspired the Buddha, and the writers of the *Upanishads*, and Moses and the great Hebrew prophets, and Confucius and Lao-Tze and Zoroaster before the common era, as well as Muhammad, Guru Nanak, Ramakrishna and many others since. But this Christ figure, or Logos, operating before and thus independently of the historical life and death of Jesus of Nazareth, then becomes in effect a name for the world-wide and history-long presence and impact upon human life of the Divine, the Transcendent, the Ultimate, the Real. In other words, in order to make sense of the idea that the great world religions are all inspired and made salvific by the same transcendent influence we have to go beyond the historical figure of Jesus to a universal source of all salvific transformation. Christians may call this the cosmic Christ or the eternal Logos; Hindus and Buddhists may call it the Dharma; Muslims may call it Allah; Taoists may call it the Tao; and so on. But what we then have is no longer (to put it paradoxically) an exclusively Christian inclusivism, but a plurality of mutually inclusive inclusivisms which is close to the kind of pluralism I want to recommend... . (pp. 22–3)

The hypothesis to which these analogies point is that of an ultimate ineffable Reality which is the source and ground of everything, and which is such that in so far as the religious traditions are in soteriological alignment with it they are contexts of salvation/liberation. These traditions involve different human conceptions of the Real, with correspondingly different forms of experience of the Real, and correspondingly different forms of life in response to the Real... . (p. 27)

If we are Christians, accepting our own tradition as one valid response among others to the Real, we should continue within it, living in relation to that 'face' of the Real that we know as the heavenly Father of Jesus' teaching – or, if we think of Christianity as a developed theological tradition, as the Holy Trinity of later church teaching. And hopefully one should have begun, in this nurturing context, to undergo the salvific transformation from natural self-centredness to a new orientation centred in God. And the same, of course, applies to the people of the other great world faiths. Each tradition will continue in its concrete particularity as its own unique response to the Real. As the sense of rivalry between them diminishes and they participate increasingly in interfaith dialogue they will increasingly affect one another and each is likely to undergo change as a result, both influencing and being influenced by the others. (pp. 29–30)

John Hick, *The Rainbow of Faiths* (London: SCM Press, 1995).

Eugene Hillman

Eugene Hillman, formerly African missioner of the Holy Ghost Fathers, argues in Many Paths: A Catholic Approach to Religious Pluralism *that the wider ecumenism to which Christians were called by Vatican II demands a re-examination of christology, ecclesiology and missiology, and a coming to terms with the reality of religious pluralism.*

An incarnational missionary approach, as we know from the life and death of Jesus, accepts the religious experience of, and enters into crucial dialogue with, the people to whom the missionary is sent. Does the church that calls itself 'essentially missionary' accept and enter into dialogue with the religio-cultural worlds of those for whom the Christian faith community exists, namely, all the peoples of the world to whom the church is sent and from whom the church is called forth? ... Does the church's official missionary practice positively encourage these diverse peoples to understand and express the meaning of Christianity in the culture-specific and historically conditioned terms of their own respective and vastly differentiated social, economic, artistic and religious experiences? ... (p. 69)

What God has done in Jesus Christ 'once and for all' (Heb. 7:27; 9:26–28) in the historico-cultural terms of one particular people, the church must do in sacramentality among all the peoples who, with their varied historical experiences, myriad cultures and social structures, constitute the whole of humanity in its spatio-temporal reality. After the manner of the divine Logos the church must go out of herself, emptying herself of power, foreign riches and alien accretions, thus opening herself to modes of human existence, experience, expression and celebration that were not previously hers.

The church, in other words, is to make herself completely at home among each people in the same authentically human way that Jesus was at home in Nazareth. To ignore the missionary implications of belief in the incarnation in relation to humankind's cultural pluriformity is to foreclose the church's real growth in genuine catholicity. This is why cultures, far from being despised or ignored by missionaries, must be evangelized, as Pope Paul VI said, 'not in a purely decorative way as it were by applying a thin veneer but in a vital way, in depth and right to their very roots, in the wide and rich sense which these terms have in *Gaudium et Spes*'.... (p. 73)

Dialogue is not a technique or a device for leading people along the path of conversion from one faith community to another. While the option must always be open for Christians as well as non-Christians to change their religious orientation by entering a different faith community, all forms of calculated persuasion or manipulation remain completely incompatible with the mutual freedom and respect required for honest interreligious dialogue. In this regard, Christians need to remind themselves that their own firm beliefs about Jesus Christ as the incarnate Word of God, the Lord of history, and the unique Saviour of the whole world, are internal faith claims, based on interpretations of a historical revelation peculiar to their own community of faith. These beliefs have their counterparts, but not their equivalents, in other religious systems. So we must always beware of the 'supercilious condescension' with which Christians often disregard the subjective faith claims of others, while expecting the others to appreciate the subjective faith claims of Christians. (p. 75)

Such a dialogue, courageously open to new beginnings, can be mutually enriching; it holds the promise of increasing unity and fuller life for all of humankind. From a specifically Christian viewpoint the dialogue may be understood also as evangelical. It is in no way opposed to the church's missionary ministry; rather, it is a more appropriate way for the church to be 'essentially missionary', reaching out to the ends of the earth not in some imperial posture but in response to the summons of the Holy Spirit who is already present among all peoples. The ecumenical purpose of the church, sent by Jesus Christ and moved by the Holy Spirit, is to make itself 'fully present to all persons and peoples'.... This mission, directed outward to the nations, even to the ends of the earth, is a call to leave behind the cultural accoutrements and historical accretions of Christianity's European past. It is a call for new beginnings, for speaking in strange tongues and expressing Christ's 'good news' through different religious symbols in the more numerous and vastly diverse cultural worlds of peoples living outside the walls of ancient Christendom. (pp. 76–7)

Eugene Hillman, *Many Paths: A Catholic Approach to Religious Pluralism* (Maryknoll, NY: Orbis, 1989).

William Ernst Hocking

William Ernst Hocking, formerly Professor at Harvard, in 'Living Religions and a World Faith' argues that a person's conception of his own faith can be deepened by contact with other religions. According to Hocking, all religions contain a common core of truth.

In the natural order of experience, broadening is preliminary to deepening.

The first business of childhood is the accumulation of riches – wide collection of facts, names, ideas, with no particular concern for their order or their nature. The state of insight which we call 'understanding' follows slowly; the ambition to master things by penetrating their 'nature' arrives with maturity.

The religious experience of the race follows a similar pattern. The many gods of the early world belong to the stage of accumulation: they are records of the wide variety of primitive religious experience, care-free in respect to order, careful only for the faithful preservation of every inkling of the divine. They are preparations for that stage of 'understanding' which discerns that many gods are one. This rhythm of broadening and deepening recurs. In the later world, when the several great systems of faith are brought, as now, into intimate contact, there is a new era of broadening, in which each religion extends its base to comprise what it finds valid in other strands of tradition. But this also must serve as preliminary to that deepening which is a search for better grasp of its own essence.

For broadening necessarily stimulates the deepening process. One's conceptions have been inadequate; they have not anticipated these new vistas and motives: we require to understand our own religion better – we must reconceive it – then we shall see how the new perspectives belong quite naturally to what has always been present in its nature, unnoticed or unappreciated by us.

We are at the dawn of this new stage of deepening. In the contemporary epoch, in which the position and meaning of religion are in constant question, inclusiveness in the content of faith becomes a secondary aim. All the sails of the mind have for some time been set for exploration and acquisition; there are really few who need any longer to be admonished not to reject what is good in what to them is foreign. The great effort now required is the effort to discern the substance of the matter underlying all this profusion of religious expression to apprehend the generating principle of religious life and of each particular form of it. (pp. 135–6)

In preparation as any religion grows in self-understanding through grasping its own essence, it grasps the essence of all religion, and gains in power to interpret its various forms.

To interpret is the best gift which one religion can bring to another. Power to interpret is the power to say more truly or in more understandable language what an idea or a usage 'means'; to interpret is to give a voice to what is relatively inarticulate and defenceless. It is indeed to some extent to improve and alter, in so far as it separates the chaff from the wheat; but it does keep the wheat and bring it to market. The interpreter is able to save a great deal which the honest but rude excluder feels impelled to throw away.

In this sense, Reconception is the way of true conservatism; it conserves as much as possible of what is worth conserving in other faiths; it provides a permanent frame for all those scattered 'accents of the Holy Ghost' which, treasured in local traditions here and there, are robbed by their separateness of their due force.

There is, one feels, a certain *noblesse oblige* in the relations among religions; those who have travelled far in the path of self-understanding have an obligation to those less skilled in self-explanation. Instead of using this advantage to beat their opponents down, it becomes a matter of chivalry to express for them their meanings better than they themselves could express them. The joy of refutation is a poor and cheap-bought joy in comparison with the joy of lifting a struggling thought to a new level of self-understanding.

Thus, instead of attempting to shut other religions up in metaphysical compartments, and then destroying the compartments, it would certainly be fairer – not to say more honourable – if we were to attempt rather to anticipate for them what they mean, opening to them that larger room toward which they trend. (pp. 142–3)

How does this method make for a world faith?

Evidently, if one and only one religion could succeed in absorbing into its own essence the meaning of all the others that religion would attract the free suffrage of mankind to itself. Any such result would necessarily be remote, since the essence cannot be taken by storm; light upon its nature will appear only gradually, and through the slow intimations of meaning as intuitive understanding of the expressions of other faiths is increased. The specific social and historical functions of the local religions could in their nature never be completely replaced by the essence of a universal religion; a truly universal religion would provide a place for such local functions. (p. 144)

William Ernst Hocking, 'Living Religions and a World Faith', in Owen C. Thomas, *Attitudes Toward Other Religions*, (London: SCM Press, 1969).

I

Kenneth K. Inada

The Buddhist scholar Kenneth K. Inada studied in the United States and Japan and has served as Professor of Philosophy at the State University of New York at Buffalo. In 'Christocentrism–Buddhacentrism' he proposes a model for dialogue which is based on the notion of flexible hypotheses as a point of departure.

Speaking on behalf of Buddhists, I may respond very positively by endorsing the proposal and simultaneously counterproposing an analogous position for Buddhism – a Buddhacentrism. This is not to be presumptuous or to counter Christocentrism as such, but rather to clarify the position of a dialogic partner.... . It is to create an ideal situation in which the dialogue partners may function fully as equals in all respects, for to understand a partner's viewpoint is to work toward an intimate feel for that person's 'centric' nature, which may be vague and unclear at the beginning, but as the dialogue proceeds should become clear.

The proposal for Buddhacentrism is really nothing new, for the whole history of Buddhism is a manifestation of such a centrism. It will be recalled that Buddhism appeared in an Indian climate of ideological pluralism, in the presence of Hinduism, Jainism and Samkhya-yoga, and that its own doctrines were framed within the prevailing philosophical and religious context – that is, with respect to the contemporaneous knowledge of metaphysics, epistemology and yoga practice. It did not make a big splash from the start, but continued to borrow, adapt and incorporate ideas from other systems and traditions throughout its long history within and without India. This does not mean, however, that Buddhism became merely a synthetic way of life, in which its original doctrines were no longer discernible, for it stood its ground and guarded carefully the core of the Buddha's enlightenment. But it was flexible and resilient enough to expound its teachings in ways that always 'fitted the case', in accordance with the Buddha's own many-sided approach to suit his listeners' respective capabilities.

The conservative streak in Buddhism solidified early on, and has continued up to the present day in the form of Theravada Buddhism. The more liberal streak sped northward, principally to Tibet, China, Korea and Japan. It not only spread but developed its doctrines by direct contact with the diverse indigenous cultures that came in its path. Buddhacentric dialogue was a huge success in China, though it met hostile forces at the outset in the forms of Confucianism and Taoism. In the process, however, Buddhism transformed itself into Chinese Buddhism, enriching and deepening thereby the whole complex of Chinese thought and culture. The same process was duplicated in Korea and Japan. And now it is happening in America... . (pp. 104–5)

In order to come to grips with this philosophical approach, I have devised a very simple diagram to illustrate the dialogic area. I call this the 'H-bar Diagram'. It is provisional and needs to be modified as we go along in dialogue... .

1. The diagram is constituted by two centric systems, Buddhacentrism and Christocentrism, with a horizontal bar that brings them in contact. It depicts contacts in a pluralistic world.
2. The bar that connects both centrisms is mobile – it may move down toward the sense level or up toward the level of wisdom. Figuratively speaking, it is on rollers.
3. The bar is where all dialogues take place and therefore it may be called the dialogic bar.
4. The nature of a dialogue is essentially philosophical in order to maintain the sense of neutrality, rationality, objectivity and realization of wisdom.
5. The dialogic bar must be kept in balance or horizontal as much as possible in order to produce fruitful results.
6. Any undue imbalance or disruption of the dialogic bar means that there is a 'derailment' in the dialogue, which must be adjusted immediately. Ideally, a dialogue must manifest a 'self-corrective mechanism'. (pp. 106–7)

H-BAR DIAGRAM

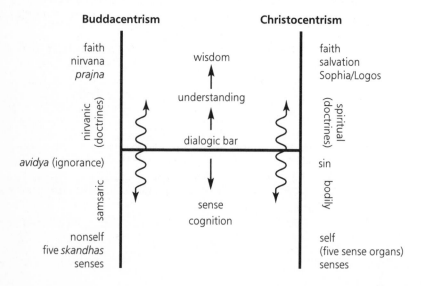

Needless to say dialogue carried on according to the H-bar Diagram requires utmost co-operation, openness and understanding by the partners involved.... . My personal observation on the concept of ultimate reality is that it is a problem, albeit a crucial one, belonging to the respective religions within their own cultural settings and need not enter in the dialogue from the beginning; that is to say, to introduce it at the very outset will only bring on metaphysical difficulties and confusion, which would not be conducive to the discussion of the more practical aspect of life, which is already burned by matters that are still being probed. (p. 107)

Kenneth K. Inada, 'Christocentrism–Buddhacentrism', in Leonard Swidler (ed.), *Toward a Universal Theology of Religion* (Maryknoll, NY: Orbis, 1987).

Muhammad Iqbal

Born in 1876, Muhammad Iqbal studied at Punjab University and later at Lahore Government College. He served as Reader in the Punjab University Oriental College, and later taught at Lahore Government College. In 'Islam as a Moral and Political Ideal', he compares the central religious assumptions of Islam with those of other faiths.

To begin with, we have to recognize that every great religious system starts with certain propositions concerning the nature of man and the universe. The psychological implication of Buddhism, for instance, is the central fact of pain as a dominating element in the constitution of the universe. Man, regarded as an individuality, is helpless against the forces of pain, according to the teachings of Buddhism. There is an indissoluble relation between pain and the individual consciousness which, as such, is nothing but a constant possibility of pain. Freedom from pain means freedom from individuality. Starting from the fact of pain, Buddhism is quite consistent in placing before man the ideal of self-destruction. Of the two terms of this relation, pain and the sense of personality, one (i.e. pain) is ultimate; the other is a delusion from which it is possible to emancipate ourselves by ceasing to act on those lines of activity, which have a tendency to intensify the sense of personality. Salvation, then, according to Buddhism is inaction; renunciation of self and unworldliness are the principal virtues. Similarly, Christianity, as a religious system, is based on the fact of sin. The world is regarded as evil and the taint of sin is regarded as hereditary to man, who, as an individuality is insufficient and stands in need of some supernatural personality to intervene between him and his Creator. Christianity, unlike Buddhism, regards human personality as something real, but agrees with

Buddhism in holding that man, as a force against sin, is insufficient. There is, however, a subtle difference in the agreement. We can, according to Christianity, get rid of sin by depending upon a Redeemer; we can free ourselves from pain, according to Buddhism, by letting this insufficient force dissipate or lose itself in the universal energy of nature. Both agree in the fact of insufficiency and both agree in holding that this insufficiency is an evil; but while the one makes up the deficiency by bringing in the force of a redeeming personality, the other prescribes its gradual reduction until it is annihilated altogether. Again, Zoroastrianism looks upon nature as a scene of endless struggle between the powers of evil and the powers of good, and recognizes in man the power to choose any course of action he likes. The universe, according to Zoroastrianism, is partly evil, partly good; man is neither wholly good nor wholly evil, but a combination of the two principles – light and darkness continually fighting against each other for universal supremacy. We see then that the fundamental pre-suppositions, with regard to the nature of the universe and man, in Buddhism, Christianity and Zoroastrianism, respectively are the following:

1. There is pain in nature and man regarded as an individual is evil (Buddhism).
2. There is sin in nature and the taint of sin is fatal to man (Christianity).
3. There is struggle in nature; man is a mixture of the struggling forces and is free to range himself on the side of the powers of good which will eventually prevail (Zoroastrianism).

The question now is, what is the Muslim view of the universe and man? What is the central idea in Islam which determines the structure of the entire system? We know that sin, pain and sorrow are constantly mentioned in the Quran. The truth is that Islam looks upon the universe as a reality and consequently recognizes as reality all that is in it. Sin, pain, sorrow, struggle are certainly real, but Islam teaches that evil is not essential to the universe; the universe can be reformed; the elements of sin and evil can be gradually eliminated. All that is in the universe is God's, and the seemingly destructive forces of nature become sources of life, if properly controlled by man, who is endowed with the power to understand and to control them... .

Man is a responsible being, he is the maker of his own destiny, his salvation is his own business. There is no mediator between God and man. God is the birthright of every man. The Quran, therefore, while it looks upon Jesus Christ as the spirit of God, strongly protests against the Christian doctrine of Redemption as well as the doctrine of an infallible visible head of the Church – doctrines which proceed upon the assumption of the insufficiency of human personality and tend to create in man a sense of dependence, which is regarded by Islam as a force obstructing the ethical progress of man. (pp. 32–8)

Muhammad Iqbal, 'Islam as a Moral and Political Ideal', in Syed Abdul Vahid (ed.), *Thoughts and Reflections of Iqbal* (Lahore: Ashraf, 1964).

J

Louis Jacobs

Louis Jacobs, formerly Visiting Professor at the University of Lancaster, argues in A Jewish Theology *that while Judaism contains more truth than other faiths, members of other faiths can enter into the World to Come.*

Sweeping though it may seem there is no escaping the truth which Judaism enunciates, and for which Jews have been ready to suffer martyrdom, that there is only One God and that the Torah ... has not been superseded by any other religion. This compels us, if we are adherents of Judaism, frankly to declare that the positions other religions take on these questions are false. Far Eastern faiths are either polytheistic or atheistic. The Christian concept of God is false from the Jewish point of view. Judaism similarly denies that Muhammad received a revelation from God which made him the last of the prophets with the Koran in the place of the Torah. Yet for all the lack of compromise in such an attitude it should not lead Jews to conclude that God has not revealed Himself to others or that the religions of the world have no truth in them. The position one ought to adopt is that there is more truth in Judaism than in other religions... .

Certain conclusions would seem to follow from the adoption of such an attitude. Such are the realities of the situation that hardly anyone born in the Far East, for example, is likely to have Judaism presented to him as a live option and since even in the West very few Christians or Muslims are likely to embrace Judaism, then it must follow that while Judaism will continue to accept converts and while it will not give up its Messianic hope of an eventual conversion to the truth by all men, it must believe that the good man of whatever faith (or, for that matter, none) will be counted among what the Rabbis call 'the righteous of the nations of the world'. The Rabbis of the early second century debated whether Gentiles have a share in the World to Come but the view adopted was that of R. Joshua who taught that the righteous of the nations of the world have a share in the World to Come. Maimonides' formulation of this is as follows:

> Whoever accepts upon himself the seven precepts (of the sons of Noah) and keeps them belongs to the saints of the nations of the world and has a share in

the World to Come. But this only applies if he accepts them and keeps them because the Holy One, blessed be He, commanded them in the Torah and informed us through Moses our teacher that the sons of Noah of old had been commanded to keep them. If, however, he keeps them because his reason tells him so he is not a 'proselyte of the gate' and is neither of the saints of the nations of the world nor of their sages.

To adopt this exceedingly narrow view which, incidentally, is Maimonides' own and finds no support in the Rabbinic sources, would mean that for Judaism the majority of mankind is denied spiritual bliss in the Hereafter. Even if Maimonides' view is rejected and the 'righteous of the nations of the world' means those who keep the 'seven precepts of the sons of Noah', even if they keep them because it seems right to do so not because of a belief in their revealed character, it would still rule out all polytheists and presumably all atheists and agnostics since one of the seven is aimed against idolatry and polytheism. But even according to the traditional Halakhah, there is the notion, helpful here, that a child brought up among heathen is not held responsible for pagan acts he performs when an adult because he has been trained to do them and cannot help himself. This doctrine of the 'child captured by heathen' is applied in the Rabbinic sources to a Jew but by the same token it would apply to anyone brought up in a polytheistic faith or an atheistic background who cannot be held responsible unless he had the opportunities of knowing the truth and wilfully rejects it and this is known only to God. In any event it seems reasonable to conclude that the 'good man' of the nations is to be understood in the purely ethical sense and that in this sense, therefore, it does not matter whether a man has been brought up in this religion or the other or in no religion at all provided that he leads a good ethical life. Admittedly this is speculative but Judaism does, after all, affirm that God is the Father of all mankind and it is very hard to believe that He will deprive any of His children of spiritual bliss because, by an accident of birth, there were no opportunities of fully knowing the truth. Indeed, it would seem to be necessary, granted our premises, to make the even bolder suggestion that the religious classics of mankind, insofar as they are monotheistic, or, at least, not polytheistic, are themselves God's way of teaching His truth to some of His children. One would presumably have to go even further than this and admit that Jews can learn from the religious classics of other faiths as they can learn from secular works. (pp. 289–91)

Louis Jacobs, *A Jewish Theology* (London: Darton, Longman and Todd,1973).

K. N. Jayatilleke

Trained in Buddhist learning in Sri Lanka as well as the kind of philosophy taught in English universities in the 1950s and 1960s, K. N. Jayatilleke is the author of Early Buddhist Theory of Knowledge. *In 'The Buddhist Attitude toward Other Religions', he provides a Theravada Buddhist view of other faiths. In his view, Buddhism is tolerant of other religions, but not relativistic.*

The concept of the Buddha as one who discovers the truth rather than as one who has a monopoly of the truth is clearly a source of tolerance. It leaves open the possibility for others to discover aspects of the truth, or even the whole truth, for themselves. The Buddhist acceptance of *Pacceka-Buddhas*, who discover the truth for themselves, is a clear admission of this fact. Referring to certain sages (*munayo*), who had comprehended the nature of their desires and had eliminated them, crossing over the waves of samsaric existence, the Buddha says: 'I do not declare that all these religious men are sunk in repeated birth and decay.' Yet, as it is pointed out, the *Dhamma* is to be preached to all beings though all beings may not profit by it just as much as all sick people are to be treated although some may get well or succumb to their illnesses despite the medicines given. This is because there are beings who would profit only from the *Dhamma*.

This assertion of the possibility of salvation or spiritual growth outside Buddhism does not mean that Buddhism values all religions alike and considers them equally true... . (p. 144)

We note here that the relativist valuation of religion in early Buddhism does not presuppose or imply the truth of all religions or religion-surrogates. Some types of religion are clearly condemned as false and undesirable, while others are satisfactory to the extent to which they contain the essential core of beliefs and values central to religion, whatever their epistemic foundations may be. Those based on claims to omniscience on the part of the founder, revelation or tradition, metaphysical speculation or pragmatic scepticism, being unsatisfactory insofar as they are based on uncertain foundations.

Revelations and revelational traditions contradict each other and it is said that they may contain propositions which may be true or false. In the case of religions based on metaphysical argument and speculation, 'the reasoning may be valid or invalid and the conclusions true or false'. Buddhism is, therefore, by implication a religion which asserts survival, moral values, freedom and responsibility, the non-inevitability of salvation, and is also verifiably true. (pp. 145–6)

I do not propose in this lecture to examine any of the specific doctrines of another religion and compare or contrast them with Buddhism but it will be observed that the definition of the Buddhist 'right view of life' (*samma ditthi*) comprehends the basic beliefs and values of the higher religions. The definition reads as follows:

There is value in alms, sacrifices and oblations; there is survival and recompense for good and evil deeds; there are moral obligations and there are religious teachers, who have led a good life and who have proclaimed with their
superior insight and personal understanding the nature of this world and the
world beyond.

This 'right view of life' (*samma ditthi*) is said to be of two sorts: (a) one of which is
mixed up with the inflowing impulses (*sasava*) and (b) the other not so mixed up.
These impulses are the desire for sensuous gratification (*kamasava*), the desire for
self-centred pursuits (*bhavasava*) and illusions (*avijjasava*). Thus a right view of
life mixed up with a desire for a belief in personal immortality in heaven or a belief
in sensuous heavens would be a *sasava sammaditthi*.

The above summary of the right philosophy of life, it may be observed, is
comprehensive enough to contain, recognize and respect the basic truths of all
higher religions. All these religions believe in a Transcendent, characterized by
Nirvana which is beyond time, space and causation in Buddhism, as an
Impersonal Monistic principle such as Brahman or Tao in some religions, and as a
Personal God in others. They all assert survival, moral recompense and responsibility. They all preach a 'good life', which has much in common and whose culmi-
nation is communion or union with or the attainment of this Transcendent. The
early Buddhist conception of the nature and destiny of man in the universe is,
therefore, not in basic conflict with the beliefs and values of the founders of the
great religions so long as they assert some sort of survival, moral values, freedom
and responsibility and the non-inevitability of salvation. But at the same time it is
not possible to say that in all their phases of development and in all their several
strands of belief in varying social contexts they have stood for the central core of
beliefs and values. (p. 146)

K. N. Jayatilleke, 'The Buddhist Attitude to Other Religions', in Paul J. Griffiths
(ed.), *Christianity Through Non-Christian Eyes* (Maryknoll, NY: Orbis 1990).

K

David Kerr

Formerly Director of the Centre for the Study of Islam and Christian Muslim Relations and Professor of Islamic Studies at Hartford Seminary, David Kerr is Professor at the University of Edinburgh. In 'The Prophet Mohammad in Christian Theological Perspective', he argues that the image of Mohammad has been distorted within the Christian tradition. What is now required is a revision of this understanding for fruitful dialogue to take place.

This study would suggest, by way of conclusion, that a modern Christian theological response to the Muslim question 'Do you accept Mohammad as a prophet?' might be formulated upon the following considerations:

- God's revelation of his Word as the power over, within and beyond creation is universal, and is universally performative of his purposes in achieving what the Bible terms 'the Kingdom of God' (which in meaning is by no means strange to the vision of the Qur'an);
- divine revelation is evidenced universally in nature and in human history, through communities and individuals, and in the deepest apprehensions of the religious traditions which have evolved around them;
- the Bible, in its Hebrew and Greek parts, provides us with a centuries-long set of interpretations of divine revelation through the graphic record of God's actions in the history of Israel, exemplifying the universal pattern of divine activity in the analysis of a particular people and, in the New Testament, a particular person, Jesus, and the apostolic Church;
- the Gospel in Christ, for the Christian, signifies the performative pattern of universal divine revelation of which the Church is called to be the doxological sign in the world, pointing however wretchedly in its history to the ontological dynamics of the Kingdom of God;
- as God has left no people without witnesses to his divine revelation, so the Church in the power of the Holy Spirit should explore the many extra-biblical testimonies positively and with imagination, searching them for complementary

signs of the mystery of divine providence and critically adopting them into its own doxology;

- Mohammad is manifestly such a sign 'in the way of the prophets', the Qur'an witnessing the universality of divine revelation, reiterating many of the fundamental perceptions of the Bible, and providing as it were a critical commentary on the more dogmatic aspects of particularly New Testament belief, and Mohammad exemplifying the application of the Qur'anic vision in society.

Along these lines may not the Christian with integrity join with the Muslim in responding to the Qur'an's invitation to 'ask blessings upon him (Mohammad) and salute him with a worthy salutation', in the spirit of Jesus' own command: 'Let there be no limit to your salutation as your heavenly Father's goodness knows no bounds.' Such salutation commits us, however, to work together as Christians and Muslims, together with all other human respondents to the universal divine revelation, for the fuller realization of God's rule on earth. It is not a concession to the dogmatic postulates of a particular religious tradition, nor of 'finality' in revelation for another. Rather it is to participate creatively in the universal activity of God, which challenges us to re-live the experience of all the prophets, particularly Moses, Jesus and Mohammad as they wrestled with the task of 'creating peace in the city' – Moses as he withdrew from the tyranny of Pharaonic Egypt in an exodus which brought the Children of Israel to the land of Canaan and eventually Jerusalem; Jesus as, entering upon the climax of his ministry, 'he drew near and saw the city and wept over it, saying: "Would that even today you knew the things that make for peace"'; and Mohammad as he made his *hijra* (migration) to Medina in his search for the *umma muslima*. Only thus, in the streets of our modern cities, laboratories of religious, ethnic, social and political pluralism, can we authenticate the meaning of prophethood in our contemporary world. (pp. 129–31)

David Kerr, 'The Prophet Mohammad in Christian Theological Perspective', in Dan Cohn-Sherbok (ed.), *Islam in a World of Diverse Faiths* (London: Macmillan, 1991).

Ursula King

Born in 1938, Ursula King has served as Professor of Theology and Religious Studies at the University of Bristol. In 'Models of Interreligious Communication', she stresses that interfaith dialogue has important implications for the theological task. In her view, the traditional teachings of Christianity need to be reformulated in the light of knowledge of other faiths.

Each tradition will have to explore the implications of religious pluralism and interfaith dialogue for its own theological thinking. From the perspective of the Christian tradition ... one could summarize the theological task as one of reformulating the traditional teachings on 'God, man and the world' (or more specifically 'God, the human being, nature and society'). Or what Teilhard de Chardin in his inquiry into the spiritual energy resources of Eastern and Western religions for 'building the earth' called the problems of 'God and his transcendence: the world and its value; the individual and the importance of the person; mankind and social requirements', all of which have found particular formulations in different theologies, but so far no overall synthesis and integrated approach have been attempted which are commensurate to our contemporary experience of history, society, and new consciousness and realization of the common destiny of humankind.... (p. 113)

Interfaith dialogue can lead participants to the existential realization that each religious tradition has received a valuable glimpse – perhaps some more, some less – of the total vision, and in dialogue we can learn to complement each other's insight and disclosure of the Divine. It is thus not a question of competition, but of the complementarity of different visions which, when related to each other, can grow into greater fullness. Without losing our respective identities, the task of integration, of relating our respective visions to teach other, can enlarge and enrich us all together and give us access to greater splendour and deeper understanding.... (p. 114)

Members of different faiths have to learn to see through each other's eyes and feel with each other's senses. Perhaps the term 'global theology' still sounds too absolutist, too unacceptable to people outside the Christian tradition, too much like a grand synthesis which leaves no room for internal differentiation. Perhaps another term has to be found – 'multilateral theologies', or something similar – to reflect at the linguistic and conceptual level the pluralistic complexities, the variety of approaches to truth and ultimate reality in their historical and contemporary forms. Such a theology must be free from any apologetics and imperialistic claims; it has to remain open-ended, always open in the search for further truth. It has profound implications for what is traditionally called the 'theology of missions' and also what is currently termed 'theology of religions'.... (p. 115)

While questions about the significance of Christ raise important historical and theoretical issues relating to a differentiated theological methodology and hermeneutics, we must not forget that much of Western Christian theology needs to be freed from what has been called its 'Latin captivity' or bondage. We need to examine our traditional theological modes of thinking from a critical distance: how far has the Western theological mode too much insisted on conceptual distinctions and separations, with an emphasis on otherness and exclusiveness rather than on the relatedness of all things, the connections between different levels of reality and experience. Here too Hindu perspectives can provide a wholesome corrective.... (pp. 117–18)

We have to learn to live in and respond creatively to a completely new context of religious and social complexity which poses a tremendous intellectual challenge to our traditional mode of doing theology. It is not our task to affirm the sheer plurality of religious experiences and revelations and then let them stand side by side. On the contrary, we need to pursue a genuine theological probing of the religious meaning of pluralism by relating our seeing, feeling, thinking, acting and praying to more than one mode of being. Hinduism has a rich tradition in dealing with complexity by approaching all realities from more than one perspective. Perhaps Christians can learn from Hindu experience that the very richness of the mystery of Christ consists precisely in allowing us to fathom its significance in many different and hitherto unknown ways.

It will not be easy to develop new theological modes of thinking and new modes of interreligious communication. All the powers of our intellect and imagination and the resources of our faith are called upon to bring to fruition the spiritual insights of our world religious heritage, to develop a theological vision which can help to build a world community on earth. Interfaith communication and dialogue can also help to remove unfavourable intergroup images and stereotypes, wrongly grounded philosophical categories and evaluative theological statements which hinder rather than help understanding. (p. 121)

Ursula King, 'Models of Interreligious Communication', in Dan Cohn-Sherbok, *Many Mansions* (London: Bellew, 1992).

Paul F. Knitter

Paul F. Knitter, Professor of Theology at Xavier University, argues that religious pluralism must now be placed within the context of human liberation. As outlined in 'Toward a Liberation Theology of Religions', such a new orientation should be grounded in a recognition of the centrality of praxis.

Besides clarifying the context and starting point for a genuinely pluralistic interreligous dialogue – beyond both exclusivism and inclusivism – the method of liberation theology can also help resolve the even more knotty problem of the uniqueness of Christ. In order to avoid pre-established absolutist positions that prevent a genuinely pluralistic dialogue, Christians must, it seems, revamp or even reject their traditional understanding of Jesus Christ as God's final, definitive, normative voice. Can they do this and still call themselves Christians? To show how a liberation theology of religions can help answer such christological quandaries, I offer the following four considerations:

1. Liberation theology insists that *praxis* is both the origin and confirmation of theory or doctrine. All Christian beliefs and truth claims must grow out of and

then be reconfirmed in the *praxis* or lived experience of these truths. According to liberation theology, one does not first know the truth and then apply it in *praxis*; it is in action, in doing, that truth is really known and validated... . *Praxis*, therefore, was the starting point of all christology. And it remains the criterion of all christology, for everything we know or say about Jesus must be continually confirmed, clarified, and perhaps corrected in the *praxis* of living his vision within the changing contexts of history... . (pp. 191–2)

2. Another related ingredient in the theology of liberation – the primacy of orthopraxis over orthodoxy – assures Christians that if claims about the finality of Christ/Christianity are not presently possible, neither are they necessary. The primary concern of a soteriocentric liberation theology of religions is not 'right belief' about the uniqueness of Christ, but the 'right practice', with other religions, of furthering the kingdom and its *Soteria*. Clarity about whether and how Christ is one Lord and Saviour, as well as clarity about any other doctrine, may be important, but it is subordinate to carrying out the preferential treatment of the poor and nonpersons. Orthodoxy becomes a pressing concern only when it is necessary for orthopraxis – for carrying out the preferential option and promoting the kingdom. (p. 192)

3. The possibilities ... of using the preferential option for the poor as a working criterion for 'grading the religions' contains further christological implications. If liberating *praxis* with and for the poor and nonpersons is an indicator and measure of authentic revelation and religious experience then Christians, whether they like it or not, have the means to discern not only whether but how much other religious beliefs and practices may be genuine 'ways of salvation' – and further, whether and how much other religious figures may be genuine liberators and 'saviours'. In other words, the soteriocentric criteria for religious dialogue contained in the preferential option for the oppressed offer Christians the tools to critically examine and possibly revise the traditional understanding of the uniqueness of Christ.

   Simply stated, for their ethical, soteriological fruits we shall know them – we shall be able to judge whether and how much other religious paths and their mediators are salvific. (p. 193)

4. A liberation theology of religions offers help in dealing with another obstacle facing those who are exploring possibilities of a nonabsolutist or nondefinitive understanding of Christ. The final touchstone, it can be said, for the validity and appropriateness of a new understanding of Christ as 'one among many', in a relationship of 'complementary uniqueness' with others, is whether such a view will, eventually, be received by the faithful. Reception by the faithful was the final criterion for the validity of the early ecumenical councils, and it remains such a criterion today for popes, councils and theologians. Christian theologians, in other words, cannot ply their trade in well-padded ivory towers, belonging as they do to the 'public of the academy', they must also be able to communicate and find a home in the 'public of the church'. (p. 194)

It might be argued today such a recognition of others is necessary for remaining faithful to the original witness about Jesus. Theologians who are exploring a pluralist theology of religions and a nonabsolutist christology are doing so not merely for the sake of novelty or for the sake of joining the excitement of a truly pluralist interreligious dialogue; rather, they do so because 'the love of Christ urges them' (2 Cor. 5:14). They want to be faithful to the original message of the Nazarean – that to which Jesus always subordinated himself: the kingdom of love, unity and justice.

In order to serve and promote that kingdom, we want to dialogue and work with others and be open to the possibility that there are other teachers and liberators and saviours who can help us understand and work for that kingdom in ways as yet beyond our hearing or imagination. 'Anyone who is not against us is with us' (Mark 9:40). (pp. 196–7)

Paul Knitter, 'Toward a Liberation Theology of Religions', in John Hick and Paul F. Knitter (eds), *The Myth of Christian Uniqueness* (London: SCM Press, 1987).

Hendrik Kraemer

Hendrik Kraemer, born in 1888, served as Professor of the History and Phenomenology of Religions in Leiden. In The Christian Message in a Non-Christian World, *he argues that each situation has its own particular nature. Yet, the belief that salvation is found only through the grace of God in Christ must serve as the point of departure for mission.*

Every religion is a living, indivisible unity. Every part of it – a dogma, a rite, a myth, an institution, a cult – is so vitally related to the whole that it can never be understood in its real function, significance and tendency, as these occur in the reality of life, without keeping constantly in mind the vast and living unity of existential apprehension in which this part moves and has its being. It is only for the sake of scientific analysis that we are allowed to break up a religion into conceptions about God, man, sin, redemption, soul, etc. This scientific method, properly speaking, is a great distortion and disregard of living and actual reality. It is, however, indispensable to get an intellectual command of the material and is therefore, at least to a certain extent, necessary as an instrument. As a guide for the adequate apprehension of religion as a living and thriving reality it is less than useless.

Now, missions have to do with religions as thriving and living realities, and in the problem of concrete points of contact to keep this incessantly in mind is the key of the whole matter. The many false hopes and reasonings that have been and are entertained on this subject in missionary circles are due to the neglect of this point. Many attempts made in missionary literature to build up various points of contact with different religions proceed on this intellectualist and analytic line of approach, which is applied by science in her own way and for a different and more legitimate end.... .

One might state this important aspect of the problem of concrete points of contact in this somewhat unusual way: that there is only one point of contact, and if that one point really exists, then there are many points of contact. This one point of contact is the disposition and the attitude of the missionary. It seems rather upsetting to make the missionary the point of contact. Nevertheless it is true, as practice teaches. The strategic and absolutely dominant point in this whole important problem, when it has to be discussed in general terms, is the missionary worker himself. Such is the golden rule, or, if one prefers, the iron law, in this whole matter. The way to live up to this rule is to have an untiring and genuine interest in the religion, the ideas, the sentiments, the institutions – in short, in the whole range of life of the people among whom one works, for Christ's sake and for the sake of those people. Whosoever disobeys this rule does not find any real point of contact. Whosoever obeys it becomes one with his environment, and has and finds contacts. Obedience to it is implied in the prime missionary obligation and passion, to wit, preparing the way for Christ and being by God's grace a pointer to him. Only a genuine and continuous interest in the people as they are creates real points of contact, because man everywhere intuitively knows that, only when his actual being is the object of humane interest and love, is he looked upon in actual fact, and not theoretically, as a fellow man. As long as a man feels he is the object of interest only for reasons of intellectual curiosity or for purposes of conversion, and not because of himself as he is in his total empirical reality, there cannot arise that humane natural contact which is the indispensable condition of all real religious meeting of man with man. In these conditions the door to such a man and to the world he lives in remains locked, and the love of Christ remains for him remote and abstract. It needs translation by the manifestation of the missionary's genuine interest in the whole life of the people to whom he goes.

The problem of the concrete points of contact is thus in its practical aspect to a very great extent a problem of missionary ethics, and not only a problem of insight and knowledge. (pp. 135–41)

The object we had in view in our stocktaking and drawing of conclusions was to emphasize the fact that the essential meaning of Christianity is to witness to the world of divine and human realities as revealed in Jesus Christ.... . Without this fundamental clearness about what Christianity is in the sense of the prophetic religion of Biblical realism, and what it is after, all approach to the non-Christian religions results in confusion of ends and methods. In our sketch of the Christian faith and the Christian ethic we have tried to effect this fundamental clarification. This statement of Christian truth, in accordance with the character of biblical realism as being the tale of God's self-disclosure and of the disclosure of the genuine condition of man and the world in the light of divine Self-disclosure, is the standard of reference for the religious life of all mankind. (p. 299)

Hendrik Kraemer, *The Christian Message in a Non-Christian World* (London: The Edinburgh House Press, 1938).

Hans Küng

Hans Küng, born in 1938 in Switzerland, studied at the Pontifical Gregorian University in Rome and later in Paris. He served as Professor of Fundamental Theology and later Professor of Dogmatic and Ecumenical Theology at the Institute for Ecumenical Research at the University of Tübingen. In Global Responsibility: In Search of a New World Ethic, *he outlines an ethical manifesto for believers in all traditions.*

But do the adherents of the various religions know equally well precisely what they have in common ethically? Not at all. So what unites all the great religions would have to be worked out carefully in detail on the basis of the sources – a significant and enjoyable task for the scholars of the different religions! But even at the present stage of the investigation some significant common views may be brought out briefly. It is not a matter of working out the differences and contra-dictions, the features of the great world religions which are exclusive and cannot be reconciled, but of working out what holds them together in spite of everything – with a view to the principle of responsibility. My question is: what can religions contribute to the furthering of an ethic, despite their very different systems of dogmas and symbols?... (p. 55)

ETHICAL PERSPECTIVES OF THE WORLD RELIGIONS

(a) Human well-being

Certainly, religions were and still are tempted to gather round themselves in order to preserve the power of their institutions, constitutions and hierarchies. And yet where they so wish, they can still credibly convey to the world, with a different moral power from that of many international organizations, that they are concerned with human well-being. For all the great religions authoritatively offer a basic religious orientation – support, help and hope in the face of the mecha-nism of all human institutions, in the face of the self-interest of the various indi-viduals and groups, and in the face of the excess of information provided by the media... .

(b) Maxims of basic humanity

Certainly religions were and always are tempted to fix themselves on and encapsulate themselves in special traditions, mysterious dogmas and ritual precepts. And yet where they wish, they can establish the validity of fundamental maxims of basic humanity with quite a different authority and power of conviction from that of politicians, lawyers and philosophers. For all the great religions in fact call for particular 'non-negotiable standards', basic ethical norms and maxims for guiding action, which are grounded in an Unconditioned, an Absolute, and therefore are also to hold unconditionally for hundreds of millions of people... .

(c) A reasonable middle way

Certainly, religions were and still are tempted legalistically to harp on some rigorist extreme positions, in both individual and social ethics, in both sexual and business and state ethics. And yet where they want to, they can win over hundreds of millions of people on this earth for a reasonable middle way between libertinism and legalism. For all the great religions in fact encourage models for action which indicate a middle way... .

(d) The golden rule

Certainly, religions were and still are tempted to lose themselves in an endless tangle of commandments and precepts, canons and paragraphs. And yet where they so will, they can explain with quite a different authority from that of any philosophy why the application of their norms does not apply from case to case, but categorically. Religions can provide a supreme norm for conscience, that categorical imperative which is immensely important for today's society, an imperative which obligates in quite a different depth and fundamental way. For all the great religions require observance of something like a 'golden rule' – a norm which is not just hypothetical and conditioned but is categorical, apodeictic and unconditioned – utterly practicable in the face of the extremely complex situation in which the individual or groups must often act... .

(e) Moral motivations

Certainly, religions were and still are tempted to command people in an authoritarian way, to call for blind obedience and to violate the conscience. And yet where they so will they can offer convincing moral motivations. For in the face of so much frustration, lethargy and apathy, especially in today's younger generation, they can offer convincing motives for action on the basis of age-old tradition in a contemporary form: not only eternal ideas, abstract principles and general norms, like philosophy, but also the living embodiment of a new attitude to life and a new lifestyle... .

(f) A horizon of meaning and identification of a goal

Certainly, religions were and still are tempted to have a double morality, namely to preach ethical demands only to others and not first apply them self-critically to themselves. But if they so will, even today – or again today – in the face of emptiness and meaninglessness for hundreds of millions of people they can credibly demonstrate with a unique power of conviction a horizon of meaning on this earth – and also a final goal. (pp. 56–60)

Hans Küng, *Global Responsibility: In Search of a New World Ethic* (London: SCM Press, 1990).

Karl-Josef Kuschel

Karl-Josef Kuschel received a doctorate and habilitation in Catholic theology from the University of Tübingen, and became Professor of the Theology of Culture and Interreligious Dialogue at the same university. In "'Faithful" to the New Testament?', he stresses that faithfulness to New Testament teaching does not rule out the possibility of interreligious encounter.

If, however, as a Christian I accept the New Testament as the normative original document, it is my duty to affirm it, whether I like it or not. Christians simply do not merely believe in God as 'an unsurpassable Mystery, one which can never totally be comprehended or contained in human thought or construct', as Knitter contends. As he had already done in his earlier works, Knitter here proposes an anthropological–epistemological notion of mystery that is alien to the New Testament. The New Testament posits instead an '*anthropos*–critical' christological notion of mystery, according to which no human (*anthropos*) has ever seen God (this is 'anthropos–critical' insisted upon) except Christ, the Son, who is 'in the bosom of the Father' (John 1:18). For Paul as well, the 'depths' of God are unfathomable, but at the same time the Apostle leaves no doubt that God revealed his mystery in Jesus Christ, who may therefore be called 'the mystery of the hidden wisdom of God' (1 Cor. 2:7). According to the New Testament, Christians who depend on Jesus as the Christ may trust that this God does not want to be an impenetrable, unfathomable riddle; that God has revealed his secret, and has done so in Jesus Christ. To say that 'Jesus is not God's total, definitive, unsurpassable truth' does not do justice to the New Testament (not to mention the creeds of the early church).

Undeniably these christological statements are awkward for interreligious dialogue and difficult to communicate. But I would also expect my non-Christian dialogue partners to express those core beliefs that are most deeply theirs even if these beliefs should be in glaring contradiction to Christian claims and demands. As Jesus Christ is for a Christian 'the way, the truth and the life', analogously for a

Jew it is the Torah, for a Muslim the Qur'an, and for a Buddhist the Buddha's Eight-fold Path. Why should dialogue become impossible if the partners set out from such opposed starting points, even if such firm claims at first appear to subordinate the other to one's own truth claims? This does not mean that the non-Christian partner is thereby rendered an unequal partner, as Knitter contends, as if all participants in the dialogue did not have the same rights. As a Christian I must put up with the possibility that a representative of Hinduism (for example, someone from the Vedantic tradition) might call me naive and superficial in my understanding of God, or that a Buddhist might tell me that the Christian image of God is far too anthropomorphic (in comparison with *Sunyata*, the Buddhist notion of Ultimate Reality). This would not make me feel in any manner discriminated against or unequally treated. According to my understanding, of course, witnesses to the truth and respect for contrary witnesses to the truth are not mutually exclusive. The decisive question is whether there is the will to dialogue, that is, a will to engage one's own truth claims in conversation with competing truth claims of others. Whoever enters an interreligious dialogue must be prepared to do this.

Knitter, however, disputes this contention: he portrays as incapable of dialogue those who want to find ways of communicating their witness to the truth. This is unfair and does not even correspond to the facts. It is not the case that my confession of Christ prevents respect for other confessions of faith, even if I am of the opinion that other faith witnesses do not reveal the same encompassing depth of truth as does the Christian. Non-Christians will not be denied the 'right' to bring their truth witness to the dialogue. And non-Christians will surely have enough self-confidence critically to examine my truth claim. Interreligious dialogue does not presuppose the suspension of the truth question but a wrestling for the truth, which I hope to grasp with greater depth and comprehension through dialogue. (pp. 90–2)

Karl-Josef Kuschel, '"Faithful" to the New Testament?' in Leonard Swidler and Paul Mojzes (eds), *The Uniqueness of Jesus: A Dialogue with Paul F. Knitter* (Maryknoll, NY: Orbis, 1997).

L

Christopher Lamb

Christopher Lamb has served as Head of the Centre for Inter Faith Dialogue at Middlesex University. In 'A Future Perspective for Inter Faith Dialogue', he stresses that religious dialogue must in the future focus on moral precepts which transcend religious dogma.

All Buddhist teaching is seen as curative – the Buddha is the Doctor for the Ills of the World – accepting that in certain circumstances an antinomian approach might provide the cure, a kind of homoeopathy... . In Buddhism moral conduct is seen as a foundation to the spiritual path, though not too much, because over-attachment to the idea of vows and precepts will be just as much a hindrance to liberation as immorality. The basis for moral conduct lies in the five precepts that every Buddhist tries to keep. All ethical conduct is measured in terms of its harm-lessness. The precepts are expressed in terms of avoidance of behaviours that will harm others (and oneself)... .

The five precepts, flowing from this single principle of *ahimasa*, summarize the ethical practice of all Buddhists in body, speech and mind. Practice fosters compassion and friendliness to all living beings through generosity, sincerity and mindfulness. The precepts abjure killing (including incitement to violent action), taking what is not freely given (harming someone through their possessions or by exploitation), sexual misconduct (another kind of harming), false speech (including lying, backbiting and harsh words), partaking of intoxicating substances (dulling the mind so as to allow heedless actions).

When it comes to the third precept, restraining sexual action, there is no absolute rule. Marriage is seen as a secular contract rather than a religious one, and different forms depend on cultural differences. Thus, besides the usual monogamy, there is found sororal polygyny and fraternal polyandry, with its distinct advance of limiting the birth rate in areas that could not support a popu-lation explosion... .

Buddhism's contribution to interreligious dialogue for world peace must be its preference for spiritual experience over adherence to dogmas. Its ethic, based on non-harming, places the final responsibility for all actions on the human being. This is why only humans can achieve nirvana – the gods must be reborn as humans first. All sentient beings have this potential by virtue of the Buddha-nature, without reference to an external creator-God who sets laws that have to be obeyed without question. Avoiding a separate entity or soul underpinning the psycho-physical processes of living beings, Buddhism asserts that every living thing can only do so through the process of change – the exchange of gases, the metabolic conversion of food, cell regeneration and so on. (pp. 208–11)

The Buddhist understanding of ethics may help to shed some light on the current dilemma facing the Christian churches. Don Cupitt has recognized that the old commitment to one set of conditions for life – be it job, vocation, marriage or religious affiliation – is now a thing of the past, however much we may lament its passing. People cross over the boundaries that separate religions, sometimes more than once in their lifetime... . He says that the religions of Asia, especially Buddhism, will contribute greatly to helping us escape from the tribalism of the past... .

The Judaeo–Christian tradition is so far the only one that has had to face up to the critical findings of science; but David Hart warns that though the other traditions have yet to be exposed to the 'searing blasts of critical appraisal', it is inevitable that they will receive similar treatment before long.

There seems to be a choice for the future to recognize that faith is not ultimately defined in mythological or credal terms, because nothing can be predicated of God and, following Kierkegaard, 'Subjectivity is the way of deliverance – that is, God as the infinitely compelling subjectivity'; in other words, we should do as Buddhism does, place humanity centre-stage.

Rather than the discussion of doctrines on which people will never agree dialogue should centre on the great moral question of our times – the question that David Hart calls the 'ontological question of what it means to be created as a mortal human'.

The choice is a stark one because religions between them have the power to produce the highest and the best in humanity, and also the cruellest and most destructive behaviour. Here then, is a future for religion: there is no confusion in the ethics of the five precepts because they do not contain promulgations of religious law, or focus on parental and godly authority and private property. As Thomas Merton recognized, Zen does not belong just to Buddhism: in so far as these traditions self-evidently transcend all dogmas and taboos they belong to all faiths. (pp. 208–14)

Christopher Lamb, 'A Future Perspective for Inter Faith Dialogue' in Christopher Lamb and Dan Cohn-Sherbok (eds), *The Future of Religion: Postmodern Perspectives* (London: Middlesex University Press, 1999).

M

John Macquarrie

Born in Scotland, the Christian theologian John Macquarrie was Professor at Oxford University. In 'Revisiting the Christological Dimensions of Uniqueness', he stresses that Christ can be definitive for him without making comparisons with other traditions.

Given the ethical imperative of dialogue, previous understandings of the uniqueness of Jesus must be reinterpreted.

It seems to me that Knitter's second thesis is again one that will command wide assent. There is however, an irony in the way in which the thesis has been stated. The first reason given for the need of dialogue is the fact that we have been forced to recognize our interdependence and the need for co-operation because of the threats to the future of the human race. The irony is that not the visions of saviour figures, not the sacrifices of their disciples in spreading the vision, not the wisdom of philosophers, have brought about a consciousness of human solidarity, but rather the deterioration of the earth through human exploitation, the oppression of some through the aggression of others, the threat of war in a destructive form without parallel, the sheer aggregation of numbers forcing us closer and closer together. This may well suggest a pessimistic view of the future, with Jesus Christ, the Buddha, Muhammad, and all the other mediators fading out of the picture, while the course of history is determined by purely material forces. This is an irony that was well portrayed by a British scientist some years ago when he wrote a novel in which the appearance of a dark cloud from space caused an immediate cessation of national rivalries as earth's peoples faced the common threat. When the cloud eventually receded without having revealed any hostile intent or inflicted any damage, the earthlings promptly returned to their former nasty ways. Or could it happen that the accumulated threats that are driving us together may awaken deeper desires for a salvation such as the religions have long promised.

At any rate, we can agree with Knitter that verbal proclamation in itself will hardly be enough, and perhaps past failures have been in large measure due to proclamation not backed up by obedience to an ethical imperative. The question is one of mission. What does that word mean for Christianity today and for other religions that are also missionary in outlook?

I do not say that proclamation is simply a thing of the past. There probably is still a place for the old-fashioned type of missionary proclamation, especially in the secularized nations of Europe and North America.

As far as Christian mission in other parts of the world is concerned, I fully agree with Knitter that it should take the form of open dialogue rather than proclamation. I have learned the lesson taught me by my Indian friend – in India, christology must take the form of krishnology... .

Jesus' salvific role can be reinterpreted in terms of truly but not only.

Here again I would have no basic disagreement with Knitter, though I would wish to use a somewhat different vocabulary. He is correct in saying that in Jesus there is not, and indeed cannot be, a full revelation of God, for the infinite cannot be fully comprehended in the finite. But Christian dogma has never claimed that the whole of God was incarnate in Christ. It was the Word, the Second Person of the Trinity, who is said to have been incarnated. Even at that, Calvin maintained that something of the Logos remained outside of Christ – a doctrine known as *illud extra Calvinisticum*, intended to counter the Lutheran tendency to maintain that the Logos was wholly contained in Christ. On the other hand, I do not go along with Knitter in rejecting the word definitive. It seems to me, this word always implies definitive for someone (or some community). I confess that Christ is definitive for me, both in the sense that he defines for me (and presumably for Christians generally) the true nature of a human being, and also the nature of God, whose image ... is revealed in him.

In this connection, I think we must notice that the same finitude which prevents us from saying that God is wholly revealed in Christ also prevents us from embracing an unlimited pluralism. Though I can be open to the truth in other faiths, both my life and my intellectual powers are too limited for me to reach even a moderately adequate understanding of all the religions that might bring spiritual enrichment. Those of us who are Christians recognize that there is much in our own faith and much in Jesus Christ with which we have failed to come to terms. Some people do acquire – through long study, dialogue and social intercourse – a living knowledge of perhaps one religion other than their own... .

So when I say that Christianity is definitive for me, I am not, as Knitter seems to think, making a boastful or arrogant claim. I am not making a comparison with another faith. I am simply saying that within my limited faith and experience, Jesus Christ is sufficient. Through him I think I have been brought into relation to God. (96–8)

John Macquarrie, 'Revisiting the Christological Dimensions of Uniqueness' in Leonard Swidler and Paul Mojzes (eds), *The Uniqueness of Jesus: A Dialogue with Paul F. Knitter* (Maryknoll, NY: Orbis, 1997).

John Mbiti

John Mbiti, a teacher at the University of Bern, argues in 'Asian and African Voices on the Uniqueness of Jesus', that in both Asia and Africa Jesus is being reinterpreted in a variety of ways that provide spiritual sustenance for the peoples in these continents.

I hear voices which are articulating loudly or feebly how Jesus encounters people in their different situations in Africa and Asia. It is at the point of these encounters that I find meaning in talking about the uniqueness of Jesus. Somehow he penetrates into their being, into their concerns, into their joys and problems. He becomes a companion in the wide sense; they feel his presence in what he was and did during his earthly life. He does not necessarily perform wonders out of the blue to rescue them, but he is with the people, understands their situation, shares their concerns, and gives them hope for the future. This is not a theoretical uniqueness, but a genuine presence at the historical level in which Jesus shares our life. It is down to earth. At the same time, in that awareness of him (through different images) there is a deeper and spiritual presence which uplifts human life and sets it reaching toward a higher ground – whether one of hope, freedom, justice, dignity, harmony, or being oneself.

There are many examples of this multiplicity of experiencing, responding to, or reinterpreting Jesus Christ in more ways than, and besides, the traditional images. Naturally, some of those inherited christological images or symbols remain meaningful, but they are also being recast, reinterpreted. The uniqueness of Jesus cannot be isolated from traditional and new images of Jesus because, in the final analysis, it is probably their sum total which makes Jesus so unequivocally unique.

In the Asian situation, characterized by, among other things, poverty and religious plurality, we hear that

> God addresses the experience of suffering through a 'gravity-bound' love that draws God into human history and into the historical lives of human persons.... This is not God's suffering 'on behalf of' in order to solve the conundrum of human suffering; rather, God suffers 'with' humankind. Here vicariousness is replaced by identification. The crucified God is the God who identifies all the way with us in our suffering and death. He suffers with us and dies with us.

> God's love for humanity and God's suffering with humanity coalesce in the term 'pain-love'. This suffering God feels pain-love; that is, God loves people to the extent of feeling their pain, as a mother feels pain in childbirth for the child whom she loves. Jesus was the pain-love of God in his earthly life. (pp. 100–1)

Let us move from Asian to African voices and take only a limited number of examples. The Ghanaian–Nigerian theologian Mercy Amba Oduyoye, like many other women theologians concerned about patriarchal domination in church and society, focuses on the liberating work of Jesus. She writes: 'The Christ of

Christianity touches human needs at all levels... . We find Jesus in the New Testament snatching women and men away from all domination, even from the jaws of death.'

Another understanding of the saving presence of Jesus comes from the East African Revival Movement, which started in Rwanda and Uganda in 1929 and spread widely all over eastern Africa and beyond. Its emphasis is upon a brokenness of heart before Christ, who removes barriers, according to Colossians 3:11.

> That Christ is a revolutionary who over-turned man-made structures, obliterating racial, ethnic, sectarian and other barriers is a message the East African Revival has taught and upheld... . It challenged the *status quo* in the African mission field... . Due to its vision of brokenness at the foot of the Cross the story of the Revival is a testimony of how the Revival vision of Christ and His achievement at the Cross has brought down blockades of colour, class, status, ethnicity, sex and education, and how it has merged pulpit and pew.
> (pp. 103–4)

These are but a few among many serious voices depicting Jesus Christ in Africa and Asia. What do they attempt to say concerning him? They are partly reinterpreting his uniqueness. At the same time they are pointing to a complexity of christological dimensions, some of which are treasured as ancient images, some of which are largely or entirely new, and others which had apparently been neglected by the church at various times in its history but are being rediscovered. All these add up to the many faces of Jesus Christ, to his 'flexibility' to be all things to all people, in all places, and at all times. He is unique in that he cannot be possessed or monopolized by any one set of images or symbols; he cannot be contained in his entirety in one place; and he cannot be exhaustively interpreted or understood. He is unique in that it is possible for him to be and not to be, to appear and to disappear. That is the unique nature of Christ, which spans time and space – yet makes him present everywhere. He may be briefly or indefinitely 'hidden', as he was from the followers who walked with him on the day of the resurrection from Jerusalem to Emmaus (Luke 24:13–35). But in that encounter he may also be recognized and named, especially at the breaking of bread, which he gives to all. (p. 106)

John Mbiti, 'Asian and African Voices on the Uniqueness of Jesus', in Leonard Swidler and Paul Mojzes (eds), *The Uniqueness of Jesus: A Dialogue with Paul F. Knitter* (Maryknoll, NY: Orbis, 1997).

Kana Mitra

The Hindu scholar Kana Mitra received an MA in philosophy from Calcutta University and a Ph.D. in religion from Temple University. She has been on the religion faculties of Vilanova and La Salle Universities, and served as an Associate Editor of the Journal of Ecumenical Studies. *In 'Theologizing through History?', she states that religious pluralism has been a constant feature of Hinduism through the centuries.*

We Hindus, especially the modern intellectual ones, proudly proclaim that our theologians recognized religious plurality from our earliest history and formulated comprehensive and perceptive theoretical interpretations for religious diversity; Westerners are still struggling with it! Taking history seriously will make us more humble – a virtue we profess, but do not always practice! Plurality of religions is integral to the entire history of the Indian subcontinent. There have been and still are worshippers of Vishnu, Shiva, Krishna, Gopala, Durga, Chandi, and other gods – the 330 million gods, as they are sometimes referred to. Never in the entire history of India has there been a Hindu religion. It is commonly said today that there are Hindus but no Hindu religion, and that the name 'Hindu' was given to us by non-Hindus. Recognition of the plurality of religions by our theologians is historically conditioned; and we need to attend to that historical conditionedness.

The general model for dealing with the plurality of religions is the Rg Vedic statement, *Ekam sat vipra vahudha vadanti* – truth is one; people call it by various names. But the theologians of different historical periods have differed in their specific arguments and orientations. If we take the examples of rather well-known theologians of Hinduism, Sankara and Ramanuja, we can see that their theological thinking was based in their historical surroundings.

Sankara handled plurality by recognizing two levels of truth – phenomenal and transcendental. Plurality is true on the phenomenal level, not on the transcendental. Sankara reconciled plurality by an ultimate denial of it. He even subordinated all personalisitc forms of belief under the suprapersonal Brahman. Even though there is no unanimity as to exactly when Sankara lived, at least there is no denial that he was not pre-sixth century CE... .

Buddhism became a dominant religion of India via the Maurya King Ashoka (273–232 BCE). The Buddhist refusal to deal with metaphysical questions or the God question and its practical denial of the caste system posed a challenge for Hinduism. Eventually the Madhyamika School of Buddhism came into being, particularly with the help of Nagarjuna (second century CE). He developed his ingenious logical scheme of *chbatuskoti* or fourfold negations to demonstrate the inconceivability of the ultimate. Sankara utilized Nagarjuna's logical scheme – which was not in opposition to the *Upanishad* tradition of *neti neti* ('not this, not that') – to develop the idea of suprapersonal Brahman, which could accommodate the Buddhist refusal to talk about God. On the level of practice, he established monastic orders to transcend caste problems. Before Sankara there were individual monks but no monastic orders in Hinduism. In accordance with the four stages of life, in the last stage Hindus often became wandering monks. Monasticism, thus, was not quite alien to Hindu traditions, although it was only for the last stage of life. Sankara, however, established four monasteries to introduce monastic orders in Hinduism. Thus, clearly much of Sankara's system, theoretical and practical, was heavily influenced by the historical circumstances of his time.

The situation of the eleventh-century Ramanuja was different. He was post-*advaita Vedanta* and post-Muslim encounter. Sankara's philosophical system appealed to the intellect but could not fulfil the emotional needs of many. Meanwhile, Islam was presenting a majestic, magnificent, benevolent, personal God, which was not foreign to the devotional trends of Hinduism. Ramanuja subordinated Sankara's nonpersonal Brahman as a way of knowledge to the personal deity Vishnu – and one could live in the eternal bliss of his presence through devotion. Again, historical circumstances played a central role in the development of the system of a major Hindu thinker.

A. L. Basham shows that the thirteenth-century theologian Madhva developed his dualistic theology in an encounter with Christianity. In more recent times, in the thought of Tagore, Aurobindo, Radha-Krishnan and others, we can see the impact of global thought. (pp. 82–3)

Kana Mitra, 'Theologizing Through History', in Leonard Swidler (ed.), *Toward a Universal Theology of Religion* (Maryknoll, NY: Orbis, 1987).

Jürgen Moltmann

Jürgen Moltmann, Professor at Tübingen University, argues in 'Christianity and the World Religions' that dialogue with other faiths must be based on Christian special promises concerning God's kingdom.

What task can Christianity have toward the other world religions? It is one goal of mission to awaken faith, to baptize, to found churches and to form a new life under the lordship of Christ. Geographically this mission proceeds to the ends of the earth. It proceeds numerically and tries to reach as many people as possible. It thinks in terms of quantity and evolves strategies for 'church growth'. We have no intention of disputing this or belittling it. But mission has another goal as well. It lies in the qualitative alteration of life's atmosphere – of trust, feelings, thinking and acting. We might call this missionary aim to 'infect' people, whatever their religion, with the spirit of hope, love and responsibility for the world. Up to now this qualitative mission has taken place by the way and unconsciously, as it were, in the wake of the 'quantitative' mission. In the new world situation in which all religions find themselves, and the new situation of Christianity in particular, the qualitative mission directed towards an alteration of the whole atmosphere of life should be pursued consciously and responsibly. It will not be able to diffuse *en passant* the atmosphere of the Christian West, nor will it desire to do so. For this is neither particularly 'Christian' nor very helpful; and it is not what is wanted. But it will have to direct its energies towards the climate which is essential if solutions are to be found to the most serious problems which face mankind today – famine, domination of one class by another, ideological imperialism, atomic wars and the destruction of the environment.

Qualitative mission takes place in dialogue. If it is a serious dialogue about the most fundamental problems, then it does not lead to non-committal permanent conversations. In dialogue the religions change, Christianity included, just as in personal conversations the expressions, attitudes and views of the partners alter. The dialogue of world religions is a process into which we can only enter if we make ourselves vulnerable in openness, and if we come away from the dialogue changed. We do not lose our identity, but we acquire a new profile in the confrontation with our partner. The world religions will emerge from the dialogues with a new profile. It may be said that Christians hope that these profiles will be turned towards suffering men and women and their future, towards life and towards peace. (pp. 193–5)

If Christianity renounces its exclusive claim in relation to the other religions, and if it does not assume an inclusive claim either, then the formula of the critical catalyst suggests itself as a new model for its post-absolutist era. A catalyst causes elements to combine simply through its presence. The simple presence of Christians in environments determined by other religions provokes effects of this kind, provided that Christians live, think and act differently. This can be called the indirect infection of other religions with Christian ideas, values and principles. If it is true that the Indian religions think 'unhistorically', then their world picture is altered by the experience of reality as history which Christians present to them. This is already taking place through the historical investigation of Hinduism and Buddhism, through the introduction of, and stress on, the future tense in the Indian languages, and, finally, through the different relationship Christians have to time. If it is true that Islam produces a fatalistic attitude, then the encounter with Christianity brings about the discovery that the world can be changed and that people have a responsibility for changing it. If it is true that many religions have their faces so turned away from the world that they disseminate social indifference, then the presence of Christians makes them recognize social responsibility and the activities appropriate to it. But these indirect catalytic influences of

Christianity on other religions are never unequivocal; they are always ambiguous, especially when they are linked with the spread of Western science and technology. Science and technology, capitalism or socialism, cannot be viewed as an indirect 'Christianization' of other religions. But these effects are there and must be noted. We must become conscious of them today so that the catalytic influences of the Christian faith can be less ambiguous than they have been, and are not confused with the influence of the West, merely under Christian auspices. (pp. 202–3)

Jürgen Moltmann, 'Christianity and the World Religions', in John Hick and Brian Hebblethwaite (eds), *Christianity and Other Religions* (London: Collins, 1980).

Moojan Momen

Born in Iran and educated in England, Moojan Momen is a physician by profession. He has written academic papers and books on the history and teachings of Islam and the Bahá'í Faith. In his view, all religions offer only partial glimpses of the nature of ultimate reality.

The concept of the unity of religions is one of the key doctrines of the Bahá'í Faith. At its most basic level, this doctrine can be expressed as the belief that the different religious systems of the world merely reflect different stages in a single process, the progressive unfoldment of religious 'Truth'. The observable differences between the various religions are regarded as only a function of the different social conditions that prevailed at the time and place that these religions first appeared.

However, this doctrine is open to some serious questions. It appears to work well enough when applied to the different religions in the Western Judaeo–Christian–Muslim tradition. One can easily conceive (whether one chooses to believe it or not) that a succession of prophets, each claiming to be a representative of God and each having a particular holy book, holy law, prophecies and teachings, were in fact successive teachers in a chain sent by a Creator God and intended to take man through progressive stages in his social and spiritual evolution. Indeed, what may make this concept particularly attractive to many converts to the Bahá'í Faith is the manner in which such an idea fits into the general schema of evolutionary thought that predominates in the biological and social sciences. If man has evolved biologically and socially, then it makes sense to conceive of his religious life as having evolved also. Problems arise, however, when the theory is applied to other religious systems, in particular the Eastern systems: Indian,

Chinese and Japanese religion. In these systems there is frequently no concept of a Creator God, of prophethood, or of the revelation of a holy law and divine teachings.

The question that arises, therefore, is: how can the Bahá'í Faith resolve its teaching of the underlying unity of all religions in view of the marked differences between them? The starting point for this resolution must be the affirmation by Bahá'u'lláh, the founder of the Bahá'í Faith, that human beings are limited in their ability to conceptualize. An absolute knowledge of the metaphysical structure of the cosmos is, Bahá'u'lláh states, impossible for human beings to achieve because of the finite nature of the human mind. Human beings 'can never hope to transcend the limitations imposed upon' them and thus will never be able to 'unravel' the 'mystery' or 'even to hint at the nature of' the Ultimate Reality which is called God in the Western religions and by various names such as Brahman, the Tao, Nirvana, or Shunyata in the Eastern religions.

As a consequence, whatever concepts and formulations have been derived for describing the Ultimate Reality 'are all the product of man's finite mind and are conditioned by its limitations'. No absolute knowledge of the cosmos being available to man, all descriptions, all schemata, all attempts to portray the metaphysical basis of the universe, are necessarily limited by the viewpoint of the particular person making them.

> To whatever heights the mind of the most exalted of men may soar, however great the depths which the detached and understanding heart can penetrate, such mind and heart can never transcend that which is the creature of their own thoughts. The meditations of the profoundest thinker, the devotions of the holiest of saints, the highest expressions of praise from either human pen or tongue, are but a reflection of that which hath been created within themselves.

The cosmological and metaphysical doctrines that have been the source of much religious dispute and disagreement are thus reduced by Bahá'u'lláh to being a product of different cultures, different religious worlds which human beings have created, different soul/psyche complexes in individuals. 'Abdu'l-Bahá, the son and successor of Bahá'u'lláh says: 'The differences among the religions of the world are due to the varying types of minds.' Each individual and each religious tradition sees the Ultimate Reality from its own particular viewpoint and describes it from this limited angle. This, of course, applies just as much to the conception of God formed in the Western religions as it does to the various concepts of the Ultimate Reality found in the Eastern religions. All human speculation and conceptualization of the Ultimate Reality is reduced to the same level: they are all relative truths – relative to different cultures and religious worlds – but none of them can encompass the whole truth about the Ultimate Reality, which is, and will always remain, beyond human comprehension.

If the goal of knowledge of the Ultimate Reality is, in the final analysis, beyond human attainment, what then is the purpose of striving along the spiritual path described in every religion? What is the purpose of the prayers and meditations that are enjoined in the religious traditions? Bahá'u'lláh says that although our efforts will not give us an absolute knowledge of the Ultimate Reality, they do help us to attain a knowledge of our own selves: 'Whatever duty Thou hast prescribed unto Thy servants of extolling to the utmost Thy majesty and glory is but a token of Thy grace unto them, that they may be enabled to ascend unto the station conferred upon their own inmost being, the station of the knowledge of their own selves.' By spiritual striving and effort to attain spiritual insight, the individual is freeing the inner self, the heart, from attachment to the things of this world. Once the dross of material attachment is cleared, the inner nature of the human being which is inherently spiritual becomes apparent. Another way of putting this, which can be found in the different religious traditions of the world, is that as one peels away the layers of the self and discards the ephemeral and superficial, what one finds within is the eternal; one uncovers the Divine or the Absolute Reality within.

'Abdu'l-Bahá likens this state of affairs to a compass: no matter how far the compass travels, it is only going around the point at its centre: however much men may strive and achieve within the realms of spiritual knowledge, ultimately they are only achieving a better and greater knowledge of themselves (or of the Absolute manifested within themselves), not of any exterior Absolute.

What then are the consequences of this cognitive relativism of metaphysics within the Bahá'í system? First, it may be said that if all metaphysical viewpoints and dogmatic positions are ultimately relative and reflect only the soul/psyche composition of the individual rather than any absolute Truth, there must be a change of emphasis in what is considered important. In most religions, metaphysics – the structure of the spiritual world – is considered of primary importance. The doctrine of the religion about these matters is considered to reveal an absolute and unchanging truth. However, if it is considered that the truth of all metaphysical systems is only a provisional, partial, relative truth, the importance of metaphysics lessens considerably. Interest is no longer primarily in the structures of metaphysics, but rather in relationships. That is to say that the focus of interest is no longer so much in what the Absolute is, but in what the individual's relationship with the Absolute should be, and what the consequences of that relationship are. The emphasis has shifted from structures to processes and relationships. And therefore ethics and a concern for the pathway of spiritual development come to the forefront of consideration. (pp. 185–217)

'Relativism: A Basis for Metaphysics', in *Studies in Honor of the Late Hasan M. Balyuzi* (ed. Moojan Momen), Studies in the Babi and Bahá'í Religions, vol. 5 (Los Angeles: Kalimat Press, 1988).

Bithika Mukerji

Born in India, Bithika Mukerji taught at universities in North America, Europe and at Banaras Hindu University. In 'Christianity in the Reflection of Hinduism', she argues that all religions in different ways seek to attain God-realization.

Revelation pertains to the unmanifest, the unspoken, the ultimately hidden mystery of existence. The stirring of interest in the meaning of the givenness of the many-splendoured universe is felt within the heart. The Indian scriptures always mention the heart in this context possibly because the brain is too ready with resolutions which makes opaque what it seeks to understand. It is not in the nature of reason to await answers. Thus an inwardization of the questing spirit marks the beginning of an awareness of the longing for penetrating the mystery of existence.

The heart experiences a yearning for the supreme felicity of a 'home coming' which is endemic to the human condition itself. It is natural for the traveller, who finds himself out of tune with his surroundings, to seek to return whence he came and where he could be himself. To such a pilgrim the scriptures speak of the final state of self-realization which is in the nature of a supreme gain.

The nature of this 'supreme gain' is stated obliquely in many ways, in paradoxes, in anecdotes and also in the form of the dialogue between teacher and disciple. The 'Unknown-ness' of the nature of the final finding is not disclosed because in the ultimate analysis the supreme living experience cannot be communicated as a commensurable commodity. It is felt within the being of the aspirant and needs no confirmation because the experience is self-authenticating. The man of enlightenment, thereafter, by his way of being in the world forges another link in the chain of living exemplars in the tradition who inspire other pilgrims toward the way of spiritual life.

The man of realization is a seer, a sage who can bear witness to the reality of the dimension of the unspoken, but eminently speakable which manifests itself in the unity of soundless resonance and the vision of divine prefigurement of letters known as the mantra. The mantra, a pulsating unity of sound and vision, by flashing into the consciousness of the seer, irradiates his understanding so that he is in tune with the cosmic rhythm of the universe. The experiencing of the unveiling of the ultimate mystery is celebrated in the sacred language of the *Vedas*. The *Vedas* are therefore a celebration of the experience of fulfilment which imparts authenticity to the promise of 'supreme gain'. The language of the *Veda* itself is of the nature of Truth itself. It is distinguished from secular language by virtue of the particular order of the arrangement of syllables, the sequence of words and the rhythm which holds them together. The unity of all three is the mantra.

The Vedic tradition has been preserved by a very exact system of memorizing and recitation. The mantra is not created by man and has its being in the enlightened consciousness of the seer, the poet, and thus it perpetuates a living tradition of spiritual quest and its fulfilment.

Much as been written on the nature of this self-realization. For the *advaita* philosophy it is the knowledge of the unity of the self with Brahman. All other vedantic traditions, which comprise the framework of Hinduism, reject this position. All religions use the language of God-realization. The devotional prayers of God-intoxicated men have enriched all the languages of India. In the sphere of religious commitment no dogma can operate because God has infinite ways of disclosing himself to his devotee. Thus variety is a matter of celebration and rejoicing as evidence of the myriad possibilities of the coming together of man and the Person (the *Ishta*) who is dear to his heart. The wealth of man's outpourings of the heart at the feet of the Lord is truly immeasurable and no limits ought to be put to channelize them in one direction. No one can legislate for another as to the true image of God because his images are legion. All forms are his because he is formless, all auspicious qualities are his because he is the ultimate repository of all magnificence. (pp. 232–3)

Bithika Mukerji, 'Christianity in the Reflection of Hinduism', in Paul J. Griffiths (ed.), *Christianity Through Non-Christian Eyes* (Maryknoll, NY: Orbis, 1990).

N

Seyyed Hossein Nasr

Born in 1933, Seyyed Hossein Nasr was educated in the United States and has served as Professor of Islamic Studies at George Washington University. In 'The Islamic View of Christianity' he argues that there are grounds for Christians and Muslims to co-exist and for Muslims to view the Christian faith respectfully.

There is, however, on the basis of the acceptance of the Divine Origin of the Christian message and reverence of an exceptional character for Christ and the Virgin, a rejection in the Qur'an itself of both the doctrine of the Trinity and the incarnation. Since Islam is based on the Absolute and not its manifestations and seeks to return Abrahamic monotheism to its original purity as the religion of the One, any emphasis upon a particular manifestation of the One in the direction of the many is seen by Islam as a veil cast upon the plenary reality of Divine Unity which Islam seeks to assert so categorically and forcefully. Therefore, the trinitarian doctrine, not only of certain Oriental churches to which the Qur'anic account seems to be closer than Western interpretations of the doctrine, but of any other kind which would not place the trinitarian relationship below the level of Divine Oneness, is rejected by the Islamic perspective. Needless to say, Islam would accept an interpretation of the Trinity which would not in any way compromise Divine Unity, one which would consider the persons of the Trinity to be 'Aspects' or 'Names' of God standing below his essence which, being the Absolute, must be One without condition and above all relations. Likewise the idea of a Divine Descent in the form of incarnation is excluded from the Islamic point of view... .

The question thus appeared to the earliest Muslims as to why a religion revealed by God through such a major prophet as Christ to a people some of whom the Prophet of Islam met and respected, should possess such teachings which should be so directly opposed to what Muslims consider as the obvious truth concerning the nature of the Divine. Few Muslim theologians of the earlier or even later centuries sought to examine the works of Christian theologians themselves on these issues, especially writings emanating from the Latin Church, while certain

Sufis such as Ibn 'Arabi and many of the Persian Sufi poets saw both the doctrine of Trinity and incarnation as symbolic ways of speaking about the Absolute and its manifestations without in any way destroying the doctrine of Divine Unity. Moreover, a theologian and Sufi like al-Ghazzali tried expressly to absolve Christ himself from having ever taught either the trinitarian or the incarnationist doctrine, he being a prophet who cannot, according to Islam, but claim God's Oneness without any reserve or compromise. (pp. 128–9)

There are, however, those within the Islamic world who realize that the destinies of Islam and Christianity are intertwined, that God has willed both religions to exist and to be ways of salvation for millions of human beings, that the enemy of both religions is modern agnosticism, atheism and secularism, and that Christianity is a dispensation willed by heaven not only as a historical background to Islam but as a revelation destined to guide a sector of humanity until the second coming of its founder. Such Muslims can draw from a vast resource of traditional Islamic writings on Christianity, based not on reducing each religion to a bare minimum to accommodate the other, but grounded in that transcendent unity which unites all authentic religions, and especially Christianity and Islam. Such Muslims, far from surrendering to the fads and fashions of the day in the name of keeping up with the times, or of loosening the reins which control the passions in order to express anger in the name of indignation, base themselves on the eternal message of the Qur'an in their dealings with Christians. They develop, in the light of present needs, the expressly Qur'anic doctrine of the universality of revelation, and even practice the Christian virtue of turning the other cheek when it comes to the matter of religious truth; that is, they accept the validity of Christianity even if Christians deny the authenticity of the Islamic revelation. They let the matter of who is saved be decided by the Supreme Judge who judges according to the truth, not the 'fashions of the times' and expediency. The voice of such Muslims seem to be drowned out at the moment by the cry and fury of those who preach hatred in the name of justice, and who even insult other religions in direct opposition to the injunctions of the Qur'an. But the voice of understanding and harmony cannot but triumph at the end, for it is based upon the truth, and surely Christ whose second coming is accepted by both Christians and Muslims shall not come but in truth and shall not judge but by truth, that truth which he asserted himself to be, according to the Gospel statement, and which the Qur'an guarantees as being triumphant at the end for there will finally arrive the moment when it can be asserted with finality that 'the Truth has come and falsehood has perished' (Qur'an 17:81). (pp. 133–4)

Seyyed Hossein Nasr, 'The Islamic View of Christianity', in Paul J. Griffiths (ed.), *Christianity Through Non-Christian Eyes* (Maryknoll, NY: Orbis, 1990).

Michael Nazir-Ali

In 'Dialogue in an Age of Conflict', the Anglican Bishop of Rochester, Michael Nazir-Ali, argues that Christian mission and interfaith dialogue are interconnected.

On what is the Church's dialogue based? It is based first of all on the recognition that men and women everywhere are created in the image of God (Gen. 1:27). It is true that this image has to some extent been affected by human sin, both communal and personal, but nevertheless the image survives, it has not been destroyed and we have dialogue with people who are not Christians because we believe this image is there and that this image has something of God, both in communities and within individuals. Secondly, we recognize that the eternal Word, the Logos, incarnate in Jesus Christ, has illuminated all human beings everywhere, as St John tells us clearly at the beginning of his Gospel (John 1:4,9). This recognition of the universal illumination of the eternal Word was present in some of the early Fathers of the Church, in Justin Martyr and Clement of Alexandria, for example, who believed that some of the greatest achievements of their particular civilization, Stoic and Platonist philosophy, for example, were possible because of the presence of the divine word in them. (pp. 73–4)

Some remarks about dialogue, mission and indeed evangelism. The Church Missionary Society has been committed for many scores of years to the view that dialogue is the presupposition for Christian mission, for Christian witness, in other words, there can be no authentic witness without prior dialogue. Unless we understand people's beliefs, their culture, the idiom of that culture, their thought forms, the intellectual tradition, the artistic tradition, the faith tradition, unless we understand these we will not be able to witness to people authentically as Christians. This is behind the strongly incarnational approach that CMS has taken in the past and continues to take today. Mission is not hit and run. People these days are talking about 'non-resident missionaries'; well, in some cases these are necessary, of course. But that will never be, I hope, a model for CMS because mission must be incarnational and this is why so many distinguished missionaries – people like Roger Hooker and Christopher Lamb – spent years in incarnational situations learning about cultures and languages and peoples before they felt able to witness to them of Christian faith and Christian truth. This is absolutely essential. So mission cannot be hit and run. It cannot be at a distance. A great deal of time and effort is being expended in the world today in preaching the gospel to people through the mass media. Now in some ways this is necessary, some parts of the world cannot be reached in any other way. Think of the way in which the Bible was broadcast at dictation speed to the people of Albania. But again it can never be an ideal way because of the commitment to incarnation and to dialogue as the presupposition for witness.

But dialogue is not only preparatory to witness, it is also the means to witness and here I have been somewhat distressed by the ambivalence in the ecumenical movement on this question. Some documents, such as the guidelines on dialogue produced by the British Council of Churches, say clearly that dialogue is a medium for authentic witness. But other documents of the World Council deny this and make every effort to claim that the occasion of dialogue must not be an occasion for Christian witness. I think the concern behind this is that our partners should not see our efforts at dialogue as efforts at proselytization and that concern is valid. On the other hand, I cannot see dialogue in its fullness without the opportunity for both sides to witness to their faith in trust that the partners recognize each other's integrity. For Christians, dialogue will always be about listening and learning; our partner's faith may shed unexpected light on our own. We must, however, also be committed to let the light of Christ shine through our conversation and reflection. Without that, dialogue remains unfulfilled for the Christian. (pp. 80–1)

Michael Nazir-Ali, 'Dialogue in an Age of Conflict', in Dan Cohn-Sherbok, *Many Mansions* (London: Bellew, 1992).

Stephen Neill

Stephen Neill, formerly Professor of Philosophy and Religion at University College, Nairobi, argues in Christian Faith and Other Faiths *that those who engage in dialogue must learn from other religions while remaining loyal to their own faith.*

Attempts to demonstrate the 'absoluteness' of Christian faith on rational or philosophical grounds cannot be said to have been entirely successful. As long as faith is interpreted in terms of understanding it is always possible that understanding might be reached in some other way than that of the Gospel of Jesus Christ – indeed that some other form of understanding might prove in the light of modern knowledge to be more complete and more logically self-consistent. It is better, perhaps, to speak rather of the uniqueness of Christianity than of its absolute validity.

Here we are on safer ground. For the Christian gospel is rooted in event and not in idea. Now every event in history is in itself unique and unrepeatable. It is possible to find parallels to almost every saying of Jesus in the books of the Rabbis; that does not alter in the slightest the fact that each human life is distinct from every other, and that any system of religious faith which is not centrally concerned with Jesus Christ cannot be in the least like a system which is so centrally concerned.

Simply as history the event of Jesus Christ is unique. Christian faith goes a great deal further in its interpretation of that event. It maintains that in Jesus the one thing that needed to happen has happened in such a way that it need never happen again the same way. The universe has been reconciled to its God. Through the perfect obedience of one man a new and permanent relationship has been established between God and the whole human race. The bridge has been built. There is room on it for all the needed traffic in both directions, from God to man and from man to God. Why look for any other?

Christians are bound to affirm that all men need the gospel. For the human sickness there is one specific remedy, and this is it. There is no other. Therefore the gospel must be proclaimed to the ends of the earth and to the end of time. The Church cannot compromise on its missionary task without ceasing to be the Church. If it fails to see and to accept this responsibility, it is changing the gospel into something other than itself.

Naturally to the non-Christian hearer this must sound like crazy megalomania and religious imperialism of the very worst kind. We must recognize the dangers; Christians have on many occasions fallen into both of them. But we are driven back ultimately on the question of truth... . The Christian claim is very close to the claim of the chemist. It states quite simply that the universe under all its aspects has been made in one way and not in another, and that the way in which it has been made has been once for all declared in Jesus Christ. When Jesus stated that he was the truth (John 14:6), he did not mean that he was stating a number of good and true ideas; he meant that in him the total structure of the universe was for the first time and for ever disclosed. But since this truth is set forth not in propositions to which intellectual assent would be the right response, but in personal form, what it demands is not so much understanding as surrender. The man who has seen Jesus as the truth of God is thereby pledged to 'do the truth', in a self-commitment which must become ever more intelligent and ever more complete until it reaches its consummation beyond the limits of space and time.

On all this the Christian cannot compromise. Yet his approach to the other forms of human faith must be marked by the deepest humility. He must endeavour to meet them at their highest, and not cheaply to score points off them by comparing the best he knows with their weaknesses, weaknesses such as are present also in the Christian scheme as it is lived out by very imperfect Christians. He must, as far as imagination will permit, expose himself to the full force of these other faiths in all that they have that is most convincing and most alluring. He must rejoice in everything that they possess of beauty and high aspiration. He must put himself to school with them, in readiness to believe that they may have something to teach him that he has not yet learned. He must sympathize with their earnest efforts to relate themselves to the needs of men in the modern world. He must listen with respectful patience to every criticism that they have to make both of Christian thought and Christian practice.

All this can be done, if the Christian is really humble. Self-asssertion is always a sign of lack of inner confidence. If the Christian has really trusted in Christ, he can open himself without fear to any wind that blows from any quarter of the heavens. If by chance some of those winds should blow to him unexpected treasures, he will be convinced that Christ's store-houses are wide enough to gather in those treasures too, in order that in the last day nothing may be lost. (pp. 16–19)

Stephen Neill, *Christian Faith and Other Faiths* (Oxford: Oxford University Press, 1970).

Lesslie Newbigin

Lesslie Newbigin, formerly a missionary in India, argues in The Gospel in a Pluralist Society *that, as in the past, Christians today have a responsibility to proclaim the gospel to all peoples. In his view, Christians should reject religious pluralism and acknowledge Jesus as the unique revelation of God. Nonetheless, Christians should accept that there is some continuity between the gospel and those outside the church.*

We shall expect, look for, and welcome all the signs of the grace of God at work in the lives of those who do not know Jesus as Lord. In this, of course, we shall be following the example of Jesus, who was so eager to welcome the evidence of faith in those outside the household of Israel. This kind of expectancy and welcome is an implication of the greatness of God's grace as it has been shown to us in Jesus. For Jesus is the personal presence of that creative word by which all that exists was made and is sustained in being. He comes to the world as no stranger but as the source of the world's life. He is the true light of the world, and that light shines into every corner of the world in spite of all that seeks to shut it out. In our contact with people who do not acknowledge Jesus as Lord, our first business, our first privilege, is to seek out and to welcome all the reflections of that one true light in the lives of those we meet. There is something deeply repulsive in the attitude, sometimes found among Christians, which makes only grudging acknowledgement of the faith, the godliness and the nobility to be found in the lives of non-Christians. Even more repulsive is the idea that in order to communicate the gospel to them one must, as it were, ferret out their hidden sins, show that their goodness is not so good after all. As a precondition for presenting the presence of the cross we come to know that, whoever we are, we are sinners before the grace of God. But the knowledge is the result, not the precondition of grace. It is in the light of the amazing grace of God in Jesus Christ that I am compelled to say, 'God be merciful to me a sinner.' Indeed, as the Fourth Gospel teaches us, it is only the presence of the living Holy Spirit that can convict the world in respect of sin and righteousness and judgement... .

The second consequence of the approach I suggest is that the Christian will be eager to co-operate with people of all faiths and ideologies in all projects which are in line with the Christian's understanding of God's purpose in history. I have repeatedly made the point that the heart of the faith of a Christian is the belief that the true meaning of the story of which our lives are a part is that which is made known in the biblical narrative. The human story is one which we share with all other human beings – past, present and to come... .

Third, it is precisely in this kind of shared commitment to the business of the world that the context for true dialogue is provided. As we work together with people of other commitments, we shall discover the places where our ways must separate. Here is where real dialogue may begin. It is a real dialogue about real issues. It is not just a sharing of religious experience, though it may include this. At heart it will be a dialogue about the meaning and goal of the human story. If we are doing what we ought to be doing as Christians, the dialogue will be initiated by our partners, not by ourselves. They will be aware of the fact that, while we share with them in commitment to some immediate project, our action is set in a different context from theirs. It has a different motivation. It looks to a different goal. Specifically – and here I am thinking of the dialogue with secular ideologies – our partners will discover that we do not invest our ultimate confidence in the intrahistorical goal of our labours, but that for us the horizon is one that is both nearer and further away than theirs... .

Therefore, the essential contribution of the Christian to the dialogue will simply be the telling of the story, the story of Jesus, the story of the Bible. The story is itself, as Paul says, the power of God for salvation. The Christian must tell it, not because she lacks respect for the many excellencies of her companions – many of whom may be better, more godly, more worthy of respect than she is. She tells it simply as one who has been chosen and called by God to be part of the company which is entrusted with the story. It is not her business to convert the others. She will indeed – out of love for them – long that they may come to share the joy that she knows and pray that they may indeed do so. But it is only the Holy Spirit of God who can so touch the hearts and consciences of the others that they are brought to accept the story as true and to put their trust in Jesus. (pp. 180–2)

Lesslie Newbigin, *The Gospel in a Pluralist Society* (London: SPCK, 1992).

David Novak

David Novak, Professor at the University of Toronto, explores in 'A Jewish Theological Understanding of Christianity in Our Time' the nature of general revelation in rela-tion to Judaism and Christianity.

Jews and Christians have a resource for developing approaches that both respect the integrity of creation and the integrity of the unique human creature therein, one who is in some ways part of it, and in some ways is not. The question then, is: How can Jews and Christians bring these considerable resources to the world at large?...

Judaism and Christianity can jointly proclaim certain normative truths about the human condition – without the surrender demanded by proselytism, syncretism, or secularism – by affirming what Jewish and Christian traditions have taught about general revelation. The latter is historically antecedent to the special revelation each community, respectively, claims as its own basic norm. General revelation still functions even after that special revelation has occurred. For Jews, it is the affirmation of the revelation to the children of Noah, something which extends beyond the revelation to the children of Israel at Sinai. For Roman Catholics and some Anglicans, it is the affirmation of natural law, something which extends beyond the divine law. For many Protestants, certainly those of Lutheran or Reformed background, it is the affirmation of the order of creation, which extends beyond the gospel. In all these traditions, it needs to be added, what is 'beyond' is certainly not what is 'higher' on any scale of value. Quite the contrary, what is more general is lower on that scale, a point that Jews who affirm the divine election of Israel, and Christians who affirm the incarnation, can readily understand. Nevertheless, what is more general and therefore lower is not without any value at all.

This general revelation, which makes itself manifest in certain universal moral principles, is most immediately accessible to human reason. It does not require a covenantal experience wherefrom the religious community proclaims it to the world. General revelation must be discovered within ordinary human experience. It must be seen from within that experience, as creating conditions necessary for authentic human community to be sustained. Yet the religious communities do not dissolve into some general human community by affirming these moral prin-ciples. They must insist all along that these principles, though necessary for authentic human community, are not at all sufficient for authentic human fulfil-ment. That can only be commanded through revelation and consummated by salvation; the ultimate redemption of the world by its creator God.

Although the religious communities of Judaism and Christianity should not legislate this minimal human morality (indeed, when they do they most often retard its social impact, especially in a democracy), they do provide it with an overall ontological context, which is a continuing vision of its original grounds and its ultimate horizon. Without that continuing vision, the very operation of human moral reason, indeed all human reason itself, flounders. Reason cannot flourish for long in an ontological vacuum, namely, in an otherwise absurd universe and in an otherwise aimless trajectory of human history.

The constitution of the relation between God's revealed law and universal moral law is an intellectual operation, conducted not only differently by the respective religious communities themselves, but even by adherents of different theological and philosophical tendencies within those communities. Nevertheless, recognition of the similarity of the problematic, coming as it does out of that which both communities accept as sacred scripture, i.e. the Hebrew Bible, can lead to a new mutuality. Such mutuality allows each community to maintain its own faith integrity in relationship with God, with the members of its own covenant, with the members of the most proximate religion (which I hold is, for Jews, Christianity), and with the world beyond.

The final requirement is that both communities respect with theological cogency the integrity of the secular order. In America, that means respect for the *novus ordo seculorum*, carefully distinguishing its legitimate moral claims from the illegitimate philosophical claims of those who would insist that secularism can be its only sufficient foundation. This respect for the integrity of the secular order, therefore, requires Jews and Christians to eschew those ultra-traditionalist elements in either community which wish to simply annul modernity *in toto* and return to their nostalgic vision of a theocratic polity of some sort or another. Both Jews and Christians should learn from modern history that the only means now available for such a restoration of any ancient regime come from fascism in its various guises – the most hideous caricature of the kingdom of God. (pp. 96–101)

David Novak, 'A Jewish Theological Understanding of Christianity in Our Time', in Leon Klenicki (ed.), *Toward a Theological Encounter: Jewish Understandings of Christianity* (Mahway, NJ: Paulist Press, 1991).

Joseph Osei-Bonsu

Joseph Osei-Bonsu, Lecturer in the University of Ghana, argues that the traditional concept of 'no salvation outside the Church' should be abandoned in a pluralistic world.

One major factor that does not promote good relations between Christianity and the other world religions is the traditional Christian maxim *extra ecclesiam nulla salus* ('outside the church there is no salvation')... . The rigid application of the traditional maxim would mean that in our world today at best only one-third of the world's present population will attain salvation and the remaining two-thirds or more who are not Christians will not be saved... . (p. 131)

As an African Christian, or more specifically, as a Ghanaian Christian addressing this issue, I cannot help but reflect on the destiny of the millions of Africans who lived both before Christ and after Christ, who died without knowing him. After the death and the resurrection of Christ it took centuries before Christianity came to Africa south of the Sahara. Even today there are millions in Africa on whom Christianity has made little impact. It is not that they have not heard of Christianity; many of them have, but it has not made any deep impression on them, just as many of us Christians have heard of Hinduism, Buddhism, Islam, etc., but these religions have not impressed us deeply enough to make us abandon our Christian religion.

Now these people who follow the African traditional religions do believe in God. If I may take the Asante of Ghana as an example, those among them who follow the traditional religion have a concept of God. God's existence for them is axiomatic, as evidenced by the saying, '*Obi nnkyere akwadaa Nyame*', meaning 'No one need to show God to the child.' This God is believed to be the creator of the world and to be immortal, omnipotent, dependable, etc. Even if there are lesser gods who feature in the cult of the Asante, they are not worshipped. Worship is reserved only for God, or the Supreme Being. The lesser gods and the ancestors are not worshipped; they are venerated. A high ethical code is observed by the adherents of this religion. It is believed that failure to observe this will result in punishment by God. As a result many of them lead lives that put Christians to shame. In their daily lives many of them show brotherly and sisterly love in a way that sometimes makes one wonder whether they are not more Christian than many of us who are officially Christians.

I do not believe that if such people die – at least those among them who try to lead good lives in accordance with the dictates of their conscience – they will be sent to hell just because they were not members of the Christian Church. Even though they do not have the Law or Christianity, they do what the Law or Christianity require. They show the effect of the Law or Christianity, they do what the Law or Christianity require. They show the effect of the Law or of Christianity written on their hearts. What I have been saying about the devotees of the African traditional religions also applies to the adherents of the major world religions who strive in their various ways to serve God. (pp. 140–1)

The adage *extra ecclesiam nulla salus* is not biblical. It is an inference made on the basis of 1 Peter 3:18ff. but the inference is incorrect. Whereas the passage states that there is salvation within the ark i.e, the Church, it does not say that salvation is possible only in the ark; neither does it say that salvation is not possible outside the ark. It cannot be maintained that in the Bible we have an entirely negative attitude towards Gentiles and non-Christians. God is presented as the God of all humankind. God's universal salvific will is clear from 1 Timothy 2:4. We believe as Christians that Christ died for all humankind. Thus all people, Christians and non-Christians, should in principle benefit from the salvific work of Christ. The Logos who enlightens all human persons and who died for all can in ways unknown to us bring non-Christians to the Father. In this he is assisted by the Spirit who blows where he will. (p. 141)

Joseph Osei-Bonsu, '*Extra Ecclesiam Nulla Salus*': Critical Reflections from Biblical and African Perspectives', in Peter Phan (ed.), *Christianity and the Wider Ecumenism* (New York: Paragon, 1990).

P

Mahinda Palihawandana

Mahinda Palihawandana, Professor in Sri Lanka, argues in 'A Buddhist Response: Religion Beyond Ideology and Power' that faiths can undergo improvement through religious encounter.

Both in the East and West, religious societies present a rather perplexing picture today. We are all aware of the familiar signs of 'sickness' in these societies: erosion of observance, slackening of faith, loss of prestige of the elites, and so on.

Yet, this is only one side of the picture. On the other side, we have evidence of their basic strengths that have elicited profound attachments. Each one of them has come to be viewed as a treasured possession by its adherents and has in turn conferred on them a sense of identity and a civilizing worldview. Their toughness of fibre is demonstrable by their resilience and adaptability. At issue, then, is not whether religious societies are becoming extinct, but rather this problem: Which is the more significant, their signs of sickness or their continuing dynamism?

These two together, however, hardly leave in doubt the fact that religious societies have the will to live and the hope of continued life, even though there is turmoil in their souls. In the reservoir of power that the religious societies represent, the positive factor is this will to live. But the turmoil in the soul indicates the presence of a negative factor as well: elements of weakness that new challenges have brought into consciousness.... (pp. 34–5)

Though each of the religions has provided a worldview by which men and women lived, can any one of them claim to be perfect? They have all failed in one way or another. Most notably, they have failed to make people live up to their ideals. So the challenge of the other religions may make us ask ourselves: Are our ideals unattainable or unrealistic? Have we somewhere in our history failed to take note of important aspects of the tradition? How to account for our obvious failures?

Buddhists, noting that Christian societies generally have been the pioneers in advancing to massive economic successes, in eradicating disease, in achieving technological triumphs, might conceivably feel that they should seriously examine the Christian critique of what has been regarded as Buddhist pessimism, or even the basic position accorded to *dukkha* (woe or suffering) in the Buddhist view of humanity. It may be argued that it is 'constitutionally' difficult for Buddhists to develop an attitude of conquering nature and of facing up to the intractable challenges of hunger, disease, deprivation, etc. Will the Buddhists accept this criticism meekly, without a serious re-examination of the meaning of the doctrine of *dukkha*? Obviously not. No one can forecast what such re-examination will bring. But whatever it brings, it is likely to lead to religious revitalization, either via healthy changes or via healthy rediscoveries or both.

Academic students of religion have hardly to be told that in their long histories the religions have undergone more changes, or more drastic changes, than the faithful are likely to concede. It remains a task for future religious consciousness to admit this fact squarely and to be ready to take the consequences. Some fear that granting respectability to a principle of change in religious viewpoints and attitudes will be self-destructive. But, in fact, the recognition of 'changing religion' may contribute to a religion's survival, as probably it was in this way they actually survived.

I think then that by religious change, the great traditions strengthen one another by various forms of 'cross-fertilization'. Attitudes and teachings cannot be bodily taken from one tradition and planted in another, but the strengths of one tradition may become the 'conducive factor' for another tradition to examine itself. Through this interaction traditions may generate new strengths in terms of their own resources.

Thus it seems to me probably that in the next stage of the encounter of religions each tradition will internally wrestle with the weak or 'negative' side of its development. At that stage, it should appear to each tradition that it owes a serious duty to itself to inquire: 'What have we to propose to humankind? Has humankind seriously taken account of what our tradition has been proposing? Have we been taking what was proposed in the past seriously enough? Or have we drifted on to a less serious course of action, or even moved in the opposite direction?' As each tradition reviews itself, there will be at least three important 'negative developments' for each tradition to cope with internally: (1) dogmatism, (2) institutionalism, and (3) alliance with power and wealth. Religious traditions must learn to divest themselves of these 'cankers' in order to advance to a new creative phase. (pp. 36–7)

Mahinda Palihawandana, 'A Buddhist Response: Religion Beyond Ideology and Power', in Donald G. Dawe and John B. Carman, *Christian Faith in a Religiously Plural World* (Maryknoll, NY: Orbis, 1986).

Raimundo Panikkar

Formerly Professor at the University of California at Santa Barbara, Raimundo Panikkar argues in 'Whose Uniqueness?' that religious truth emerges from interreligious dialogue.

The question of the uniqueness of Christ arose from the idea of Christianity being the only one and true religion, the unique and fully saving religion. Christianity was supposed to be unique because it alone saves. This may be right or wrong, but it is not incoherent, it makes sense. Once this idea has been given up by a good number of theologians, a strategic retreat has shifted the question to Jesus: is Jesus unique? My submission is that this uniqueness may prove to be yet another pseudo-problem.... .

If I love my neighbour it is because I find my neighbour lovable. I cannot love out of an extrinsic command to love. The Christian theologian in me tells me that I find my neighbour lovable because the grace of Christ is poured on her, and so I discover his face. But the Buddhist mind, which I also have, tells me that I love her because we all have Buddha-nature. The Hindu in me leads me to discover *karma* as universal solidarity, and this links me with my neighbour as to myself. The secular person, which I also am, makes me ponder the fact that all those (and also other) traditions, in spite of their lofty words, have pretty well forgotten to love their neighbours in deed, and leads me to suspect that there is a *Zeitgeist* (not uniquely Christian), an actual *mythos*, I would rather say, which makes us realize that without such a passion for justice the world faces disaster and we harm our own humanness.

It is significant, not to say suspicious, that precisely now Christians (as well as many others) speak of salvation to 'be realized in this world through human actions', when for centuries they (and others as well) have given the impression that their 'reign is not of this world' and that faith rather than works has saving power – not to speak of connivance with the powers that be in order to preach resignation, patience, and postponement of justice until the coming world.

It is a telling 'sign of the times' that we all now seem to stress the 'Unknown Christ', the 'Universal Buddha-nature', the 'Cosmic *Karma*' and the '*Humanum*'. Where is uniqueness here? Are some more unique than others? Do we not mean perhaps distinctiveness?

For too long theologians have entrenched themselves in a specialized fortress and neglected philosophy, from which they did not want to be contaminated once the handmaid of theology came of age – so the Enlightenment saga goes.

To put it all in one sentence: identity is not synonymous with identification, nor uniqueness with distinctiveness. Christ's identity is not our identification of him, nor is his uniqueness his distinctiveness.

The uniqueness of Christ has been interpreted as meaning a unique person (Jesus, the son of Mary), with a unique message (say, the Beatitudes or love for all, including enemies), eliciting a unique *praxis* (helping the other or striving for justice), and with a unique function (salvation or liberation of humankind).

Now, the fourth uniqueness cannot be defended unless one condemns all the 'non-followers' of the unique Christ. The third and second uniquenesses are simply not the case. Many saints, prophets and traditions have uttered and practised all those sublime doctrines – independently and even before Christ. There remains only the first uniqueness, which is an obvious truth: everyone is unique.... (pp. 111–12)

We may find a transcendental relationship between what Christians call Christ and what other cultures and religions may express with a set of homeomorphic equivalents. But in this case the uniqueness of Christ has been relativized and brought into the field where it has an accepted meaning. Christ is then the logotype, as it were, of the Christian language....

Pluralism, for me, is not an attitude which posits that there are many true religions or many authentic Christs – albeit with different names. Truth itself is pluralistic, not plural. The pluralistic attitude is fruit of the experience that we are not the masters of truth and can thus only decide (about truth) in each particular case through dialogical discourse. Even in law courts one does not judge the other by sheer hearsay. This is the flaw of any single theology of religions with the claim to universal validity. Even the one Christian *logos* has spoken many *logoi*, as Christian scripture itself (and tradition) asserts. We may understand some languages of others (not all), and hear new tunes of the symphony or eliminate others, but we cannot say that all languages (religions) say the same until and unless they actually say it. (pp. 113–14)

Raimundo Panikkar, 'Whose Uniqueness?', in Leonard Swidler and Paul Mojzes (eds), *The Uniqueness of Jesus: A Dialogue with Paul F. Knitter* (Maryknoll, NY: Orbis, 1997).

Bhiku Parekh

Bhiku Parekh, formerly Professor of Political Theory at the University of Hull, was also Deputy Chairman of the Commission for Racial Equality. In 'The Concept of Interfaith Dialogue', Parekh proposes a Hindu response to the issue of religious pluralism. In his view, interfaith dialogue must be based on sympathy for one another's faith and can encourage self-critical awareness.

An interfaith dialogue might be inspired by two related but different impulses.

First, it might spring from a desire to understand other religions and to explore how and why they arrive at their distinctive conceptions of God, religion, the universe and man and his duties. Second, it might be inspired by a desire to learn from them, to acquire new insights into the nature of moral and religious sensibility. Although the two approaches are related, for understanding and learning cannot be easily separated, they have different origins and consequences. In the first approach one seeks to understand others, but does not use that knowledge better to understand and critically evaluate one's own religion. A dialogue in the second case has a different thrust. It springs from a search for critical self-understanding and acknowledges that no religion is perfect and represents total truth about the nature of the Divine. In such a view others do not remain separate but become part of oneself, and one's dialogue with them becomes an integral part of one's dialogue with oneself. In the first case, interfaith dialogue springs from and encourages tolerance and mutual respect; in the second it fosters a spirit of critical self-understanding and interreligious borrowing.

If I had to take an example of a religious man genuinely engaged in the second kind of interfaith dialogue, I would point to Gandhi. I choose him neither because he was the only man in history to engage in it nor because he was the most sophisticated, for he was neither, but because I happen to know more about him than about the others. He struck up close friendships with Jews and Christians in South Africa, lived with them on his communal farm and made a close study of their scriptures. He went to South Africa to serve a Muslim patron and had close Muslim friends. And being a Hindu deeply influenced by the three great Indian religions, he had read widely in Hinduism, Buddhism and Jainism.

For Gandhi every major religion articulated a unique vision of God and emphasized different features of the human condition. The idea of God as loving Father was most fully developed in Christianity, and the emphasis on love and suffering was also unique to it. As he put it: 'I cannot say that it is singular, or that it is not to be found in other religions. But the presentation is unique.' Austere and rigorous monotheism and the spirit of equality were 'most beautifully' articulated in and peculiar to Islam. The distinction between the impersonal and personal conceptions of God, the principle of the unity of all life and the doctrine of *ahimsa* (nonviolence) were distinctive to Hinduism. For Gandhi every religion had a distinct moral and spiritual ethos and represented a wonderful and irreplaceable 'spiritual composition'. To a truly religious man all religions should be 'equally dear'.

Gandhi argued that since God was infinite and the limited human mind could grasp only a 'fragment' of him, and that too inadequately, every religion was necessarily limited and partial. Even the religions claiming to be directly revealed by God were revealed to men with their fair share of inescapable human limitations and communicated in necessarily inadequate human languages. To claim that a particular religion offered an exhaustive or even definitive account of the nature of God was to imply both that some men were free from inescapable human limitations and that God was partial, and thus to be guilty of both spiritual arrogance and blasphemy. Since no religion was final and perfect, each greatly benefited from a dialogue with others. For Gandhi the purpose of an interreligious dialogue was threefold. First, it helped each religion understand the others better and encouraged it to feel relaxed enough to assimilate from them whatever it found worth accepting. Second, it helped each understand itself better and enabled it to appreciate both its uniqueness and similarities with the others. Third, it lifted each religion above the superficial levels of beliefs and rituals, deepened its spirituality and enabled it to catch a glimpse of the 'pure' or 'eternal' religion lying beyond all religions. (pp. 162–3)

Bhiku Parekh, 'The Concept of Interfaith Dialogue', in Dan Cohn-Sherbok, *Many Mansions* (London: Bellew, 1992).

Geoffrey Parrinder

Born in 1910, Geoffrey Parrinder was formerly Professor of the Comparative Study of Religion at King's College, London and has written numerous books dealing with the world's religions. In 'The Meeting of Religions Today', he contends that interfaith dialogue offers new opportunities for members of religious faiths to encounter one another with tolerance.

The religions of the world today face a completely new situation, and this is particularly significant for the West. Never before this century have there been such close contacts as now obtain in religious organizations, practices and thought. The 'one world' in which we live, with its close communications, makes nonsense of religious isolation. Whether it is agreeable or not, the fact is that men and women can and do now compare religious ideas with one another and often mix them together. This situation presents challenges to traditional forms of theology.

The challenges are acute for the Semitic or Western religions of Christianity, Judaism and Islam. They have been accustomed to think of themselves as supreme, in religion and culture, possessing the highest truths and the oldest and best philosophies. Many histories of philosophy, or of other aspects of culture, have considered only European or Near Eastern forms as if they were the only ones that mattered... .

We have been accustomed to speak of the rest of the world, say India or China, as isolated until our explorations in the sixteenth century and colonization in the nineteenth. In fact it is the West that has been isolated. India has long been a meeting-place for some of the greatest religions. Christianity appeared there in the early centuries and the Syrian Church has persisted along the Malabar coast, while new churches have sprung up in many parts of India. Islam entered India from the eighth century and eventually spread over much of the sub-continent, so that today rather less than one-sixth of Indians are counted as Muslims. There have long been small communities of Jews and Parsis in western India. Although the great majority of Indians are counted as followers of some form of Hindu religion there are other ancient and powerful indigenous Indian religions; as well as relatively small numbers of Jains and Sikhs, Buddhism arose in India, prospered for a thousand years, and then dispersed to take Indian religion and culture to much of the rest of Asia. So the meeting of religions today is but an acceleration in India of age-long processes. India has been used to many religions, so that Hindus tend to regard other faiths as different ways to one goal with unusual tolerance.

Western Christianity is emerging from its isolation and slowly adjusting its thinking to the fact that not only do other religions exist, but that they persist. Even more, that they are not far away, to be the subject of missionary attention, but are close at hand. The Jews have of course been long in Europe, but they have often been treated to indifference at best, and to shameful persecution at worst. Grudgingly it might be admitted that Jews had a form of religion to which they strangely held fast; their past was sacred history, but it was rarely thought that their present religion could teach anything. (pp. 95–6)

No doubt those who attend interfaith services expect and accept that different religions have different ways, names and beliefs. Acceptance of this fact is an ingredient of modern life. The cosmic Christ can be seen as inspiring and embracing all expressions of sincere faith. This cannot be put better than in a favourite passage from the great Archbishop William Temple. In his devotional commentary on St John's Gospel he wrote on the verse that speaks of the Logos as 'the true Light, which lighteth everyone'. Temple commented: 'By the word of God – that is to say by Jesus Christ – Isaiah and Plato, Zoroaster, Buddha, and Confucius, uttered and wrote such truths as they declared. There is only one Divine light, and every man in his own measure is enlightened by it.' Therefore Christians need not be afraid, as if the ark of God were trembling, when they hear other names and concepts, even in churches, for these can be taken as inspired by the one divine light.

There are some who would have no sharing or dialogue with members of other religions, regarding them as 'pagans' and 'lost' unless they submit to particular organizations and doctrines. But a better example of sharing in prayer, in a church, was given by Pope John Paul II in 1986 when he joined with hundreds of leaders of world religions, Christian, Jewish, Muslim, Hindu, Buddhist, Sikh and Shinto, to pray for peace in the basilica of St Francis in Assisi. (pp. 105–6)

Geoffrey Parrinder, 'The Meeting of Religions Today', in Dan Cohn-Sherbok, *Many Mansions* (London: Bellew, 1992).

Peter Phan

Peter Phan, Professor at the University of America, addresses the question of Jesus'
uniqueness in 'Are There Other "Saviours" for Other Peoples?' In his view, the claim of
Jesus' uniqueness should not be abandoned in religious dialogue.

In recent interreligious dialogues between Christianity and other world religions
the question has often been raised whether Christians can and must recognize that
there are, besides Jesus the Christ, other saviours, such as Gautama the Buddha
and Muhammad, who may be equal or even superior to Jesus. The question is
often couched in terms of the uniqueness of Jesus: Is Jesus so unique among the
religious figures of history as to rule out any other possible mediator of salvation?
Can and should Christians continue to affirm that Jesus the Christ is normative
for all peoples in their relationship with God, that is, ultimately decisive, definitive, archetypal for humanity's relation with God?

Answers given to this question can be grouped into three types: exclusivistic,
inclusivistic and pluralistic. The exclusivistic type affirms that only in Jesus can
true revelation and salvation be found, the Christ event being constitutive of any
authentic encounter with God, always and everywhere. The inclusivistic type
affirms the uniqueness of Jesus without denying that God's saving presence may
also be operative in other forms of religions. Proponents of this view, however,
insist that Christ includes other religions either by being present in them anony-
mously or by fulfilling them. Jesus remains, if not constitutive of, at least normative for, all religious experience. Finally, the pluralistic type affirms that Jesus is
unique, but his uniqueness includes and is included by other potentially equal
religious figures. It views Jesus as neither constitutive of nor normative for
authentic religious experience, but as theocentric, that is, as a universally relevant
manifestation, incarnation and sacrament of God's revelation and salvation in
history. Jesus may have universal relevance but not uniqueness. (pp. 163–4)

If Jesus is not identical with Christianity, then the claims to uniqueness for
Jesus and for Christianity are two different claims. They may be connected but
are not the same. Not only are they claims for two different realities, their epistemological status is different and therefore cannot be validated in the same
manner. The claim that Jesus is the only Christ is a claim of faith, a 'kerygmatic
affirmation', to use Aloysius Pieris's term, as is the claim that Gautama is the
only Buddha; whereas the claim that Christianity is the only true religion, superior to other religions, is based, or at least has traditionally been based, on
empirical evidences.

It is precisely the distinction between Jesus and Christianity, between the claim
to uniqueness for Jesus and that for Christianity, that enables some Catholic
theologians to be critical of Christianity, as a historical religion, and to recognize

that non-Christian religions can be authentic ways of salvation, and not merely that there is a general revelation in them... .

But to return to the claim to superiority and uniqueness for Christianity as a historical religion. Can such a claim be reasonably be made? The pluralists' answer is a resounding No on the basis of the three basic reasons given above. My response is both Yes and No. Lest I be accused of clever tergiversation, allow me to explain. First of all, two things must be clear. First, the claim to superiority for Christianity is, as I have said above, an empirical claim, at least that has been the way in which this claim is substantiated by the Catholic Church... .

Second, since religions are both 'gnostic' and 'agapeic' ... both enlightenment and transformation, the criteria for judging their 'truth' must be both doctrinal and praxeological. Religions are 'true' if they both teach correct doctrines and transform human lives... . On the basis of these criteria, the answer to the question whether Christianity can claim uniqueness in the sense of superiority over other religions, can only be Yes and No. No, because some of its teachings, both credal and moral, are inadequate or simply wrong. No, also because it has not always shown 'marvellous propagation', 'eminent holiness', 'inexhaustible fruitfulness', 'Catholic unity', and 'invincible stability'... . On the other hand, yes, because empirically, there are some doctrines, both credal and moral, in Christianity that are noble and uplifting and to this extent transformative of human lives, while there are others that can be shown to be 'truer', more humane and hence more liberative than those taught by other religions on the same subject matter... . Yes, also because, empirically, there have been (and will always be) some Christians who live lives of self-sacrifice and generosity... . (pp. 170–1)

But what if the claim to superiority means that Christianity has the fullness of truth, that Christians possess a full and perfect understanding of religious matters? In the light of the utterly ineffable nature of the divine Mystery, of the historically conditioned character of human understanding and language, and of the inherent limitations of the human intellect, only a fool or one totally innocent of all learning would make such a claim. (p. 172)

Peter Phan, 'Are There Other "Saviours" for Other Peoples?', in Peter Phan (ed.), *Christianity and the Wider Ecumenism* (New York: Paragon, 1990).

Aloysius Pieris

The Sri Lankan Catholic theologian Aloysius Pieris studied at the University of London and served as Director of the Tulana Research Centre in Kelaniya and Professor at the East Asian Pastoral Institute in Manila. In 'The Buddha and the Christ: Mediators of Liberation', he argues that those who engage in dialogue must seek to understand the core liberative experiences of other faiths.

Interreligious dialogue is carried out on three different, but essentially related, levels: the levels of core-experience, collective memory and interpretation.

The 'core' of any religion is the liberative experience that gave birth to that religion and continues to be available to successive generations of humankind. It is this primordial experience that functions as the core of a religion, at any time, in any given place, in the sense that it continuously re-creates the psycho-spiritual mood proper to that particular religion, imparting at the same time its own peculiar character to the socio-cultural manifestation of that religion. It is precisely through recourse to this primordial experience that a religion resolves its recurrent crises and regenerates itself in the face of new challenges. In fact, the vitality of any given religion depends on its capacity to put each successive generation in touch with the core-experience of liberation.

The medium by which the core-experience is made available to successive generations is precisely the 'collective memory' of that experience. A religion would die as soon as it is born if it failed to evolve some means of perpetuating (the accessibility of) its core-experience. Religious beliefs, practices, traditions and institutions that grow out of a particular religion go to make up a 'communication system' that links its adherents with the originating nucleus – that is, the liberative core of that religion. This is why a religion fades out of history even after centuries of existence when its symbols and institutions lose their capacity to evoke in their followers the distinctive salvific experience that defines the essence of that religion. Did this not happen to the great religions of ancient Egypt, Rome, Greece and Mesopotamia?

Integral to the functioning of the communication system of the collective memory is 'interpretation'. In order to be remembered, an experience – in its symbols, beliefs and rituals – has to be framed in terms of historical and cultural categories. Thus, the core-experience in all religions, insofar as it is remembered, tends also to be interpreted in such diverse ways as to form various philosophical, theological and exegetical schools.

In Buddhism, the core-experience lends itself to be classed as *gnosis* or 'liberative knowledge'; the corresponding Christian experience falls under the category of *agape* or 'redemptive love'. Each is salvific in that each is a self-transcending event that radically transforms the human person affected by that experience. At the same time, there is an indefinable contrast between them, which largely determines the major differences between the two religions, differences quite obvious even to the casual observer. And yet, it must be recognized that both *gnosis* and *agape* are necessary precisely because each in itself is inadequate as a medium not only for experiencing but also for expressing our intimate moments with the Ultimate Source of liberation. They are, in other words, complementary idioms that need each other to mediate the self-transcending experience called 'salvation'. Any valid spirituality, Buddhist or Christian, as the history of each religion attests, does retain both poles of religious experience – namely, the gnostic and the agapeic. The movement of the spirit progresses through the dialectical interplay of wisdom and love, or, to put it in Buddhist terms, through the complementarity between *prajna* and *karuna*, and in the Hindu tradition, the sapiential spirituality known as the *jnana-marga* and the affective-active paths called the *bhakti-* and *karma-marga*.

But in order to appreciate and dialogue about both the differences and the complementarity between the core-experiences of Buddhism and Christianity, one must enter into their collective memories. Buddhism and Christianity are both vibrant today because each has developed its own religious system (of doctrines, rites and institutions), which can make the original experience available to contemporary society. Hence the conclusion is unavoidable: a Christian who wishes to enter into a core-to-core dialogue with Buddhism must have two qualifications: (1) a preliminary empathic apprehension of the real nature of the other religion's core-experience, and (2) an uninhibited willingness to make use of the religious system that the Buddhist offers to the Christian as the only means of access to that core-experience – in other words, a readiness to enter into a *communicatio in sacris* with Buddhists. (pp. 162–3)

Aloysius Pieris, 'The Buddha and the Christ: Mediators of Liberation', in John Hick and Paul F. Knitter (eds), *The Myth of Christian Uniqueness* (London: SCM Press, 1987).

Sayyid Qutb

Sayyid Qutb, born in 1906, was a leading figure in the Muslim Brothers. Imprisoned in Egypt, he was released in 1964. Two years later he was rearrested and later executed. In 'That Hidden Schizophrenia', he argues that the message of Jesus Christ was corrupted; as a consequence, the Christian religion is unable to serve as a means of mediating God's will. In his view the West should become Islamized.

If the Christian ideological ideal had remained as sound as that expounded by Jesus Christ (peace be unto him), it could have presented still the right interpretation of the universe, of the situation of man therein and of his primary objectives in this world. It could have brought the Christians back to the law of Moses, as clarified by Jesus to ease some of the Jewish restrictions on worship and human relations.

But what happened was that the followers of Jesus were subjected to atrocious persecution by both the faithless Jews and the pagan Romans who were their temporal rulers. This led the disciples (the students of Jesus) and their followers to hide themselves and to move and act in secrecy for long periods of time. Amidst such circumstances they altered the text of their Scriptures, transmitting the history of Jesus and the events in his life in a haphazard fashion, being unable to verify freely the authenticity of those narratives. As a result, the gospel (*Injil*) as inspired by God to Jesus, was interpolated among those legends and narratives about the life of Christ – stories which came from different and conflicting sources. These hybrid compositions have been called 'Gospels' but they are for the most part the words of these students and their own versions about the biography of Jesus, with quotations here and there from what was originally the gospel. The most ancient of these 'Gospels' was written a full generation after Christ, and most Christian historians greatly differ in fixing its date, estimating it between 40 AD and 64 AD. They differ as well about the language it was originally written in, as they have found but one single translation.

It was Paul who was considered the principal propagator of the Christian faith to the Gentiles, himself being a Roman heathen converted to Christianity. Paul's conception of Christianity was adulterated by the residues of Roman mythology and Greek philosophy. That was a catastrophe which infected Christianity since its early days in Europe, over and above its disfiguration during the early period of persecution when the prevailing circumstances did not allow for examining and authenticating its religious textual bases... .

But the greatest calamity was the subsequent event which was considered, at face value, the triumph of Christianity. It happened when the Roman Emperor Constantine embraced the new religion and enabled the Christians to become the ruling party in 355 AD... . The Christian community, while powerful enough to keep Constantine king, could not crush or eradicate idolatry. Christianity's principles became muddled and transmuted as a result of its struggles and conflicts, leading to formation of a new synthetic religion displaying conspicuously equal elements of both Christianity and paganism. In this respect Islam differs from Christianity. It completely exterminated its rival (idolatry) and propagated its principles pure and without opacity. But this Emperor, Constantine, was a slave to his lusts and had no genuine religious convictions and he deemed it in his interest and the interest of the two competing ideologies (idolatry and Christianity) to have unity and reconciliation. Paradoxically, the Christians did not object to the idea! It seems that they believed the new faith would prosper if mingled with the popular pagan creeds, but would eventually rid itself of the absurdity of idolatry.

However, the religion never did rid itself of the impurities of paganism, as devoted Christians had hoped for, but continued its course polluted with heathen myths and conceptions. Still worse, it was so encumbered with political and racial differences that it used to alter and modify its basic principles in accordance with its political aims. (pp. 75–7)

The unfortunate circumstances which influenced Christianity at its very inception, then its political success ... added to the subsequent political and racial contentions, disfigurations and modifications in the creed. As a result, the ideological ideal was burdened with the elements of so-called 'mysteries' quite alien to its nature as a Divine religion. Accordingly, the Christian conception, as modulated by successsive graftings at the outset, and as edited by the general and private religious Councils later on, became unable to give authoritative Divine interpretation to the nature of existence and its genuine relation to the Creator. Nor could it elucidate the nature and attributes of the Creator, or the nature of human existence and the proper goals of mankind. These elements must be correctly assessed so that the social order deriving from and dependent upon them will be sound and correct as well. (p. 78)

Sayyid Qutb, 'That Hidden Schizophrenia', in Paul J. Griffiths (ed.), *Christianity Through Non-Christian Eyes* (Maryknoll, NY: Orbis, 1990).

R

Alan Race

Alan Race, Rector of St Andrew's Church, Aylestone, Leicester, argues that Christians must set aside absolutist claims about their faith.

The 'scandal of particularity' is a theme running through both ancient and modern Christianity. As an evocation of the absolute uniqueness of Christ, it has functioned as a rallying cry to the Christian faithful, fundamentally safeguarding their identity on theological and political fronts. Theologically, it has protected the *sui generis* nature of Jesus Christ as a saviour figure on the stage of world religious history. Politically, it has provided ideological divine sanction, at one extreme, for Christian separatism and, at the other, for exploitation, domination and imperialism... . The scandal of Christian particularity relates therefore to the sense of exclusiveness regarding the truth of its religious claims and the political use that has been made of those claims. Yet no matter how pervasive the evocation of the absolute uniqueness of Christ has been, at least three developments during this century signal the need for its careful scrutiny.

First, new encounters between people of different world faiths are demonstrating how each religious tradition provides a living context for religious aspiration, unswerving faithfulness and vibrant spirituality outside the Christian circle. Growing positive respect for these world faiths is leading some theologians to re-evaluate the concept of the absolute uniqueness of Christ in relation to other perceived revelatory visions of the divine life.

Second, historical and philosophical currents of thought have demonstrated how religious truths are more humanly constructed than we once imagined. Doctrines and patterns of meaning are not inviolable, but have been linked inextricably to the needs, institutions, perceptions and religious assumptions of a society at any one period. Historically, reality as 'a continuous connection of becoming' leaves little room for the older view of religious truth which was grounded in a supernatural interventionist account of divine activity. On the philosophical level, religious beliefs now tend to be held less as direct descriptions of the divine life, than as provisional pointers to truth using symbolic and metaphorical forms. Clearly, the doctrine of Christ is not so readily or easily circumscribed under these conditions.

Third, awareness of the ideological function of the absolute uniqueness of Christ in the missionary exploitation of other cultures and religions has rightly attracted strong criticism on moral grounds. Now, while the religious and political abuse of the uniqueness of Christ does not discredit the concept of Christ's absoluteness as such, there is no necessary connection between the 'scandal of particularity' and the Christian refusal to acquiesce in State power when the latter shows pretentions to divine triumphalism. (pp. 61–2)

As a result of this kind of analysis, my contention is this: both the internal shifts within Christian thought about the person of Jesus and the inappropriateness of the belief in final supremacy ... attached to Jesus in a culture which values religious pluralism positively, point to a profound need for reinterpreting what tradition came to call the 'scandal of particularity'. The doctrine of the incarnation cannot bear the weight which Christian thought has put on it, and nowhere is this more highlighted than from within the whole modern debate around the Christian theology of religions. Therefore the 'scandal' now is the refusal to take the necessary steps in Christian theological reconstruction in the light of changed perceptions. This is not to say that simply because Christians are learning to value the religious experience of their neighbours, therefore Christian thought about Jesus ought to change. It is claiming, however, that the factors of arbitrariness and ambiguity compound the problematic nature of traditional christology in modern debate, once the relationship between Christianity and other faiths is brought into the open. (p. 70)

The kind of epistomology required to undergird this new venture in dialogue has yet to be fully realized. Meanwhile, the experience of persisting religious pluralism entails that truth in the religious interpretation of reality can no longer remain a function of one tradition alone. Of necessity it must embrace many traditions, as well as what we know from the natural and human sciences. In this process of 'dialogue for truth', the eschatological nature of truth, itself reflected pluralistically in the world's different religious visions of the divine life, can be a bridge to any epistemological framework that might emerge. Whatever form it takes, it is committed to the belief that the 'particularities' of the world religious traditions are not isolated islands, but territories deeply and necessarily related to one another. (p. 72)

Alan Race, 'Christ and the Scandal of Particularity', in Dan Cohn-Sherbok (ed.), *Many Mansions* (London: Bellew, 1992).

Fazlur Rahman

Fazlur Rahman, Professor at the University of Chicago, argues in 'A Muslim Response: Christian Particularity and the Faith of Islam' that even though Muslims reject christological claims about Jesus, they regard him as a divinely appointed messenger of God.

Islam's attitude to Christianity is as old as Islam itself, since Islam partly took shape at the point of its very genesis by both adopting certain important ideas from Judaism and Christianity and criticizing others. Indeed, Islam's self-definition is partly the result of its attitude to these two religions and their communities.

That there was messianism present among certain Meccan Arab circles at the time Muhammad appeared is undeniable. This fact has been amply documented. And instead of accepting either Judaism or Christianity, these Arab circles were looking for a new revealed religion of their own, so that 'they might be better guided' than the two older communities. After the advent of Muhammad as God's messsenger, the Qur'an (Koran) repeatedly refers to a group of people about whom it says, 'We had already given them the Book (i.e., the Torah and/or Gospel) and they also believe in the Qur'an.' These verses clearly show the existence of some Jews or Christians or Judeo–Christians who had also entertained messianic hopes and who encouraged Muhammad in his mission. The Qur'an, indeed, taunts the Meccan pagans saying that whether they believed or not in the Qur'an (or the Prophet), 'those to whom We had already given the Book, believe in it (or him)'.... (pp. 69–70)

If Muhammad and his followers believe in all prophets, all people must also and equally believe in him. Disbelief in him would be equivalent to disbelief in all, for this would arbitrarily upset the line of prophetic succession. In the late Meccan period, however, the Prophet becomes more aware that Jews and Christians would not believe in him, nor would they recognize each other.... (p. 71)

The awareness of the diversity of religions, despite the unity of their origin, sets Muhammad a theological problem of the first order. It so persistently and painfully pressed itself on his mind that from the beginning of this awareness until well into the last phase of his life the Qur'an treats this question at various levels. The fact that religions are split, not only from each other, but even within themselves, is recurrently deplored, but a somewhat different point of view on the problem also emerges in the Qur'an. Humankind had been a unity, but this unity was split up because of the advent of divine messages at the hands of the prophets. The fact that the prophets' messages act as watersheds and divisive forces is rooted in some divine mystery, for if God so willed, he could surely bring them on one path.... (p. 72)

The Qur'an's reply to these exclusivist claims and claims of proprietorship over God's guidance, then, is absolutely unequivocal: Guidance is not the function of communities but of God and good people, and no community may lay claims to be uniquely guided and elected.... The whole mystique of election is undermined by the repeated statements of the Qur'an after mentioning biblical prophets and their people....

In conformity with this strong rejection of exclusivism and election, the Qur'an repeatedly recognizes the existence of good people in other communities – Jews, Christians and Sabbaeans – just as it recognizes the people of faith in Islam ... (p. 73)

So far as Islam is concerned, it recognized Jesus and his divine mission from the time of its birth. However, it criticized, sometimes severely, the doctrine of the incarnation of God in Jesus and, consequently, rejected trinitarianism. Christians have mostly taken this to be a rejection of Christianity itself. The Qur'an assigns to Jesus the position of a prophet, God's Word and Divine Spirit, but withholds – for reasons that are not arbitrary or fortuitous but rooted deeply in its very conception of the God–human relationship – assent to the divinity of Jesus or, indeed, of anybody else. (p. 75)

The unacceptability of Jesus' divinity and the Trinity to the Qur'an is an incontrovertible fact, as is the fact that Jesus and his followers are regarded as exceptionally charitable and self-sacrificing. The Qur'an would most probably have no objection to the Logos having become flesh if the Logos were not simply identified with God and the identification were understood less literally. For the Qur'an, the Word of God is never identified simply with God. Jesus, again, is the 'Spirit of God' in a special sense for the Qur'an, although God had breathed his spirit into Adam as well (15.29; 30–8.72). It was on the basis of some such expectations from the self-proclaimed monotheism of Christians – and of course, Jews – that the Qur'an issued its invitation: 'O People of the Book! Let us come together upon the formula which is common between us – that we shall not serve anyone but God, that we shall associate none with Him...' (3.64). This invitation, probably issued at a time when Muhammad thought not all was yet lost between the three self-proclaimed monotheistic communities, must have appeared specious to Christians. It has remained unheeded until now. But I believe something can still be worked out by way of positive co-operation provided the Muslim hearken more to the Qur'an than to the historic formulations of Islam and provided that the pioneering efforts ... continue to yield a Christian doctrine more compatible with monotheism and egalitarianism. (pp. 78–9)

Fazlur Rahman, 'A Muslim Response: Christian Particularity and the Faith of Islam', in Donald G. Dawe and John B. Carman, *Christian Faith in a Religiously Plural World* (Maryknoll, NY: Orbis, 1986).

Karl Rahner

Karl Rahner, born in Swabia in 1904, was Professor at the Universities of Innsbruck and Munich. In 'Christianity and the Non-Christian Religions', he claims that non-Christian religions can serve as authentic means of gaining a right relationship to God.

We must therefore rid ourselves of the prejudice that we can face a non-Christian religion with the dilemma that it must either come from God in everything it contains and thus correspond to God's will and positive providence, or be simply a purely human construction. If man is under God's grace even in these religions – and to deny this is certainly absolutely wrong – then the possession of this supernatural grace cannot but show itself, and cannot but become a formative factor of life in the concrete, even where (though not only where) this life turns the relationship to the absolute into an explicit theme, viz. in religion. It would perhaps be possible to say in theory that where a certain religion is not only accompanied in its concrete appearance by something false and humanly corrupted but also makes this an explicitly and consciously adopted element – an explicitly declared condition of its nature – this religion is wrong in its deepest and most specific being and hence can no longer be regarded as a lawful religion – not even in the widest sense of the word. This may be quite correct in theory. But we must surely go on to ask whether there is any religion apart from the Christian religion (meaning here even only the Catholic religion) with an authority which could elevate falsehood into one of its really essential parts and which could thus face man with an alternative of either accepting this falsehood as the most real and decisive factor of the religion or leaving this religion. Even if one could perhaps say something like this of Islam as such, it would have to be denied of the majority of religions. It would have to be asked in every case to what extent the followers of such religions would actually agree with such an interpretation of their particular religion. If one considers furthermore how easily a concrete, originally religious act can be always directed in its intention towards one and the same absolute, even when it manifests itself in the most varied forms, then it will not even be possible to say that theoretical polytheism, however deplorable and objectionable it may be, objectively must always and everywhere be an absolute obstacle to the performance in such a religion of genuinely religious acts directed to the one true God. (pp. 31–2)

Christianity does not simply confront the member of an extra-Christian religion as a mere non-Christian but as someone who can and must already be regarded in this or that respect as an anonymous Christian. It would be wrong to regard the pagan as someone who has not yet been touched in any way by God's grace and truth. If, however, he has experienced the grace of God – if, in certain circumstances, he has already accepted this grace as the ultimate, unfathomable entelechy of his existence by accepting the immeasurableness of his dying existence as opening out into infinity – then he has already been given revelation in a true sense even before he has been affected by missionary preaching from without. For this grace, understood as the *a priori* horizon of all his spiritual acts, accompanies his consciousness subjectively, even though it is not known objectively... . Such a revelation is then the expression in objective concepts of something which this person has already attained or could already have attained in the depth of his rational existence. It is not possible here to prove more exactly that this *fides implicita* is something which dogmatically speaking can occur in a so-called pagan. We can do no more here than to state our thesis and to indicate the direction in which the proof of this thesis might be found. But if it is true that a person who becomes the object of the church's missionary efforts is or may be already someone on the way towards his salvation, and someone who in certain circumstances finds it, without being reached by the proclamation of the Church's message – and if it is at the same time true that this salvation which reaches him in this way is Christ's salvation, since there is no other salvation – then it must be possible to be not only an anonymous theist but also an anonymous Christian. (pp. 35–6)

Karl Rahner, 'Christianity and the Non-Christian Religions' in John Hick and Brian Hebblethwaite (eds), *Christianity and Other Religions* (Oxford: Oneworld, 2001).

Stuart E. Rosenberg

Born in 1922 in New York, Stuart Rosenberg has served as a rabbi in New York and Toronto. In 'Christianity and the Holocaust', he stresses that the Holocaust is the logical outgrowth of Christian doctrine. Such a terrible legacy must serve as the background to Jewish–Christian dialogue.

The exceptions – the relatively few and notable 'righteous Gentiles' – help prove the rule. During the twelve years of Hitler's 'kingdom of night' which culminated in 1945, most Christian churches distanced themselves from the Holocaust, whose destructive force was moving inexorably toward the fulfilment of Hitler's 'final solution to the Jewish problem': the wholesale slaughter and destruction of that people, for no other reason than that they were Jews. But even after the war, when the work of reconstruction and reconciliation should have begun – even then, few Christians leaders or their church councils reached out to assist the remnants of European Jewry. Worse still, few, if any, actively sought to address their own crucial religious question: the meaning of the Holocaust for believing and practising Christians.

The second silence of the churches must surely be related to their first – their almost total acquiescence in, and acceptance of, Hitler's anti-Jewish measures in the 1930s and 1940s. The so-called 'European background of antisemitism' was in fact little more than its own Christian history.

Why, then, in the years immediately following World War II, did so few churches or their leaders fail to see that there was a relationship between the long and continuous history of Christian anti-Judaism and the end product of Nazism – the calculated murder of one-third of the Jewish people? Many of their communicants still hid their faces, or, even worse, placidly accepted the doom of the six million in Hitler's Europe as a divine judgement for the 'Jewish rejection of Jesus'.

Sensitive souls among them are now inquiring: how could we have failed to see that the Holocaust was a judgement upon us as Christians, and not upon the Jews as Jews? How could we not have understood that the six million unredeemed crucifixions have left us with blood on our own hands? As a Jew, I draw strength from the growing number of devoted Christians who are now willing to state, without hesitation or equivocation, that after Auschwitz, the central moral test and religious question for Christianity is the survival of the Jews in a Christian world. Indeed, all of those earlier issues relating to this question which I have called 'the Christian problem' – are now beginning to be re-examined, reviewed, and in some quarters courageously acted upon.

Yet I am convinced that Jews still have a crucial role to play in this process. Without Jews to raise these questions, to remind the churches repeatedly and tirelessly, to confront Christian conscience with the moral and religious implications of these spiritual shortfalls, there are strong signs that new silences will again prevent them from coming to terms with their 'Christian problem'.

This is what makes a thorough understanding of the Holocaust and its implications for Christianity so crucial for the outcome of any dialogue between Jews and Christians. To suppress a serious discussion and analysis of the Holocaust out of 'genteel' concerns for personal sensitivities, or out of fear of erecting barriers to ongoing and continuing encounters is to miss the point. In the language of Robert McAfee Brown, a leading Christian ecumenist, 'each partner (to the dialogue) must accept responsibility in humility and penitence for what his group has done, and is doing, to foster and perpetuate division; each partner must forthrightly face the issues that cause separation as well as those that create solidarity'. (pp. 45–6)

Stuart Rosenberg, 'Christianity and the Holocaust', in Paul J. Griffiths (ed.), *Christianity Through Non-Christian Eyes* (Maryknoll, NY: Orbis, 1990)

Franz Rosenzweig

In The Star of Redemption, *the Jewish theologian Franz Rosenzweig focuses on the relationship between Judaism and Christianity rather than the world's religions. Nonetheless, he maintains that both Judaism and Christianity in their different ways offer insights into spiritual truth.*

Before God, then, Jew and Christian both labour at the same task. He cannot dispense with either. He has set enmity between the two for all time, and withal has most intimately bound each to each. To us (Jews) he gave eternal life by kindling the fire of the Star of his truth in our hearts. Them (the Christians) he set on the eternal way by causing them to pursue the rays of that Star of his truth for all time unto the eternal end. We (Jews) thus espy in our hearts the true image of the truth, yet on the other hand we turn our backs on temporal life, and the life of the times turns away from us. They (the Christians), for their part, run after the current of time, but the truth remains at their back; though led by it, since they follow its rays, they do not see it with their eyes. The truth, the whole truth, thus belongs neither to them nor to us. For we too, though we bear it within us, must for that very reason first immerse our glance into our own interior if we would see it, and there, whilst we see the Star, we do not see – the rays. And the whole truth would demand not only seeing its light but also what was illuminated by it. They (the Christians), however, are in any event already destined for all time to see what is illuminated, and not the light.

And thus we both have but a part of the whole truth. But we know that it is in the nature of truth to be imparted, and that a truth in which no one had a part would be no truth. The 'whole' truth, too, is truth only because it is God's part. Thus it does not detract from the truth, nor from us, that it is only partially ours. A direct view of the whole truth is granted only to him who sees it in God. That, however, is a view beyond life. A living view of the truth, a view that is at the same time life, can become ours too only in image and likeness. As for the Christians, they are denied a living view altogether for the sake of a living effectiveness of the truth. Thus both of us, they as much as we, we as much as they, are creatures precisely for the reason that we do not see the whole truth. Just for this we remain within the boundaries of mortality. Just for this we – remain. And remain we would. We want to live. God does for us what we want so long as we want it. As long as we cling to life, he gives us life. Of the truth he gives us only what we, as living creatures, can bear, that is our portion. Were he to give us more, to give us his portion, the whole truth, he would be hoisting us beyond the boundaries of humanity. But precisely as long as he does not do this, just so long too we harbour no desire for it. We cling to our creatureliness. We do not gladly relinquish it. And our creatureliness is determined by the fact that we only take part, only are part.

Life had celebrated the ultimate triumph over death in the Truly with which it verifies the personally vouchsafed truth imparted to it as its portion in eternal truth. With this Truly, the creature fastens itself to its portion in eternal truth. In this Truly, it is creature. The Truly passes as a mute mystery through the whole chain of beings; it acquires speech in man. And in the Star it flares up into visible, self-illuminating existence. But it remains ever within the boundaries of creatureliness. Truth itself still says Truly when it steps before God. But God himself no longer says Truly. He is beyond all that can be imparted, he is above even the whole, for this too is but a part with him; even about the Whole, he is the One. (pp. 415–17)

Franz Rosenzweig, *The Star of Redemption* (Holt, Rinehart and Winston, 1970).

Rosemary Radford Ruether

After studying at Claremont Graduate School, Rosemary Radford Ruether served as Professor at Garrett Evangelical Theological Seminary. In 'Feminism and Jewish–Christian Dialogue', she argues that women have been prevented from playing a central role in the religious life of the world's faiths.

Feminism is a new challenge to Christian claims of universalism that poses different problems from those of interreligious relationships. Interreligous relationships speak of many different ways in which experience of the Divine has been localized in human experience and the mutual recognition of these historico-cultural configurations by each other. Feminism speaks of new contexts where the Divine needs to be localized. By and large, not only Judaism and Christianity, Islam and Buddhism, but even ancient tribal religions have not allowed the Divine to be experienced in a way defined by women. Feminism looks back at the history of all religions as expressions of male-dominated cultures that have marginalized women to some extent, although women have been more radically and totally marginalized in some religious systems than in others.... .

In Judaism and Christianity this exclusion of women from the shaping of tradition and the handling of sacred objects has been particularly marked. Women, of course, have been worshippers in both religions, but primarily as passive recipients of traditions; they were not allowed to teach or even learn on the scholarly level. Both religions symbolize God as single male being, although both have vestigial remnants of feminine aspects of God as well. But these have been suppressed and denied.

This exclusion of women from shaping and teaching the tradition has meant that Judaism and Christianity have been characterized by a pervasive androcentrism. In Christianity, the understanding not only of God, but of Christ, the created nature of 'man', sin and grace, together with the symbolic and structural definition of the church, has been shaped by a male-centred perspective. Women appear around the edges as sinners, as repentant recipients of grace, or as spiritual auxiliaries; but the centre of the drama has been the male in relation to the male God.

Today for the first time in Christian history, substantial numbers of women are being ordained in various Christian churches, and the number of women in theological schools, training for ministry, has increased rapidly over the last decade. Women are also beginning to become professors in the various disciplines of theological education in seminaries as well. For the first time there are now enough women as ministers, teachers and students of the theological tradition to begin to criticize the androcentrism of the theological tradition itself and to search for alternatives.

This search for alternatives takes several forms. First, there developed a literature that documents the pervasive influence of sexism on theology and religious sciences, and analyses how it produces a biased interpretation of the tradition. Then there is a search within the tradition for alternatives, both for stories of women's actual participation in religious expression as well as for critical perspectives by which to open up more inclusive ways of developing the tradition itself. A substantial body of mature, scholarly literature has developed since the early 1970s and now provides solid resources in feminist critique of biblical studies, church history, theology, ethics and pastoral psychology. (pp. 140–2)

This new feminist *midrash* on patriarchal texts and traditions will not only enter into dialogue and controversy with patriarchal religion. It must also open itself to dialogue with feminist exploration of religion in other traditions. There must certainly be a dialogue between Christian and Jewish feminists, and also with Muslim feminists as well. There must also be dialogue between feminists engaged in the transformation of historical religions and feminists who break with these historical religions and seek to revive, from repressed memories of ancient goddesses and burned witches, visions of new possibilities for women's spirituality today.

This does not mean that such a dialogue between feminists in historical faiths and pagan feminists will be easy. There are many barriers to communication to be cleared away, questions about the historical interpretation of ancient religions and the relationship of female divinity symbols to modern post-Christian patterns of thought. There are also questions about reverse exclusivism and separatism, as well as about exclusivism on the Jewish and Christian side, which is often reinforced today by accusations from male Jewish and Christian theologians who define feminism as 'paganism' in order to frighten Jewish and Christian women away from any feminist analysis of patriarchal religion. It may be that feminism done in the context of historical faiths and feminism done in the context of religions of nature-renewal are working with different paradigms of religious experience, so that each side lacks, fundamentally, certain categories that the other sees as essential. (pp. 147–8)

Rosemary Radford Ruether, 'Feminism and Jewish–Christian Dialogue', in John Hick and Paul Knitter (eds), *The Myth of Christian Uniqueness* (London: SCM Press, 1987).

Robert Runcie

Robert Runcie, former Archbishop of Canterbury, argues in 'Christianity and World Religions' that Christian faith can be transformed by encounter with other religions.

I cannot speak here about the impact of interreligious dialogue on other religions, but must restrict my remarks to reflections made from a Christian perspective. Certainly, given the experience and witness of Christian faith, encounter with other faiths can deepen and enrich us, and make us reflect anew on matters central to our own faith. It should not be forgotten that Christianity itself was formed in dialogue with Judaism. Jesus of Nazareth was himself a Jew, and always remained a Jew, regularly joining in the worship of the synagogue, regardless of how fiercely he may have criticized the establishment figures of Judaism of his time. The Christian church too first gained self-consciousness through wrestling with the pressing issue of its relation to Judaism. (p. 24)

For Christians, the person of Jesus Christ, his life and suffering, his death and resurrection, will always remain the primary source of knowledge and truth about God. The central message of the Christian gospel is the message of love, love poured out in the complete and self-giving of God in his Son for the sake of all life and creation. For the Christian, this is firm and fundamental – it is not negotiable. None the less, Christians recognize that other faiths reveal other aspects of God which may enrich and enlarge our Christian understanding... .

One of the greatest challenges of interfaith dialogue which Christian theology must face is the question of the universality of Christ and his mission: the question as to the meaning and significance of the incarnation within the context of religious pluralism. There exists no easy answer to these questions, and it would take time before Christians can accept that there may be a plurality of answers within Christian theology itself, even before one moves to the wider pluralism of interfaith experience.

What is at stake in our understanding of the finality and significance of Christ's life and work, of, to use F. D. Maurice's term, 'the universalism of the Kingdom of

Christ' at the centre and heart of the Christian faith? For Christians the coming of Christ is the ultimate sign of the fullness of God's grace. But in an age of radical historical consciousness an understanding of the incarnation as the central Christian event must also be linked to an understanding of the historical circumstances in which this belief first took root and developed.

Theological reflection must take account also of contemporary circumstances to which this message must now relate. These are not only questions of theological import but also of pastoral concern. An honest attempt to seek for answers would require an attitude of love and respect towards neighbours of other faiths. It would also open up new possibilities for mutual witness. If we would want to find viable and helpful answers in a situation of great need, we will have to abandon any narrowly conceived Christian apologetic, based on a sense of superiority and an exclusive claim to truth. Instead of triumphalism and rejection, Christians must practise reconciliation. We need to hear afresh the call of our Lord to follow his example of generous self-giving and loving service, his example of compassion and suffering, of help and hope for the poor, of strength for the weak. There is a call to universalism here, to the universal power of love and forgiveness which can transform the world. (pp. 28–9)

I am not advocating a single-minded and synthetic model of world religion.... What I want is for each tradition, and especially my own, 'to break through its own particularity'....

Our world is in desperate need of a new and larger vision of unity which transcends our differences. All people of faith possess potential for seeking greater unity through dialogue, through bonds of fellowship and through shared service of the wider community. Is not the communion experienced in interfaith dialogue ultimately about a new way of life, a new mode of being, where we no longer see each other as competitors but as partners and fellow pilgrims called to bear witness to the same spirit among all peoples? (p. 29)

Robert Runcie, 'Christianity and World Religions', in Dan Cohn-Sherbok (ed.), *Many Mansions* (London: Bellew, 1992).

S

Stanley Samartha

In 'The Cross and the Rainbow', Stanley Samartha, formerly Visiting Professor at the United Theological College, argues that Christian exclusivism must now give way to a pluralistic understanding of the world's religions.

Although most Christians today are unwilling to take a totally negative attitude toward neighbours of other faiths, there seems to be a good deal of hesitation on the part of many to re-examine the basis of their exclusive claims on behalf of Christ. The place of Christ in a multi-religious society becomes, therefore, an important issue in the search for a new theology of religions.... .

Through the incarnation in Jesus Christ, God has relativized God's self in history. Christian theologians should therefore ask themselves whether they are justified in absolutizing in doctrine him whom God has relativized in history. Today's questions regarding the relationship of Jesus Christ to God are very different from those asked in earlier centuries. In many ways, they are new questions that need new solutions. These new solutions, however, must be theologically credible, spiritually satisfying and pastorally helpful.

A process of rejecting exclusive claims and seeking new ways of understanding the relationship of Jesus Christ to humanity is already underway. From what may be described as 'normative exclusivism' Christians are moving toward a position of relational distinctiveness of Christ, relational because Christ does not remain unrelated to neighbours of other faiths, and distinctive because, without recognizing the distinctiveness of the great religious traditions as different responses to the Mystery of God, no mutual enrichment is possible.

Such efforts toward a new Christian theology are taking place in India. Christian theological reflection in India obviously cannot be carried on in isolation and must take into account what is happening in different parts of the world church, but at the same time Indian theologians cannot go on as if, in the long centuries of religious life in India, there had been no theological reflection whatsoever on issues of interreligious relationships. More precisely, the Hindu response to religious pluralism should become a part of Indian Christian theological reflection.... . (pp. 69–70)

Any attempt to formulate such a christology should take into account at least two factors that have emerged out of India's long history of multi-religious life. One is the acceptance of a sense of Mystery and the other the rejection of an exclusive attitude where ultimate matters are concerned. Mystery is not something to be used to fill the gaps in rational knowledge. Mystery provides the ontological basis for tolerance, which would otherwise run the risk of becoming uncritical friendliness. This Mystery, the Truth of the Truth (*Satyasya Satyam*), is the transcendent Centre that remains always beyond and greater than apprehensions of it or even the sum total of those apprehensions. It is beyond cognitive knowledge (*tarka*) but is open to vision (*dristi*) and intuition (*anubhava*). It is near yet far, knowable yet unknowable, intimate yet ultimate and, according to one particular Hindu view, cannot even be described as 'one'. It is 'not-two' (*advaita*), indicating thereby that diversity is within the heart of Being itself and therefore may be intrinsic to human nature as well.

This emphasis on Mystery is not meant as an escape from the need for rational inquiry, but it does insist that the rational is not the only way to do theology; the mystical and the aesthetic also have their necessary contributions to theology. Mystery lies beyond the theistic/nontheistic debate. Mystery is an ontological status to be accepted, not an epistemological problem to be solved. Without a sense of Mystery, *Theos* cannot remain *Theos*, nor *Sat* remain *Sat*, nor can Ultimate Reality remain ultimate.

In religious life, Mystery and meaning are related. Without a disclosure of meaning at particular points in history or in human consciousness, there can be no human response to Mystery. The history of religions shows that these responses are many and are different, sometimes even within a particular religious tradition. Quite often these differences are due to cultural and historical factors. Although each response to Mystery has a normative claim on the followers of that particular tradition, the criteria derived from one response cannot be made the norm to judge the responses of other traditions.... .

No one could have anticipated in advance the presence of God in the life and death of Jesus of Nazareth. There is an incomprehensible dimension to it. That Jesus is the Christ of God is a confession of faith by the Christian community. It does indeed remain normative to Christians everywhere, but to make it 'absolutely singular' and to maintain that the meaning of the Mystery is disclosed only in one particular person at one particular point, and nowhere else, is to ignore one's neighbours of other faiths who have other points of reference. To make exclusive claims for our particular tradition is not the best way to love our neighbours as ourselves. (pp. 75–6).

Stanley Samartha, 'The Cross and the Rainbow', in John Hick and Paul F. Knitter (eds), *The Myth of Christian Uniqueness* (London: SCM Press, 1987).

Dayananda Sarasvati

Born in 1824, Dayananda Sarasvati was the founder of the Arya Samaj in Bombay, an organization devoted to the recovery of Vedic Hinduism, and a polemicist against the British in India. Opposed to idol worship, he criticized various features of Hinduism and was also censorious of various aspects of Christianity. In 'The Light of Truth', he outlines his conception of universal religion.

I believe in a religion based on universal and all-embracing principles which have always been accepted as true by mankind, and will continue to command the allegiance of mankind in ages to come. Hence it is that the religion in question is called the primeval eternal religion, which means that it is above the hostility of all human creeds whatsoever. Whatever is believed in by those who are steeped in ignorance or have been led astray by sectaries is not worthy of being accepted by the wise. That faith alone is really true and worthy of acceptance which is followed by *Aptas*, i.e., those who are true in word, deed and thought, promote public good and are impartial and learned; but all that is discarded by such men must be considered as unworthy of belief and false.

My conception of God and all the other objects in the universe is founded on the teachings of the *Veda* and other true *Shastras*, and is in conformity with the beliefs of all the sages from Brahma down to Jaimini. I offer a statement of these beliefs for the acceptance of all good men. That alone I hold to be acceptable which is worthy of being believed by all men in all ages. I do not entertain the least idea of founding a new religion or sect. My sole aim is to believe in truth and help others to believe in it, to reject falsehood and help others to do the same. Had I been biased, I would have championed any one of the religions prevailing in India. But I have not done so. On the contrary, I do not approve of what is objectionable and false in the institutions of this or any other country, nor do I reject what is good and in harmony with the dictates of true religion, nor have I any desire to do so since a contrary conduct is wholly unworthy of man. He alone is entitled to be called a man who possesses a thoughtful nature and feels for others in the same way as he does for his own self, does not fear the unjust, however powerful, but fears the truly virtuous, however weak. Moreover, he should always exert himself to his utmost to protect the righteous and advance their good, and conduct himself worthily towards them even though they be extremely poor and weak and destitute of material resources. On the other hand, he should constantly strive to destroy, humble, and oppose the wicked, sovereign rulers of the whole earth and men of great influence and power though they be. In other words, a man should, as far as it lies in his power, constantly endeavour to undermine the power of the unjust and to strengthen that of the just, he may have to bear any amount of terrible suffering, he may even have to quaff the bitter cup of death in the performance of this duty, which devolves on him on account of being a man, but he should not shirk it.

Now I give below a brief summary of my beliefs... .

1. He who is called Brahma or the Most High, who is Paramatma or the Supreme Spirit who permeates the whole universe; who is a true personification of Existence, Consciousness, and Bliss; Whose nature, attributes, and characteristics are Holy; who is Omniscient, Formless, All-pervading, Unborn, Infinite, Almighty, Just and Merciful; who is the author of the universe, sustains and dissolves it; who awards all souls the fruits of their deeds in strict accordance with the requirements of absolute justice and is possessed of the like attributes – even him I believe to be the great God.

2. I hold that the four *Vedas* – the repository of Knowledge and Religious Truths – are the Word of God. They comprise what is known as the *Sanhita-Mantra* portion only. They are absolutely free from error and are an authority unto themselves. In other words, they do not stand in need of any other book to uphold their authority. Just as the sun (or a lamp) by his light, reveals his own nature as well as that of other objects of the universe, such as the earth – even so are the *Vedas*. (pp. 202–3)

Dayananda Sarasvati, 'The Light of Truth', in Paul J. Griffiths (ed.), *Christianity Through Non-Christian Eyes* (Maryknoll, NY: Orbis, 1990).

Henri le Saux

Born in Brittany in 1910, Henri le Saux studied at a local seminary and later at a major seminary at Rennes. He later settled in India where he founded the ashram of Shantivanam in South India, and later constructed a hermitage at Uttarkashi. In Saccidananda *he attempted to provide a synthesis of Christian and Hindu thought.*

If the Christian experience of the Trinity opens up to man new vistas of meaning in the intuition of *Saccidananda*, it is equally true that the terms *sat, cit* and *ananda*, in their turn, greatly assist the Christian in his own meditation on that central mystery of his faith. No single theological language will ever be able to express all that the gospel has revealed to us concerning God who is Father, Son and Holy Spirit. It is therefore to be expected that just as Judaism and Hellenism have made their contributions, so the divine preparation of India in its turn will serve to lead believers to contemplate the mystery in a new depth. In particular, the intuition of *Saccidananda* will be an aid in penetrating the mystery of the Spirit, which, according to St John's Gospel, relates chiefly to God's presence to men in their hearts. And if anyone comes to the Gospel with personal experience of *Vedanta*, it can be said with assurance that the Gospel words will elicit profound echoes from the intuition which he already had of *Saccidananda*; and that in turn this previous experience will cause marvellous harmonics to sound in his present faith in the Holy Trinity. This is because all things are the work of the one Spirit, who has been preparing for this man's awakening and resurrection ever since long ago he first revealed himself to the heart of the *rishis* (seers) as the infinite presence.

Here there is no question of theological theorizing or of academic comparison between the terms of the Christian revelation and those in which India has expressed its own unique mystical experience. It is rather a matter of an awakening, an awareness far beyond the reach of the intellect, an experience which springs up and erupts in the deepest recesses of the soul.

The experience of *Saccidananda* carries the soul beyond all merely intellectual knowledge to her very centre, to the source of her being. Only there is she able to hear the Word which reveals within the undivided unity and *advaita* of *Saccidananda* the mystery of the Three divine Persons; in *sat*, the Father, the absolute Beginning and Source of being; in *cit*, the Son, the divine Word, the Father's Self-knowledge; in *ananda*, the Spirit of love, Fullness and Bliss without end.

In *sat*, then, the Christian will adore especially the mystery of the First Person, the Father. The Father indeed is in himself unoriginated Being, the unmanifested Source from which his self manifestation proceeds. But if the Father alone is contemplated, then adoration must remain forever silent. For in himself, the Father is the One who has not yet spoken, who is essentially unmanifest, unknown. He is the Abyss of Silence. The Word alone makes him known, and it is only in his Word, his Son, that he is present to himself.

It is from the *sat*, the Simply Being, *san-matra* in Vedantic terms, that *cit* comes. *Cit* is the presence to itself, the consciousness of itself, the opening to itself, of *sat*. St John says of the Word that he was 'in the beginning'. Of *sat*, the Father, nothing can conceivably be said to place him anywhere at all, whether in time or in eternity. The Father is origin, source, absolutely. The spring is not the stream of water that flows from it, and yet the spring is only known by this flowing stream. So what is the spring itself, the pure source? What is Being, *sat*, in itself? What is the Father?

Cit is the self-awakening of Being, its coming to manifestation within itself. It is not merely an aspect or mode of Brahman, the Absolute. In Christian terms, it is a real procession, a real birth, first in eternity and subsequently in time. The Son is the consubstantial Word through whom the Father expresses himself within himself. And in that Word whereby the Father expresses himself, in his own self-awareness and presence to himself in the Son, everything that is has come to be. (pp. 594–5)

Henri le Saux, '*Saccidananda*' in Harvey Egan (ed.), *An Anthology of Christian Mysticism* (Collegeville, MN: The Liturgical Press, 1991).

Zalman Schachter

Zalman Schachter, of Polish origin, was ordained by the Lubavitch Hasidic Yeshivah in Brooklyn, gained a DHL from the Hebrew Union College, and has been a Professor of Judaica and Psychology of Religion at Temple University. In 'The Interior Path', he emphasizes the role of mysticism in the encounter between faiths.

In the space in which I represent the Jewish *magisterium* to my fellow believers, we are Torahcentric; without the Torah there is no place for us. It is exactly this function of *Memra*, the word, the Logos, *Sophia*, *Hokhma* that centres the process that is the basis of all our striving. Or, maybe even better put: it is the tropism in our souls that draws us closer to God, and *Hokhma* is this tropism. So if we were not to have that tropism to take us closer to God, then we would not have any ground left... .

Deep down I am convinced that there is such a thing as generic religion, no-frills religion, which comes in a plain brown wrapper. And we also have brand names: Judaism, Christianity, and the like. And all of us would not have gotten to where we are had not the brand name religions and their dogmas taken us there. But somehow there is something to generic religion. And this is perhaps where that universal theology is. There is *Sophia* drawing us to that also. It is the 'also' that I want to talk about.

Kabbalah and its hermeneutic help me a lot. My suggestion is that the mysticisms of all religions have given us languages and have technologies for thinking about different levels of experience dealing with different levels of alternate realities. If we are looking for an ultimate one, we need the language and experience of mystics. We need to find out what that transformative thing is for us in an experience like Meister Eckart's 'The eye with which I see God is the eye with which God sees me.' For the ultimate we want the term Godhead rather than God. Such language creates ways in which we can talk and think about that ultimate reality. It is not a reality that we can look at as an object out there. It is not even in here; it transcends both. It is the nominative case of I AM THAT I AM or – as we would say in *Kabbalah* and *Hasidism* – a way that looks at the universe from God's perspective. So, too, do I look at the function of the *Soter* (Saviour). The rationalists among us Jews have often wished to deny the *Soter* function of the *Zaddik* ('righteous one'), and Sunni Muslims do not like to deal with it, and yet Sufis talk about *Fana fi rasul*, the way to *Fana' fi'llahi* – self-effacement to the messenger as the way to self-effacement to God: that one becomes a window for the other. Hasidim talk about the *Shorest han 'shamah*, that the root of one's soul is with the *rebbe*. Often, in dialogue with Christians, I find that we share best when I sense that Christians are Nazarene Hasidim and that in Jesus they have a *rebbe*, a *Soter*... .

I find also a Trinity of three persons in one God easier to handle when I go with the Christian Kabbalist Joachim de Fiore. He says that there is an apprehension of reality which we meet in God the Father. The first two thousand years of world history (within the biblical time track) refers to that. And then comes an apprehension of reality that we meet in God as the Son, a period changing from the new era to the present. And there still is the next one to come, that of the Holy Spirit. My sense is that this is the element of *Ruah Haqodesh*, that feminine hypostasis of God, that element in which Pallas Athena is seen as springing out of the head of Zeus, or as is said, *Hokhma* comes out from the Great Nothing; no thing (*Hahokhma m'ayin timmatze*). Here perhaps *sunyata* – the Buddhist void – and *Hokhma* do have an interface and a dynamism between themselves. (pp. 101–2)

Now I want to ask myself what is the good of talking about the position of universal religion. It is the coming one knocking at our door. We throw it out the door, and it comes in through the window; it keeps on saying: 'Do something about how you talk together.' We face the issue of the paradigm shift. Every map of reality we have had up to now seems less firm. If we have to share the road together so that we can walk on the way, a good map would be helpful. The old maps have been shaken by every discipline outside the discipline of religion. We are grasping so hard to keep the old maps, the ones we are used to, playing our dialogue games, and it turns out that the maps are all rotting under our feet. There is not much left of that old reality map anymore. There are no substances and no particles and no waves, and there is so much emptiness. There is something about *sunyata* and the void and the godhead and St John of the Cross's dark night that helps us get to the unified state. This development brings us to the ultimate in religion. (pp. 102–3)

Zalman Schachter, 'The Interior Path', in Leonard Swidler (ed.), *Toward a Universal Theology of Religion* (Maryknoll, NY: Orbis, 1987).

Robert P. Scharlemann

Robert P. Scharlemann, Professor at the University of Virginia, states in 'Why Christianity Needs Other Religions' that even when Jesus is understood as the revelation of God, the non-Christian is as much a part of this revelation as is the Christian.

Even when Jesus is understood exclusively as the revelation of God (that is, as the one and only human being who is existent deity), the non-Christian is as much a part of this revelation as is the Christian, not as the reprobate or rejected one but as an equal participant in the salvation connected by Christians with the name of Jesus. The basis for this thesis is that the actuality of Jesus as the Christ involves a triadic structure constituted by the relations of Peter and Judas to each other and to Jesus. We need to forestall a possible misunderstanding by noting at the outset that the figure of Judas does not represent the reprobate, the one to be excoriated, but something else which I hope to make clear in the course of developing the proposed line of thought. From the thesis, it seems to me to follow that Christianity, even at its most exclusive, requires that there be others, not Christians, just as Jesus' living reality required that there be two, equally true responses to his appearance, those of Peter and of Judas. Understanding the Christian meaning of Jesus in this way is somewhat different not only from Troeltsch's or Schleiermacher's but also from the dialectical understanding found in the early Barth. Closer to this understanding is the one that appears in Barth of the *Church Dogmatics* where he treats of Judas, whom he distinguishes from Paul and the other apostles by saying that in Judas the 'No' to Jesus is the 'Yes', whereas in the other disciples the 'Yes' followed the 'No'.

The intention here is to indicate that, even for an exclusively understood Christianity, the plurality of religions is not a deficiency, not something which one seeks to overcome, but a fulfilment of the meaning of Jesus' being the Christ. There are some indications in the New Testament itself of the fact that the followers of Jesus should not hope for a state of affairs in which everyone would be a follower. Such an indication is contained, for example, in the image of the followers of Jesus as the salt of the earth. Salt is the seasoning that gives flavour to the food that we eat. But no one would wish to have only salt to eat. Jesus' followers may, similarly, be the salt of the earth; but no one would want to have the salt without the food seasoned by it. Christian existence comes into its own only by its relation to worldly existence. Other indications found in the sayings ascribed to Jesus in the New Testament might include Jesus' reference to there being other folds with other sheep and the parable of the last judgement, according to which every encounter with a person in need (in person, hungry, naked) is an encounter with Jesus.

But these indications in the New Testament are not clearly or explicitly concerned with the question that is posed for us today about the relation between Christianity and the other religions. (The same would be true, of course, of the passage classically used to support the claim of Jesus' exclusiveness, Acts 4:12: 'There is salvation in no one else, for there is no other name under heaven given among men by which we must be saved.') So the question must be posed carefully. It is the question whether the very structure of the affirmation of Jesus as Christ, when understood exclusivistically, does not involve the existence of at least one person who always denies what the Christian affirms. This is not to contend that the affirmation must be so understood even within the Christian community. It is, rather, to follow the methodological counsel that, in thinking through a theological matter, one takes not the easiest but the most difficult possibility. In this case the most difficult possibility is to understand how an exclusively understood Christianity can require the acknowledgement of other religions as equally participants in truth and salvation. (pp. 37–8)

Robert P. Scharlemann, 'Why Christianity Needs Other Religions' in Peter Phan (ed.), *Christianity and the Wider Ecumenism* (New York: Paragon, 1990).

Christoph Schwobel

The Christian theologian Christoph Schwobel served as a Lecturer in Theology at King's College, University of London. In 'Particularity, Universality and the Religions', he criticizes the exclusivist and pluralist stance and advances a Christian basis for interfaith dialogue based on an acknowledgement of both universality and particularity.

The conservative exclusivist and the pluralist in its different versions seem to have difficulties in providing an adequate basis for interreligious dialogue. For the exclusivist approach to dialogue is, if not expressly rejected, a means for proselytizing. The pluralist approach that associates itself programmatically with interreligious dialogue seems to see the possibility of such a dialogue only by bracketing, reinterpreting, or relativizing the particular truth claims of particular religious traditions. This immediately provokes the danger that a dialogue which suspends religious truth claims cannot even develop into a dialogue of religions, but turns into a dialogue of cultural traditions based on principles such as universal tolerance and respect, whose foundation is very often not to be seen in the religions themselves but in a humanist critique of all religions. A dialogue which is perceived along these lines can all too easily turn into a new guise of Western imperialism where subscribing to the principles of the Enlightenment becomes a precondition for participation in dialogue.

A similar difficulty occurs when one considers what both approaches could contribute to the fight for justice and peace as the common goal for humankind. The exclusivist approach tends to interpret justice and peace from an exclusivist theological perspective which excludes the non-Christian religions as long as they remain just that. The pluralist approach is in danger of eschewing any particular religious or theological justification for the common endeavour to work for justice and peace and tends to replace the missing foundation with a commitment to the secular values of an autonomous ethic, which, apart from its intrinsic difficulties, has significantly failed to gain acceptance in many of the world's major religious traditions.

These difficulties can be traced to a common problem that both approaches share: the failure to come to terms with the complex relationship of particularity and universality in the religions, and especially in Christianity. The exclusivist view can give strong expression to the particularity and distinctiveness of Christian faith while calling the universality of the activity of God it proclaims into question. The pluralist approach, contrary to its avowed intentions, seems to tend to develop a picture of the universal and ultimate noumenal focus of all religions transcending the particular concrete religions or of a common anthropological constant underlying all particular religious expressions, which allows their distinctive particularity only a penultimate and preliminary status. (p. 33)

The offensive universality of the truth claims of Christian faith is grounded in the particular self-disclosure of this particular God, Father, Son and Spirit in the spatio-temporal particularity of the Christ event in which God is disclosed as the universal source of creation, reconciliation and fulfilment for creation. This gives the understanding of the universality of God a particular content. Christian theology has expressed this particular understanding of the universality of God by interpreting love as the complete summary of the Christian understanding of God, which expresses the unity of God's will, action and being. The attributes in which the universality of God is expressed in Christian theology are therefore to be interpreted from the perspective of this understanding of God as creative, reconciling and saving love.

This understanding of the universality of God, which is grounded in the particularity of God's self-disclosure in Christ through the Spirit and which is the ultimate foundation for the universality of the truth claims of Christian faith, can neither be restricted to particular aspects of reality nor can it be reduced to an imaginative construction of 'reality'. The specific characteristic of Christian faith is that it combines the disconcerting particularity of the perspective of faith with universal truth claims about the universality of God. This implies that the whole of reality is seen as determined by God's creative, reconciling and saving agency in such a way that God's action is the condition for the possibility of all natural processes and all human activity.... .

The universality of God's agency and presence has to be taken as the theological basis for an adequate Christian understanding of the religions. On this presupposition no theological understanding of the religions can be adequate which implicitly or expressly denies the all-encompassing presence of God for his creation and which calls the universality of God's will of love for his creation into question. Moreover, on this view every theological conception of understanding the religions must be deemed insufficient which restricts the power of God to overcome the alienation of humanity from its divine ground of being and meaning to one particular sphere of reality. The basis for a theological understanding of the religions is therefore the universality of God's action and presence in the world. The religions therefore have to be seen as human responses to God's all-encompassing presence and activity in which God is active as in all forms of created being as the ground of being and meaning and as the source and end of its fulfilment... .

It must, however, be emphasized that this understanding of the universality of God's presence to his creation and of the universality of God's reconciling and saving love for his creation is for Christian theology never independent of God's self-disclosure in the particularity of the Christ event as the particular trinitarian God – Father, Son and Spirit. (pp. 38–9)

Christoph Schwobel, 'Particularity, Universality, and the Religions', in Gavin D'Costa (ed.), *Christian Uniqueness Reconsidered* (Maryknoll, NY: Orbis, 1990)

Waldron Scott

Waldron Scott served as General Secretary of the World Evangelical Fellowship. In '"No Other Name" – An Evangelical Conviction', he argues that evangelicals have an important role to play in interreligious dialogue.

I wonder if evangelicals do not have some positive contributions to make to others engaged in interreligious dialogue, even though the 'traditional' evangelical approach carries the onus of familiarity? After all, evangelicals make up the greater part of the Protestant missionary force in our time. This being so, it would seem to be advantageous for ecumenically oriented leaders to interact with evangelicals. Yet such interaction can hardly be expected if there is not a mutual readiness to listen and learn.

It is not at all uncommon to hear evangelicals express the wish that ecumenists would exhibit the same irenic spirit toward evangelicals that they do toward non-Christians... . The specific contribution evangelicals might make to the large enterprise will be evaluated ultimately by the actual participants. But if I were to suggest possible contributions, they would include our concern for faithfulness to what the Bible positively teaches on relevant subjects (e.g. dialogue), insights on the phenomenon of 'conversion' with which we have extensive experience and which should throw light both on the gospel and on other religions, and the corrective influence brought to bear by our insistence that all religious systems, including our own, carry demonic elements and therefore stand under God's judgement.

First, the positive biblical witness in relation to dialogue. It is well known that Luke, for example, frequently employs the verb *dialegomai* to describe Paul's approach to people of other faiths. Yet this is dialogue of a particular kind, significantly different from that advocated today. It is dialogue subordinate to proclamation. This shows up clearly in Paul's ministry at Thessalonica (Acts 17:1–4). Here five verbal forms are brought together: proclaim, explaining, argued (*dielexato*), proving and persuaded... .

I cite this example not to suggest that contemporary concepts of dialogue are altogether wrong, but that they do not do justice to the full biblical record and therefore are inadequate. Even if they should prove to be very useful at a certain stage of relationships between people of different faiths, it would be a pity if other biblical dimensions of dialogue were lost sight of. True dialogue inevitably leads to encounter, which may engender confrontation as well as harmony and understanding.

Second, the possibility of losing sight of the very real phenomenon of conversion... . In my own ministry as General Secretary of the World Evangelical Fellowship, I continually meet women and men of Muslim, Hindu, Buddhist and other religious backgrounds who have been converted to Jesus as Lord precisely as that has been traditionally understood by Christians for centuries and is still understood by evangelicals today. At the human level I have even been the instrument of a number of such conversions. This is a phenomenon that our contemporary generation should investigate in depth for insights that would surely emerge, and the findings applied seriously to interreligious dialogue. Are all these conversions to be regarded as blunders? Is God to be faulted for overtaking the impeccable and zealous Pharisee, Saul, and bringing him to acknowledge Jesus Christ as Lord? I do not see evidence of this kind of serious investigation in ecumenical discussion.

Third, the necessity of keeping alert to the demonic in religion. It seems to evangelicals that contemporary dialogical theology underestimates the reality of the demonic dimension. 'Even Satan disguises himself as an angel of light' (2 Cor. 11:14). Consequently God sends his messengers 'to open their eyes, that they may turn from darkness to light and from the power of Satan to God, that they may receive forgiveness of sins and a place among those who are sanctified in me' (Acts 26:17–18). Thus the evangelical emphasis on proclamation (admittedly often to the neglect of legitimate dialogue, Christian presence and social action) is nevertheless a prophetic ministry that is fully warranted, even necessitated by the biblical perspective. (pp. 70–3)

Waldron Scott, '"No Other Name" – An Evangelical Conviction', in Gerald H. Anderson and Thomas F. Stransky (eds), *Christ's Lordship and Religious Pluralism* (Maryknoll, NY: Orbis, 1981).

Ahmed Shafaat

The Muslim scholar Ahmed Shafaat argues in 'The Abrahamic Ummah' that Muhammad's goal was to draw Muslims, Christians and Jews together into one ummah, united in the worship of the true God.

Recognizing this very significant common concern on the part of the Jews, Christians and Muslims, the Prophet Muhammad actually described the community consisting of these three religious groups as an *ummah* when in Medina he attempted to create a multi-religious society. But it is not simply their concern for monotheism that can bind the three religious groups into a single *ummah*; it is also the close historical links between them – the origin of their religions from more or less the same geographical area and from culturally and ethnically related peoples and their constant involvement with each other throughout the centuries – that enables us to speak of them as a single *ummah*. We shall call this *ummah* the Abrahamic *ummah* because Abraham is the most widely recognized symbol of the close historical relationship between the three groups of which it is constituted.

In the light of the Qur'an and Bible we can go further and see a religious significance in the historical links between the three groups. We can see their religions as part of the same history of revelation and we can see their histories as linked by a divine purpose... .

We begin by describing the general way in which the whole history of revelation is linked together by the Qur'an. In Qur'an 3.81 we read:

> Behold! God took the covenant of the prophets (saying) I have given you revelation (*kitab*) and wisdom but when comes to you another apostle who will confirm what is with you (of the true religion), do believe in him and help him. God said, Do you agree and take this covenant binding on you? They said, We agree. He said, Then bear witness, and I also am a witness along with you.

Here the whole history of revelation is seen at a glance and links within it are brought out in terms of a covenant taken from the prophets before the dawn of history. This covenant binds the prophets to support those among them who preceded them in time by confirming their truth and helping those who may come after them by preparing in some fashion the way for them.

The link with the past is established by confirmation and the link with the future by preparation. This linking may be achieved either explicitly by a reference to past prophets or revelations and by predictions about the future ones or it may be achieved implicitly by the nature of the contribution made to the realization of the divine purpose in the on-going history of revelation.

Confirmation does not mean affirming continued relevance or perfection of all the other prophets' teachings: for the Qur'an makes it clear that parts of earlier revelations can cease to be relevant, get corrupted, or may be improved. Confirmation rather amounts to saying that in his own age every true prophet provided to the people to whom he was sent necessary and effective means for attaining the condition of faith, spiritual health and salvation. (pp. 188–9)

The prophet's attempt to bring together the three groups into a single *ummah* – united in faith in the one true transcendent God but following their diverse ways in worship and in running their internal affairs – was unsuccessful, it seems, because of the strong tendency in those days on the part of the Jews and Christians to consider salvation and knowledge of the true God as exclusive to themselves, and an equally strong tendency on the part of Christians to identify the one true God with Jesus Christ in more than a symbolic sense. Now that there is some questioning and even rejection of these tendencies in much Jewish and Christian thought there is hope that the Prophet's vision may be realized. However, a hurdle on the Muslim side has also to be overcome, and that is the prevalent tendency among recent generations of Muslims to identify the Prophet's mission entirely with the bringing of a mode of worship and a system of running the affairs of society, in other words, to identify the Islamic revelation with system of *Shari'a* – a tendency which often leads them to deny that salvation and authentic relationship with God is possible in other systems of *Shari'a*. (p. 200)

Ahmed Shafaat, 'The Abrahamic *Ummah*', in Dan Cohn-Sherbok (ed.), *Islam in a World of Diverse Faiths* (London: Macmillan, 1991).

Ingrid Shafer

Ingrid Shafer, born in Austria, obtained a Ph.D. from the University of Oklahoma and has served as Professor of Interdisciplinary Studies at the University of Science and Arts of Oklahoma. In 'The Incarnation as Koan or The Unique Universal Ultimate', she argues that all religious absolutes can be embraced by Christ as the Universal Ultimate.

If we go beyond the original understanding of Yeshua as teacher and prophet (reflected in the synoptic gospels) and call Jesus the Word become Flesh, the Light of the World, God Incarnate, Son of God and Son of Man, the Infinite Finite, or the Ultimate Paradox, then we already possess the key that will allow us to view him both as unique and as potentially one among other bearers of God's saving grace in history. In fact, the very uniqueness of Jesus as the Christ can be seen to flow out of and terminate in simultaneous cancellation and preservation ... of 'either-or dualism' into qualified 'both-and non-dualism'.

These opposite, dissolving and fusing 'names' given to Jesus by disciples and theologians from Paul and the editor of John's Gospel to Kierkegaard point toward Mystery: the ineffable and radically enigmatic at the heart of the incarnation. They creatively and imaginatively juxtapose, join and overcome opposites and transcend (not contradict) common sense logic. Like Zen *koans*, they hint at the elusive, always just beyond the horizon of Truth by breaking through the opaqueness of ordinary categories of reason, and rendering them translucent to the emergent meaning that illuminates its own genesis.

Jesus can best be 'grasped' with analogical language. For us he reveals both the Ground of Being beyond time and space and the screaming, nursing, gurgling, peeing, sleeping baby boy born to the young Jewish woman Mary in the reign of Caesar Augustus; he manifests at once the Absolutely Other and the utterly us. He is the dynamic flow at the still centre beyond either-or opposition. Like light, he is simultaneously quantum and wave, discrete packets and continuous flow, absence and presence, the Perfect Hologram – neither localized nor extended through space and yet both localized and extended through space. (pp. 127–8)

For us Christians, Yeshua is the one whom we must follow in order to keep from being restricted by self-centredness (not to be confused with self-acceptance, which is essential for loving others) in the sense of being deaf to the call to be open to all other beings, to be living, germinating seeds that break through the shell that separates us from others. In Yeshua the Christ, God calls us to embrace and co-create the unfolding cosmos from family to friends to strangers to the natural world and ultimately the Source of All: Love, passionate, cosmic, absolute Love, which according to Dante 'moves the sun in heaven and all the stars'. As Christians, it is by following Yeshua the Lover, who 'walked his talk', that we can become ever clearer lenses to gather and transmit God's transforming light and in the process expand ourselves to become most fully ourselves. Ultimately, humanization and divinization are the same relational process viewed from the transcendent and immanent poles. We allow ourselves to be most fully transformed into those lenses and in a sense achieve ourselves as ongoing process by returning Yeshua's love with the kind of focused passion for which the beloved is absolutely unique. This is analogous to the way humans fall in love and have eyes only for each other and want to fulfil each other's every wish. They consider their lover absolutely unique even though they rationally know that under different circumstances someone else might have taken the lover's privileged place. For Christians, Jesus is as unique a way as the Buddha is for Buddhists or Krishna for Hindus or the Tao for Taoists. (pp. 134–5)

If we can also learn to include nonhuman nature in the loving embrace of the incarnation, then, I believe, we will reach an even deeper current of the universal law of love, one that allows a confluence of the religious stream of Abraham with the rivers of India and China as we share our stories of faith.... . Then Yeshua the man who was born in the reign of Caesar Augustus and lived and was executed and became the New and Timeless Ruler by whose appearance the calendar of

Christendom would be synchronized, can indeed emerge as the standard of the Common Era as Yeshua gradually comes to unfold the *eschaton* in what Christians call Christself and symbolize the Cosmic Change Agent in ways that include, among countless others, the Christian *logos/hokmah*, the Taoist *yin/yang*, the Hindu *Atman/Brahman-Ishvara/Shakti*, and the Buddhist *Kuan-Yin* as the uniqe universal Ultimate. (p. 136)

Ingrid Shafer, 'The Incarnation as *Koan* or The Unique Univeral Ultimate', in Leonard Swidler and Paul Mojzes (eds), *The Uniqueness of Jesus: A Dialogue with Paul F. Knitter* (Maryknoll, NY: Orbis, 1997).

Ninian Smart

Ninian Smart, born in 1926, studied at Oxford and became Professor at the Universities of Birmingham, Lancaster and Santa Barbara. In Dimensions of the Sacred *he outlines the central dimensions of the world's religions.*

To return to the dimensions: in each case I give them a double name, which helps to elucidate them and sometimes to widen them.... .

1. The ritual or practical dimension. This is the aspect of religion which involves such activities as worship, meditation, pilgrimage, sacrifice, sacramental rites and healing activities. We may note that meditation is often not regarded as a ritual, though it is often strictly patterned. This is partly why I also call this dimension the practical.... .
2. The doctrinal or philosophical dimension. For different reasons religions evolve doctrines and philosophies. Thus the doctrine of impermanence is central to Buddhism. It also interacts dialectically with the ritual or practical dimension, since philosophical reflection of a certain kind aids meditation, and meditation in turn helps the individual to see existentially the force of the doctrine. Some traditions are keener on doctrinal rectitude than others: Catholicism more than Quakerism, Buddhism more than traditional African religions, Theravada more than Zen. We may note that diverse traditions put differing weights on the differing dimensions. Religions are by no means equidimensional.
3. The mythic or narrative dimension. Every religion has its stories. The story of Christ's life, death and resurrection is clearly central to the Christian faith. The story of the Buddha's life, though somewhat less central to Buddhism, is still vital to Buddhist piety. In the case of secular worldviews and to an important

degree in modernizing traditions, history is the narrative which takes the place of myth elsewhere. So the version of history taught in a nation's schools is not only a major ingredient in the national sense of identity, but enhances pride in 'our' ancestors, 'our' national heroes and heroines.

4. The experiential or emotional dimension. It is obvious that certain experiences can be important in religious history – the enlightenment of the Buddha, the prophetic visions of Muhammad, the conversion of Paul and so on. Again there are variations in the importance attached to visionary and meditative experiences: they are obviously vital to Zen and Native American classical religion (the vision quest); they are less important in Scottish Calvinism. But they or associated emotional reactions to the world and to ritual are everywhere more or less dynamic, and have been studied extensively... .

5. The ethical or legal dimensions. A religious tradition or sub-tradition affirms not only a number of doctrines and myths but some ethical and often legal imperatives. The Torah as a set of injunctions is central to orthodox Judaism; the Shari'a is integral to Islam; Buddhism affirms the four great virtues (*brahmaviharas*); Confucianism lays down the desired attitudes of the gentleman; and so on. Again, the degree of investment in ideal human behaviour varies: it is central to Quakerism, less important in the Shinto tradition (though Shinto ritual was tied to the notion of the *kokutai* or national essence during the Meiji era and into the between-wars period). In modern national states certain norms of civil behaviour tend to be prescribed in schools.

6. The organizational or social component. Any tradition will manifest itself in society, either as a separate organization with priests or other religious specialists (gurus, lawyers, pastors, rabbis, *imams*, shamans and so on), or as coterminous with society. Embedded in a social context, a tradition will take on aspects of that context (thus the Church of England cleric begins to play a part in the English class system).

7. The material or artistic dimension. A religion or worldview will express itself typically in material creations, from chapels to cathedrals to temples to mosques, from icons and divine statuary to books and pulpits. Such concrete expressions are important in varying ways. If you only have to carry around a book (like an evangelical preacher in Communist Eastern Europe) you are freer than if you have a great monastery or convent to occupy. (pp. 10–11)

The phenomenology of religion seeks to draw out varying patterns, and these are important. What I have tried to do in this volume is to use a dimensional shape to exhibit these patterns, but I recognize that there are other ways of going about the task. Moreover, I have not always been as detailed in dealing with all the dimensions. But I hope that, if others feel the need for a different approach, they will not be hesitant in trying it out... . I consider that the task of understanding patterns in religion is not at all an easy one. But we can all benefit from grasping some of the major themes in what has, after all, been a pervasive feature of human history and life. By reflecting on the past of the human race we may gain better insight into our present and future. We may also, in having a clearer picture of human patterns of symbols and of the taxonomy of the sacred, clarify what the major concerns are in the differing cultures of the human race. (p. 298)

Ninian Smart, *Dimensions of the Sacred* (London: Harper Collins, 1996).

Huston Smith

Huston Smith, a leading figure in the history of religions, served as a professor at the University of California, Berkeley. In The Illustrated World's Religions, *he argues that the wisdom traditions of the world's faiths provide a framework for under- standing the unity of all things and their estimable worth as well as the mystery of the world.*

Looking back on the road we have travelled, three questions suggest themselves. We have met the world's religions individually; how should we configure them – see them as related to one another? Second, have they anything to say to the world collectively, in concert? And third, how should we comport ourselves in the world they make pluralistic?

To the question of configuration, three answers come to mind.

The first holds that one religion is superior to the others. There is nothing in this book to suggest that this is the case; but equally, nothing that argues against it, for comparisons have not been its province.

A second and opposite position holds that religions are basically alike. Their differences are incidental compared with the towering truths on which they unite. This appeals to our yen for togetherness, but on inspection it proves to be the trickiest position of the three. For as soon as it moves beyond vague generalities – 'every religion has some version of the Golden Rule' – it founders on the fact that the religions differ in what they consider essential and nonnegotiable.

A third conception likens religions to stained glass windows that refract sunlight in different shapes and colours. This analogy allows for significant differ- ences between the religions without pronouncing on their relative worth. If peoples of different cultures have different temperaments, God may have taken those into account in addressing them.

Leaving to the reader to configure the religions as seems appropriate, we proceed to the second question. Have they anything to say to the world concert- edly – in a single voice? (p. 245)

Mortal life gives no view of the whole; we see things in dribs and drabs, and self-interest skews perspective grotesquely. It is as if life were a great tapestry which we face from its wrong side. This gives it the appearance of a maze of knots and threads that look chaotic. From a purely human standpoint, the wisdom traditions are the species' most prolonged and serious attempts to infer from the hind side of life's tapestry its frontal design. As the beauty and harmony of the design derives from the way its parts interweave, the design confers on those parts a significance they are denied in isolation. We could almost say that seeing ourselves as belonging to the whole is what religion – *religio*, rebinding – is. It is mankind's fundamental thrust at unification.

The first motif – unity – leads to a second. If things are more integrated than they seem, they are also better than they seem. Paralleling the astrophysicists' report that the world is bigger than it looks to our unaided eyes, the wisdom traditions report that it is better than it feels to our unregenerated hearts. And in comparable degree we should add, which means that we are talking about light years. Yahweh, God and Allah; T'ien and the Tao; Brahman and Nirvana, carry the signature of the *ens perfectissium* – perfect being. This perfection floods the wisdom traditions with an exuberance nowhere else to be found... .

To the unity of things and their inestimable worth, the wisdom traditions add (as their third surmise) mystery. Murder mysteries have debased that word, for detective mysteries are not mysteries at all for having solutions. A mystery is that special kind of problem which has no solutions because the more we understand it, the more we see that we don't understand. In mysteries, knowledge and ignorance advance lockstep. As known unknowns become known, unknown unknowns proliferate; the larger the island of knowledge, the longer the shoreline of wonder... .

Things are more integrated than they seem, they are better than they seem, and they are more mysterious than they seem; this is the vision that the wisdom traditions bequeath us. When we add to this the baseline they establish for ethical conduct and their account of the human virtues, one wonders if a wiser platform for human life has been envisioned. At the centre of the religious life is a particular kind of joy, the prospect of a happy ending that blossoms from necessarily painful beginning, the promise of human difficulties embraced and overcome. In daily life we have only hints of this joy. When they arrive, we do not know whether our happiness is the rarest or the commonest thing on earth, for in all earthly things we find it, give it, and receive it, but cannot hold onto it. When we possess those intimations, it seems in no way strange to be happy, but in retrospect we wonder how such gold of Eden could have been ours. Religiously conceived, the human opportunity is to transform epiphanies into abiding light. (p. 248)

If one of the wisdom traditions claims us, we begin by listening to it. Not uncritically, for new occasions teach new duties; but nevertheless expectantly, realizing that it houses more truth than a single lifetime could fathom, let alone enact.

But in addition to our own traditions, we listen to the faith of others, including the secularists. We listen first because our times require it. Daily the world grows smaller, leaving understanding the only place where peace can find a home. Those who listen work for peace, a peace built not on religious or political hegemonies, but on mutual awareness and concern. For understanding brings respect, and respect prepares the way for a higher capacity, which is love. (p. 249)

Huston Smith, *The Illustrated World's Religions* (San Francisco: Harper Collins, 1994).

Wilfred Cantwell Smith

Wilfred Cantwell Smith, born in 1916, was Professor of the Comparative History of Religion at Harvard University. In 'The Christian in a Religiously Plural World' he argues that modern Christian theologians must have an awareness of the world's religions, and that religious harmony is central to world peace.

I suggest that we are about to enter a comparable situation with regard to the other religious traditions of mankind. The time will soon be with us when a theologian who attempts to work out his position unaware that he does so as a member of a world society in which other theologians equally intelligent, equally devout, equally moral, are Hindus, Buddhists, Muslims, and unaware that his readers are likely perhaps to be Buddhists or to have Muslim husbands or Hindu colleagues – such a theologian is as out of date as is one who attempts to construct an intellectual position unaware that Aristotle has thought about the world or that existentialists have raised new orientations, or unaware that the earth is a minor planet in a galaxy that is vast only by terrestrial standards. Philosophy and science have impinged so far on theological thought more effectively than has comparative religion, but this will not last. (p. 48)

Men have yet to learn our new task of living together as partners in a world of religious and cultural plurality. The technological and economic aspects of 'one world', of a humanity in process of global integration, are proceeding apace, and at the least are receiving the attention of many of our best minds and most influential groups. The political aspects also are under active and constant consideration, even though success here is not so evident, except in the supremely important day to day staving off of disaster. The ideological and cultural question of human cohesion, on the other hand, has received little attention, and relatively little progress can be reported, even though in the long run it may prove utterly crucial, and is already basic to much else. Unless men can learn to understand and to be loyal to each other across religious frontiers, unless we can build a world in which people of profoundly different faiths can live together and work together, then the prospects for our planet's future are not bright.

My own view is that the task of constructing even that minimum degree of world fellowship that will be necessary for man to survive at all is far too great to be accomplished on any other than a religious basis. From no other source than his faith, I believe, can man muster the energy, devotion, vision, resolution, the capacity to survive disappointment, that will be necessary – that are necessary – for this challenge. Co-operation among men of diverse religions is a moral imperative, even at the lowest level of social and political life.... .

If we must have rivalry among the religious communities of earth, might we not for the moment at least rival each other in our determination and capacity to promote reconciliation? Christians, Muslims and Buddhists each believe that only they are able to do this. Rather than arguing this point ideologically, let us strive in a friendly race to see which can implement it most effectively and vigorously in practice – each recognizing that any success of the other is to be applauded, not decried. (pp. 50–1)

I rather feel that the final doctrine on this matter may perhaps run along the lines of affirming that a Buddhist who is saved, or a Hindu or a Muslim or whoever, is saved, and is saved only, because God is the kind of God whom Jesus Christ has revealed him to be. This is not exclusivist; indeed, it coheres, I feel, with the points that I have made above in dissenting from exclusivism. If the Christian revelation were not true, then it might be possible to imagine that God would allow Hindus to worship him or Muslims to obey him or Buddhists to feel compassionate towards their fellows, without his responding, without his reaching out to hold them in his arms. But because God is what he is, because he is what Christ has shown him to be, therefore other men do live in his presence. Also, therefore, we (as Christians) know this to be so.... .

We are saved by our knowledge; we are not saved by our membership in the Church; we are not saved by anything of our doing. We are saved, rather, by the only thing that could possibly save us, the anguish and the love of God. While we have no final way of knowing with assurance how God deals or acts in other men's lives, and therefore cannot make any final pronouncement ... none the less we must perhaps be at least hesitant in setting boundaries to that anguish and that love.

The God whom we have come to know, so far as we can sense his action, reaches out after all men everywhere, and speaks to all who will listen. Both within and without the Church men listen all too dimly. Yet both within and without the Church, so far as we can see, God does somehow enter into men's hearts. (pp. 57–8)

Wilfred Cantwell Smith, 'The Christian in a Religiously Plural World', in John Hick and Brian Hebblethwaite (eds), *Christianity and Other Religions* (Oxford: Oneworld, 2001).

Norman Solomon

Born in 1933, Norman Solomon served as a rabbi in London, and was the Director of the Centre for the Study of Judaism and Jewish Christian Relations at Selly Oak College, Birmingham, and Lecturer in Modern Judaism at Oxford University. In Judaism and World Religion *he argues that Jews must be open to religious experience in other traditions.*

Today, the traditional readiness ... makes it natural for Jews to appreciate that others have a 'share in God'.

This need not create pressure towards relativism, for the recognition that others can know and be faithful to God has never been understood as implying that all that they do and believe is correct ... there is no necessary connection between accurate knowledge of God's nature or revelation ... and the 'portion in the world to come'.... .

Perhaps a few constructive words on Judaism's relationship with Hinduism and Buddhism will not be out of place here. The historical and theological entanglements that blight the interrelationships of the three monotheistic faiths have no place here, and the main obstacle to a constructive relationship comes from the inherited monotheistic insistence that God is 'jealous' and that all who 'worship sticks and stones' are extremely wicked. The modern worldview and situation must enable us to transcend this attitude, and it is good to remark that the few Jewish thinkers who have seriously addressed themselves to the 'Eastern' religions have revealed rich areas for exploration.... . (p. 242)

Religions do make truth claims, such as that the Torah came from Heaven, that Jesus was the incarnation of God, born of a virgin, or that people are reborn in various forms until they attain nirvana, and many of these claims are contradictory. They also make practical claims, such as that one ought not to worship idols or that one ought to celebrate festivals or to marry or not to marry this one or that.

It would be wrong to gloss over any of this. The first task is to achieve a harmonious society, and in the light of all we have said this should be possible, under secular government, even with a plurality of religious faiths, communities and practices.

After that, there is a search for truth. Truth is delicate, too delicate for warring communities, but in a peaceful community there may be a common search for truth. The community must be very peaceful, though, with a positive peace, not just an absence of fighting. Truth can only emerge where those who search for it do not feel threatened, and are not browbeaten by those who think they already possess the truth, and who insist on 'sharing' it whether or not anyone wants to listen. So the society in which truth is to be sought will allow for distinctiveness, for commitments, for witness, but not for pressurizing and aggressive proselytizing.

I have aimed to portray Judaism as a religion with a commitment, a mission, to the world. This sense of responsibility has often been dimmed by the emphasis

our leaders, in times of persecution, have had to put on the preservation of identity and distinctiveness so necessary for our survival in a hostile world, yet it has
never been allowed to disappear. In bad times the sense of mission focuses on the
messianic future: in enlightened times it is expressed in the Jewish desire to play a
full part in the social and spiritual improvement of mankind. The 'covenant of
Noah' offers a pattern for us to seek from others not necessarily conversion to
Judaism, but rather that faithfulness to the highest principles of justice and
morality which we perceive as the essence of revealed religion. The dialogue of
faiths becomes in this way an imperative arising through our common mission
with, rather than against, other faiths.

So we take joy in the bond that unites humankind, as descendants of the 'first
created pair', Adam and Eve, and look forward to the restoration of that universal
bond in time to come, when 'the earth shall be full of the knowledge of the Lord, as
the waters cover the sea' (Isaiah 11:9).

Yet there is truth, there is distinction between true and false, between right and
wrong, this world is not beyond good and evil, and so there must be demarcation,
and this is reflected both in our teaching and in our society. We cannot set the
bounds of truth; we must listen and try to learn, grow in experience and forge
language, remain open to the world around us with its myriad peoples and ways,
and read and interpret the words of scripture and sage constantly, critically, in the
context of our own age and society.

Tradition can only be captured for the present by a critical and creative process
which does not shirk novel moral decisions. It is too tempting to evade responsibility for those decisions by deceiving oneself that there is some simple direct
guiding line from ancient text to contemporary reality. (pp. 243–4)

Norman Solomon, *Judaism and World Religion* (London: Macmillan, 1991).

Mary Ann Stenger

*The Christian scholar Mary Ann Stenger has been a visiting Assistant Professor of
Religious Studies at the University of Louisville, Kentucky. In 'The Understanding of
Christ as Final Revelation', she outlines various approaches to interreligious dialogue
from within the Christian tradition.*

From our discussion of Barth, Rahner, Tillich and Hick, we can clearly see the
tensions between final revelation in Christ and a desire to be open to truth in non-
Christian religions. For those who want to retain the centrality of final revelation
in Christ and a close tie to the historical Jesus Christ, openness will most likely be

expressed as some form of Christian inclusivism, including non-Christians under Christian rubrics. Even most of Tillich's writings, although more open than Barth or Rahner because of his formal abstractions of universal meaning, basically express a Christian inclusivism centred in Jesus as the Christ as final revelation.

Although I am more sympathetic to Tillich's more open position than Barth's more closed stance, I see problems with any form of Christian inclusivism. Such a position fails to take the non-Christian religions seriously, on their own terms. It really dismisses their teachers, Scriptures, prophets, deities and ultimates as secondary and really irrelevant to Christian truths. With such a position, dialogue is a sharing of ideas but not an openness to new ideas. But if we really engage with another person, we are open to adjusting our ideas.

In fact, both Tillich and Hick have engaged in dialogue with non-Christians, and one can see ongoing shifts in their thought as a result of those conversations. In fact, both make similar moves in their thinking, toward one underlying Reality or depth beneath the particular phenomena of the religions. They, like some others, have found a form of theocentrism as a solution to their acceptance of truths outside Christianity. Such a position has the advantage of allowing individual religions to have their truths but makes all religious truths relative to the one underlying or centring Real or depth.

Such a position does not destroy the acceptance of final revelation in Christ, but it does relativize it in relation to other revelations in non-Christian traditions. Christians can still retain the absoluteness of Christ for them, but they do not assert it in relation to the non-Christian.

One can develop criteria out of one's own tradition and state them in ways that are not tied to the particular tradition.... But the real test of such criteria is not just how they can be in dialogue with non-Christians. Many traditions might agree on Tillich's critique of idolatry or Barth's critique of religion in relation to God's revelation, even though they would not accept the concrete content from which these critiques arise.

Our future, then, is not to abandon our Christian centring in Christ as final revelation but to relate that centre finally to ultimacy which is beyond finite expressions and forms. I recognize that there are some who call for an even more radical relativism, seeing each tradition operating within its historical–cultural context, without claiming one underlying absolute. But I see the direction toward ultimacy and truth in all religions as a structural commonality even if we do not agree on the nature of that ultimacy. Consequently, we can only work out of our own traditions and cultures, but we must continue in conversation and dialogue that is based on our common search for truth and transcendence. As we do so, core doctrines like final revelation in Christ are not abandoned but interpreted anew for our present pluralistic situation. (pp. 202–3)

Mary Ann Stenger, 'The Understanding of Christ as Final Revelation', in Peter Phan (ed.), *Christianity and the Wider Ecumenism* (New York: Paragon, 1990).

Marjorie Hewitt Suchowcki

In the view of Marjorie Hewitt Suchowcki, formerly Dean at Wesley Theological Seminary, feminism demands the acceptance of religious pluralism. In 'In Search of Justice', she argues that religious pluralism is now the only position that can be integrated within a feministic perspective on world religions.

A feminist perspective ... suggests that one must radically affirm religious pluralism, but not without bringing a critical consciousness of well-being in human community to interreligious and intrareligious discussion. Justice is thus to be the fundamental criterion of value and the focus of dialogue and action among religions.

To develop and hold such a position raises interesting problems. First, is it not the case that establishing justice as a norm whereby all religions are judged simply introduces one universal for another, and hence continues the pattern of oppression? Second, and closely related to this, who defines 'well-being'? Justice is a concept closely aligned to religious convictions, and each concept of justice reflects the religious sensitivities and suppositions of the culture that gave it birth. Third, if the first and second problems cannot be answered adequately, then we must face the situation of religious relativism, which would follow were there no acceptable norms of discernment to be applied to religious positions.... (pp. 149–50)

I suggest ... that there is another base of contact among the religions that allows a nonimperialistic criterion of justice. Oddly enough, the contact puts us back again in the ideological realm we supposedly left behind in calling for justice rather than doctrine as the basis of dialogue. If it is the case that interpretations of well-being are rooted in the salvific interaction of religion with ordinary and extraordinary problems of existence, then it is possible that each religion's deepest valuation of what physical existence should be lies, not in its coping with the exigencies of history, but in its projection of the ideal. By looking at each religion's vision of the ultimately perfect mode of existence for its saints or holy ones, whether that vision be otherworldly or not, we might find some echo of unanimity on the value of freedom from suffering.

My point is that justice is not given a universally acceptable content, not even with regard to physical well-being. Some of the variances in definition may be traceable to the ways in which religions have interpreted and dealt with negative factors in existence. We must be sensitive to these variances, but they do not require a full relativization of justice such that it is rendered useless as a norm to judge that which is of greater or lesser value in and among religions. On the contrary, we must look to the heart of justice in each religion as that which renders life meaningful in light of a vision of what existence should be. Using justice as a norm means that the primary visions within each religion of what societal life should be in a 'perfect' world is a source of judgement that can be used internally within each religion to judge its present societal forms of justice. Dialogue among the religions can likewise proceed from the development of mutual concerns for justice that can lead to concerted actions for justice in the world. Justice is a dynamic and transformative notion, capable of being used even to judge itself.

I recognize, of course, that my own determination to ground at least physical well-being as a norm inherently contained within every notion of justice is hardly an impartial or unconditioned determination. My approach is from a feminist perspective, and I have learned the content of justice from experiences of injustice, or that which makes for ill-being. Valuing well-being in the threefold sense outlined earlier means that I look for its traces within that which is given ultimate value in each religion. Nonetheless, I recognize that only the first – physical well-being – can come close to finding common agreement, and even that level has problematic aspects.

What is necessary, then, in looking for a nonimperialistic mode of justice is to look at ultimate rather than penultimate visions of justice. The determinate mode of justice must be drawn from the vision of the termination of adversity, or the ideal form of human existence envisioned in each religion. This vision is far more likely to yield agreement on the value of at least the basic forms of justice dealing with physical existence. If so, then the criterion of justice in that minimal mode can appeal to an internal norm within each religion. This mitigates the charge that the norm of justice as a basis for making value judgements concerning religions is as imperialistic as doctrinal norms....

Affirming religious pluralism within the context of justice shifts the focus of dialogue to the concreteness of human well-being. The very exploration of human well-being, however, inevitably directs our attention to questions concerning how we determine what constitutes well-being, or into the heart of the ideological nature of the religions. Interreligious dialogue focused on justice promotes intrareligious dialogue concerning ultimate and penultimate values. (pp. 159–60).

Marjorie Hewitt Suchowcki, 'In Search of Justice', in John Hick and Paul F. Knitter (eds), *The Myth of Christian Uniqueness* (London: SCM Press, 1987).

Leonard Swidler

The Catholic theologian, Leonard Swidler, received a Ph.D. in history and philosophy from the University of Wisconsin, and an STL from the Catholic Theology Faculty of the University of Tübingen. He has served as Professor of Catholic Thought and Interreligious Dialogue at Temple University. In 'Interreligious and Interideological Dialogue', he argues that interreligious and interideological dialogue is the most suitable matrix within which theology should currently operate.

Why, indeed, should one pursue the truth in the area of religion and ideology by way of dialogue? A fundamental answer to these questions lies in the even more dramatic shift in the understanding of truth that has taken place first in Western civilization, and now beyond it, throughout the nineteenth and twentieth centuries, making dialogue not only possible but necessary.

Whereas the notion of truth was largely absolute, static and exclusive up to the last century, it has subsequently become deabsolutized, dynamic and dialogic – in a word, 'relational'. This new view of truth came about in at least four different, but closely related, ways:

1. Historicization of truth: truth is deabsolutized and dynamized in terms of time, both past and future, with intentionality and action playing a major role in the latter.
2. Sociology of knowledge: truth is deabsolutized in terms of geography, culture and social standing.
3. Limits of language: truth as the meaning of something, and especially as talk about the transcendent, is deabsolutized by the nature of human language.
4. Hermeneutics: all truth, all knowledge, is seen as interpreted truth and knowledge, and hence is deabsolutized by the observer, who always is also interpreter. (p. 7)

The following are some basic ground rules of interreligious, interideological dialogue that must be observed if dialogue is actually to take place. These are not theoretical rules given from 'on high', but ones that have been learned from hard evidence.

First Rule: The primary purpose of dialogue is to learn – that is, to change and grow in the perception and understanding of reality, and then to act accordingly... .

Second Rule: Interreligious, ideological dialogue must be a two-sided project – within each religious or ideological community, and between religious or ideological communities... .

Third Rule: Each participant must come to the dialogue with complete honesty and sincerity.

Fourth Rule: In interreligious, interideological dialogue we must not compare our ideals with our partner's practice... .

Fifth Rule: All participants must define themselves... .

Sixth Rule: Each participant must come to the dialogue with no hard-and-fast assumptions as to points of disagreement... .

Seventh Rule: Dialogue can take place only between equals... .

Eighth Rule: Dialogue can take place only on the basis of mutual trust... .

Ninth Rule: Persons entering into interreligious, interideological dialogue must be at least minimally self-critical of both themselves and their own religious or ideological tradition... .

Tenth Rule: Each participant eventually must attempt to experience the partner's religion or ideology 'from within'. (pp. 13–16)

It should be apparent that Christians need not, should not, take a condemnatory attitude toward non-Christians, particularly those who are adherents of other religions or ideologies, for fear that they would be disloyal to their Christian commitment. Rather, they would be disloyal to their Christian commitment ... if they did not seek to recognize the same truths, the same insights, wherever they find them. This immediately implies that Christians ought to take a stance not of debate, but rather of dialogue with non-Christians. In this dialogue they will doubtless learn that there are many valuable insights in their own Christian tradition that they had overlooked, or suppressed, or distorted, and they can be brought to this rediscovery of their own treasures through finding those very same insights held forth in another religion or ideology in exemplary fashion.

Moreover, is it not also possible that they will discover in another religious, ideological tradition insights that in fact do not seem to have been expressed in their own Christian tradition? If they can resist the temptation to be doctrinaire and triumphalistic, they will have to say yes, it is possible; we can hope to gain truly new insights into the meaning of life.

What does this do to the Christian notion that Jesus Christ is somehow the fullness of what it means to be human? For one thing, it would be said that presumably none of the new insights gathered would in fact run contrary to what had already been exemplified ... in Jesus Christ. Further, one can speak of a development of unfolding, an evolution. One can take the language of a Teilhard de Chardin and speak of moving from the Alpha to the Omega point. Is it not the case that even the early Christians spoke of another coming of the Christ? Surely another coming is not going to be identical with the first coming. If it were, it would not be another coming; it would be the first coming. There will of course be profound similarities, but if it is to be another, then there must also be some differences. Might not these 'new insights' constitute part of these differences? If in fact Christians come to be persuaded that Muhammad and Marx, for example, provided some 'new insights', might they not be seen and understood only in terms of being at a specific time at the end of history. Obviously that is not necessary, for here clearly we are again dealing with metaphorical, hyperbolic, poetic, mythic language. The *eschaton* is clearly beyond our everyday experience. However, cannot events within history be taken to be stages toward, even constitutive elements leading to, that *eschaton*, that Omega point, to again use Teilhardian language? If so, then there need be no opposition ultimately between the Christian understanding of how the world is 'reconciled to God through Christ' and how many persons will in fact experience this reconciliation to God, this learning of the ultimate meaning of human life, through means other than Jesus Christ. (pp. 45–6)

Leonard Swidler, 'Interreligious and Interideological Dialogue', in Leonard Swidler (ed.), *Toward a Universal Theology of Religion* (Maryknoll, NY: Orbis, 1987).

T

Mohammed Talbi

Born in 1921, Mohammed Talbi was a Professor at the University of Tunis, and directed the history department at the Centre d'Etudes et de Recherches Economiques et Sociales in Tunis. In 'Islam and Dialogue – Some Reflections on a Current Topic', he states that despite theological obstacles Muslims and Christians should engage in dialogue in the modern world.

Dialogue for Islam is first and foremost a necessary and vital reestablishment of contact with the world at large. This is still more urgent and beneficial for Islam than for other religions, such as Christianity, which has never really lost such contact, something which puts Christianity in a relatively privileged position today. It is also, in a certain sense, a revival of an old tradition. In fact the whole of Revelation invites us to do just this ... the Revelation invites the Prophet and the Muslim to discuss and to enter into dialogue with men in general, and especially with the faithful of the biblical religions. (pp. 82–3)

This attitude implies, however, if ambiguity is to be avoided, that we admit that there are several ways to salvation... . With very few exceptions the theological systems of all religious confessions have been based on the axiom, expressed in different ways, that 'outside the Church there is no salvation'. Within each faith the group of faithful to benefit by salvation has been still more restricted by the rejection of various heresies whose followers have been consigned to eternal damnation. This leads to the conclusion that apart from certain chosen ones, the vast majority of human beings are destined for perdition. And yet all faiths proclaim that God is Justice, Mercy and Love! It is precisely in this area that we need a real theological renewal and a radical change of mentality. For what chance is there of an open-minded dialogue free of distrust if, from the very beginning, we lay down the absolute principle that those on the other side will inevitably be condemned to hell solely on account of their convictions?...

It is not impossible, therefore, either for Islam or for Christianity, or indeed for the other main religions, on the basis of their texts and with the support even of certain ancient theological tradition to elaborate a theology which would allow for a certain degree of plurality in the ways of salvation, where it is only because one cannot forbid Divine Goodness from overflowing, in a gesture of justice, of mercy and of love, beyond the strict limits of any given Church in order to embrace all men of good will who live exemplary lives. (pp. 91–3)

As far as classical Muslim theology is concerned, it has always proclaimed that the Light of God will finally disperse all darkness and will shine equally for all. 'They desire to extinguish with their mouths the Light of God; but God will perfect His light, though the unbelievers be adverse' (Qur'an 61.8).

Meanwhile divergences continue and show little sign of fading away, at least in the foreseeable future. One must believe that they have their role to play in the economy of salvation, and of the world, among other things by giving an impetus to evolution.... .

> Mankind were only one community, then they fell into variance. But for a word that proceeded from thy Lord, it had been decided between them already touching their differences. They say: 'If only a sign (casting light on this mystery) had been sent down on him from his Lord.' Say: 'The mystery (*ghayb*) of God is inscrutable. Then watch and wait; I shall be with you watching and waiting' (Qur'an 10.18–19).

> Say: 'O my God, Creator of the Heavens and the Earth, who knowest all things visible and invisible. Thou wilt judge in the end between Thy servants touching that whereon they are at variance' (Qur'an 39.46).

Thus when all is said and done we find ourselves faced with the unfathomable mystery of God's Plan and man's condition. So we must accept our differences and disagreements, and by competing with one another in good works, shorten the time in which the trial of our disagreements will come to an end. We must also forego expecting too much from dialogue if we are to avoid bitterness and discouragement and be able to make progress, come wind or wild weather. For we must not have any illusions on this point: whatever the precautions we take there will be many discordant voices. Nobody has ever found in the past a magic wand which could eliminate misunderstandings and radically change the world. We should not expect one to turn up in the future. Dialogue means unending patience. If it helps us to draw gradually nearer to one another, to replace indifference or hostile reserve by real friendship, by true brotherhood even, in spite of our different beliefs and opinions, it will have already accomplished much. Dialogue does not necessarily mean finding a common solution; still less does it imply an absolute need to come to an agreement. Its role is rather to clarify and open up the debate still more, allowing all those engaged to progress, instead of becoming immutably fixed in their own convictions. The way towards the Kingdom of Light will prove to be a long one, and God has chosen to enshroud it in mystery. (pp. 100–1)

Mohammed Talbi, 'Islam and Dialogue – Some Reflections on a Current Topic', in Paul J. Griffiths (ed.), *Christianity Through Non-Christian Eyes* (Maryknoll, NY: Orbis, 1990).

John V. Taylor

John V. Taylor, formerly Anglican Bishop of Winchester, argues in 'The Theological Basis of Interfaith Dialogue' that Christians must overcome their past isolation and engage in encounter with other faiths. Dialogue, he states, offers a new beginning.

We come to the dialogue, therefore, lumbered with our past histories and the fears they have engendered in us. But if we are to go forward history must be forgotten, or at least forgiven. For dialogue is between the living, the people of here and now. Dialogue seeks a new beginning. Dialogue also has to take account mainly of the normal adherents of the different faiths, not the great saints nor the great sinners, for in a sense they prove very little.... .

For I believe we should think of every religion as a people's particular tradition of response to the reality which the Holy Spirit of God has set before their eyes. I am deliberately not saying that any religion is the truth which the Spirit has disclosed, nor even that it contains that truth. I think it may often be misleading to speak of the various religions as revelations of God, for that suggests that God has disclosed part of himself to one people and a different part to others. Is that how a compassionate father loves the various children of his family? It is surely truer to believe that God's self-revelation and self-giving is consistent for all, but that different peoples have responded differently. (pp. 216–17)

But since every religion is a historically determined tradition of response to what the Spirit of God has forever been setting before men's eyes, we must expect to find that each religion has become a self-consistent and almost closed system of culture and language. Communication between one such system and another is fraught with difficulty which must not be underestimated. As dialogue begins, therefore, we shall frequently find that the same word carries an entirely different cluster of meanings in the different traditions; we may also discover with surprise that quite different words are used to mean the same thing. (p. 208)

I have again been talking as a Christian to Christians, aware that others have been overhearing our debate on a central theme of our faith. But I make no apology for that because I believe that, if interfaith dialogue is to become sincere and deep, we have got to expose to one another the ways in which, within our separate households of faith, we wrestle with the questions that other religions put to us. To be overheard as we face up to these disconcerting questions will make us very vulnerable to one another. But if we are not ready to lower our defences, if in fact we are more interested in scoring points than in knowing one another, we may as well give up dialogue altogether.

So, besides letting one another know the absolutes in their own faith that may not be surrendered, the partners in the dialogue must also give serious reflection to the critique which each inevitably brings to bear upon the convictions of the others, however painful and disturbing this may be. If, as I have said, our irreducible loyalties belong to our experiences, and only secondarily to the doctrines that enshrine them, then we must be prepared to have the experiences questioned. Christians, for example, must allow their discourse with Jews to re-open a question which has troubled us from the earliest days: How can Jesus be Messiah and agent of the eschatological kingdom, when it is so patent that things are not made new and the End is still awaited? Defensiveness ought not to make us unwilling to admit that this constitutes a real problem for us. Jewish experience through history may have a lot of light to throw upon the mystery of non-fulfilment in the covenants of God, and the hiddenness of God's victories. The Jewish–Christian dialogue, if pursued with mutual compassion, might blossom into a new theological understanding of the meaning of hope.

Or, again, the questions that Hinduism asks about the true definition of Christ's relation to God – asked in unaffected concern as often as in dispute – should send the Christians back not to abandon their claims but to a fresh exploration of terms and metaphors, just as the challenge of Greek philosophy did in the early centuries... .

To reformulate involves risking the loss of the original truth, yet it is also the only way in which that truth can live and grow into fuller comprehension. Reappraisal of one's own tradition and reformulation of one's own fidelities calls for an extraordinary mixture of humility and boldness. I have to put the question: Do all the partners in the interfaith dialogue come with an equal degree of self-questioning? I sometimes wonder, from what I have seen, whether Christians, for all our past aggressiveness, are not now exhibiting a greater share of self-criticism and mobility of dogma than those who meet us in debate. However that may be – and I could be wrong about it – a genuine openness to the questions that another faith poses can mean, for the believer of any religion, a deeper entry into one's own faith. (pp. 230–1).

John V. Taylor, 'The Theological Basis of Interfaith Dialogue', in John Hick and Brian Hebblethwaite (eds), *Christianity and Other Religions* (London: Collins, 1980).

Paul Tillich

Paul Tillich, formerly Professor at Harvard University and the University of Chicago, argues in 'Christianity Judging Itself in the Light of its Encounter with the World Religions' that ultimate concern is a major feature of all religions. Thus Christians should engage in dialogue with members of other faiths.

I want now to give examples of the way in which Christianity both judged other religions and accepted judgement from them, and finally to show the inner-Christian struggle against itself as a religion, and the new vistas which open up in consequence of these struggles for the future encounters of Christianity with the world religions.

What is the consequence of this judgement of Christianity of itself for its dealing with the world religions? We have seen, first of all, that it is a mutual judging which opens the way for a fair valuation of the encountered religions and quasi-religions.

Such an attitude prevents contemporary Christianity from attempting to 'convert' in the traditional and depreciated sense of this word. Many Christians feel that it is a questionable thing, for instance, to try to convert Jews. They have lived and spoken with their Jewish friends for decades. They have not converted them, but they have created a community of conversation which has changed both sides of the dialogue. Some day this ought to happen also with people of Islamic faith. Most attempts to convert them have failed, but we may try to reach them on the basis of their growing insecurity in face of the secular world, and they may come to self-criticism in analogy to our own self-criticism.

Finally, in relation to Hinduism, Buddhism and Taoism, we should continue the dialogue which has already started and of which I tried to give an example in the third chapter: not conversion, but dialogue. It would be a tremendous step forward if Christianity were to accept this! It would mean that Christianity would judge itself when it judges the others in the present encounter of the world religions.

But it would do even more. It would give a new valuation to secularism. The attack of secularism on all present-day religions would not appear as something merely negative. If Christianity denies itself as a religion, the secular development could be understood in a new sense, namely as the indirect way which historical destiny takes to unite mankind religiously, and this would mean, if we include the quasi religions, also politically. When we look at the formerly pagan, now Communist, peoples, we may venture the idea that the secularization of the main groups of present-day mankind may be the way to their religious transformation.

This leads to the last and most universal problem of our subject: does our analysis demand either a mixture of religions or the victory of one religion, or the end of the religious age altogether? We answer: none of these alternatives! A mixture of religions destroys in each of them the concreteness which gives it its dynamic power. The victory of one religion would impose a particular religious answer on all other particular answers. The end of the religious age – one has already spoken of the end of the Christian or the Protestant age – is an impossible concept. The religious principle cannot come to an end. For the question of the ultimate meaning of life cannot be silenced as long as men are men. Religion cannot come to an end, and a particular religion will be lasting to the degree in which it negates itself as a religion. Thus Christianity will be a bearer of the religious answer as long as it breaks through its own particularlity.

The way to achieve this is not to relinquish one's religious tradition for the sake of a universal concept which would be nothing but a concept. The way is to penetrate into the depth of one's own religion, in devotion, thought and action. In the depth of every living religion there is a point at which the religion itself loses its importance and that to which it points breaks through its particularity, elevating it to spiritual freedom and with it to a vision of the spiritual presence in other expressions of the ultimate meaning of man's existence. (pp. 120–1)

Paul Tillich, 'Christianity Judging Itself in the Light of Its Encounter with the World Religions', in John Hick and Brian Hebblethwaite (eds), *Christianity and Other Religions* (London: Collins, 1980).

Arnold Toynbee

The historian Arnold Toynbee, in 'Christianity Among the Religions of the World', argues that Christianity should rid itself of its exclusivist claims.

My first suggestion would be that we in the West should try to purge our Christianity of its Western accessories. Here an admirable example has been set by the Western Christian missionaries in the earliest wave of Western missionary work in modern times: the Jesuit missionaries in China and India in the sixteenth and seventeenth centuries. The Jesuits were, of course, highly cultivated men. They were masters of all the resources of Western Christendom, which, by that time, was a highly cultivated civilization. And when they came upon the civilizations of China and India they were able to appreciate the fact that here they were in the presence of great cultures, which, on the secular side, were built upon different foundations from the Western culture – upon different philosophies, for instance. The Jesuits were not unmindful of the fact that, in the early centuries of the life of the Christian Church in the Graeco–Roman World, the fathers of the Church – especially the Alexandrian fathers, Clement and Origen, in the second and early third centuries of the Christian Era – had been aware of the same problem of having to express Christianity in terms familiar to the people to whom they were addressing themselves. In that time and place, Christianity had to be interpreted to people with a Greek philosophical education. The Jesuit missionaries realized that the Greek terms in which Christianity had been expressed from the time of the Roman Empire onwards were not the best terms for making it acceptable to the minds and the hearts of Chinese and Indians. So they deliberately set themselves to divest their Christianity of its Western and its Graeco–Roman accessories and to put it to the Chinese and the Indians in their own terms.

This operation is one that is necessary at all times, because we are always relapsing from the worship of God into the worship of our tribe or of ourselves; and therefore we Christians, whether we are Western Christians or Eastern Christians, tend to treat Christianity as if it were the tribal religion of our particular civilization. In the West we tend to treat it as something that is inseparable from the West, and even as something that derives its virtue not so much from being Christian as from being Western. (pp. 158–9)

My next suggestion is more controversial, because it raises a more crucial issue. We ought also, I should say, to try to purge our Christianity of the traditional Christian belief that Christianity is unique. This is not just a Western Christian belief; it is intrinsic to Christianity itself. All the same, I suggest that we have to do this if we are to purge Christianity of the exclusive-mindedness and intolerance that follows from a belief in Christianity's uniqueness.

Here I should like to draw a distinction which, I think, is all-important, though also, no doubt, debatable. I should say that one can be convinced of the essential truth and rightness and value of what one believes to be the fundamental points in one's own religion – and can believe that these tenets have been received by one as a revelation from God – and at the same time not believe that I, my church, my people, have the sole and unique revelation. If one accepts, and builds on, the Jewish and Christian vision of God as being love, one would feel it unlikely, no doubt, that I and my church and my people had not had some revelation from God. If God loves mankind, He would have made a revelation to us among other people. But, on the same ground and in virtue of the same vision of what God's nature is, it would also seem unlikely that He would not have made other revelations to other people as well. And it would seem unlikely that He would not have given His revelation in different forms, with different facets, and to different degrees, according to the difference in the nature of individual souls and in the nature of the local tradition of civilization.... (pp. 160–1)

What, then, should be the attitude of contrite Christians toward the other higher religions and their followers? I think that it is possible for us, while holding that our own convictions are true and right, to recognize that, in some measure, all the higher religions are also revelations of what is true and right. They also come from God, and each presents some facet of God's truth. They may and do differ in the content and degree of the revelation that has been given to mankind through them. They may also differ in the extent to which this revelation has been translated by their followers into practice, both individual practice and social practice. But we should recognize that they, too, are light radiating from the same source from which our own religion derives its spiritual light. (p. 163)

Arnold Toynbee, 'Christianity Among the Religions of the World', in Owen C. Thomas, *Attitudes toward other Religions* (London: SCM Press, 1969).

Leo Trepp

The Jewish scholar, Leo Trepp, served as Professor of Philosophy and Humanities at Napa College, California. In 'Judaism and the Religions of Humanity', he argues that Judaism accepts that righteous Gentiles can be saved.

Judaism perceives itself as unique among the religions of the world, because it is both a faith and a people; both of these elements interact. Standing under God, it draws its character from revelation brought into history, evolving in the people's law, ordinances and traditions, and manifesting itself in a diaspora–homeland community, in which once again both societies of the one people interact. A two-way street exists. In Israel the Jewish mind unfolds predominately not exclusively from internal forces, in the diaspora from exposure to surrounding cultures. By its very character Judaism considers itself and its contribution to be essential for all humanity. By the same token, it denies any exclusiveness as a road to God. As Israel is unique, its being inimitable, there must be other avenues to God, each of them unique and inimitable. The conclusion is formulated in the rabbinic dictum: 'All the righteous of the nations of the world have a share in the world to come' (Tosefta Sanhedrin, 13:21).

There are however certain guidelines, commandments that make for righteousness. They are technically known as the seven Noachide Commandments given to the ancestor of humanity after the flood and binding on all his descendants. They are: prohibition of idolatry, unchastity, shedding of blood, profanation of God's name, robbery, mutilation of animals, and the obligation to establish justice and administer it in just courts (Gen. Rabb., Noah: 34:8). Idolatry, the worship of human achievement as the ultimate, is the key element; humanity fashions its god out of its own desires. This is perversion that leads to the profanation of the Name of God, whenever human ambitions and human aggressiveness are carried out as a divine 'mandate'. (Seeing in an image only a symbol that leads to God is not idolatry; although such worship of images is forbidden the Jew.) A resolute turning away from such idolatry leads prosperously on the road to God. 'He who renounces idolatry may be regarded as a Jew' (Megillah, 15a). He travels the same road as the Jew. (pp. 34–5)

In spite of their shortcomings in practice religions are vital for human survival; on account of their shortcomings they have to sustain each other. Rabbi Akiba rests human dignity squarely on religious foundations: 'God has granted a great gift to man, in creating him in his image, but he granted man an even greater gift, in making it known to him that he was created in God's image' (Abot, 3:18). We also learn: 'God created only one human being, in order that no one might say to his neighbour: "My ancestors were greater than yours"' (Sanhedrin, 4:5). Although the rabbis believed in the historicity of the biblical creation story, and merely added a moral lesson, we may be permitted to regard the statement as an instance of early 'demythologization' – (even as some rabbis held that Job never existed [Baba Batra, 15a]). It holds for us the admonition to separate '*Geschichte*' from '*Heilsgeschichte*'. Whatever is unverifiable, holds truth only for the adherents of a given religion; it is '*Heilsgeschichte*'. Only insofar as we may draw from it a universal, ethical message, unencumbered by dogma, may we apply it generally... .

Judging religions 'by their fruits', Judaism has developed a certain immunity against the arguments of modern philosophy from Hume to logical positivism. God may not be verifiable, but the difference a belief in God and in certain tenets of faith makes is verifiable. Philosophy from Philo to Spinoza was the handmaiden of religion, but has become its severe critic. This has a double advantage. It serves as a rebuke to those philosophers and scholars, including Kant and Hegel, who built into their thought a 'proof' of the pre-eminence of Christianity, or presumed it, as did Wellhausen, Noth and others. It serves as an incentive to the religious bodies in their diversity to demonstrate to the world that faith makes a positive difference in human affairs. (pp. 38–40)

Leo Trepp, 'Judaism and the Religions of Humanity', in John Hick and Hasan Askari (eds), *The Religious Experience of Diversity* (Maryknoll, NY: Orbis, 1985).

Ernst Troeltsch

In 'The Place of Christianity Among the World Religions', the Christian theologian Ernst Troeltsch, formerly Professor at the Universities of Heidelberg and Berlin, outlines his earlier view and argues that religion is a participation in the presence of the Divine. Hence, Christianity should be understood as simply one form of the religious life.

Now, the naive claim to absolute validity made by Christianity is of quite a different kind. All limitation to a particular race or nation is excluded on principle, and this exclusion illustrates the purely human character of its religious ideal, which appeals only to the simplest, the most general, the most personal and spiritual needs of mankind. Moreover, it does not depend in any way upon human reflection or a laborious process of reasoning, but upon an overwhelming manifestation of God in the persons and lives of the great prophets. Thus it was not a theory but a life – not a social order but a power. It owes its claim to universal validity not to the correctness of its reasoning nor to the conclusiveness of its proofs, but to God's revelation of Himself in human hearts and lives. Thus the naive claim to absolute validity of Christianity is as unique as its conception of God. It is indeed a corollary of its belief in a revelation within the depths of the soul, awakening men to a new and higher quality of life, breaking down the barriers which the sense of guilt would otherwise set up, and making a final breach with the egoism obstinately centred on the individual self. It is from this point of view that its claim to absolute validity, following as it does from the content of its religious ideal, appears to be vindicated. It possesses the highest claim to universality of all the religions, for this its claim is based upon the deepest foundations, the nature of God and of man.

Hence we may simply leave aside the question of the measure of validity possessed by the other religions. Nor need we trouble ourselves with the question of the possible further development of religion itself. It suffices that Christianity is itself a developing religion, constantly striving toward a fresh and fuller expression. We may content ourselves with acknowledging that it possesses the highest degree of validity attained among all the historical religions which we are able to examine. We shall not wish to become Jews, nor Zoroastrians, nor Mohammadans, nor again Confucianists, nor Buddhists. We shall rather strive continually to bring our Christianity into harmony with the changing conditions of life, and to bring its human and divine potentialities to the fullest possible fruition. It is the loftiest and most spiritual revelation we know at all. It has the highest validity.... . Such was the conclusion I reached in the book which I wrote some twenty years ago.... . (pp. 82–3)

Christianity could not be the religion of such a highly developed racial group if it did not possess a mighty spiritual power and truth; in short, if it were not, in some degree, a manifestation of the Divine Life itself. The evidence we have for this remains essentially the same, whatever may be our theory concerning absolute validity – it is the evidence of a profound inner experience. This experience is undoubtedly the criterion of its validity, but, be it noted, only of its validity for us. It is God's countenance as revealed to us; it is the way in which, being what we are, we receive, and react to, the revelation of God. It is binding upon us, and it brings us deliverance. It is final and unconditional for us, because we have nothing else, and because in what we have we can recognize the accents of the divine voice.

But this does not preclude the possibility that other racial groups, living under entirely different cultural conditions, may experience their contact with the Divine Life in quite a different way, and may themselves also possess a religion which has grown up with them, and from which they cannot sever themselves so long as they remain what they are. And they may quite sincerely regard this as absolutely valid for them and give expression to this absolute validity according to the demands of their own religious feeling. We shall, of course, assume something of this kind only among nations which have reached a relatively high stage of civilization, and whose whole mental life has been intimately connected with their religion through a long period of discipline. We shall not assume it among the less developed races, where many religious cults are followed side by side, nor in the simple animism of heathen tribes, which is so monotonous in spite of its many variations. (pp. 85–6)

As all religion has thus a common goal in the Unknown, the Future, perchance in the Beyond, so, too, it has a common ground in the Divine Spirit ever pressing the finite mind onward toward further light and fuller consciousness, a Spirit which indwells the finite spirit, and whose ultimate union with it is the purpose of the whole many-sided process. (p. 89)

Ernst Troeltsch, 'The Place of Christianity Among the World Religions', in Owen C. Thomas, *Attitudes Toward Other Religions* (London: SCM Press, 1969).

V

Vivekananda

The Hindu theologian Vivekananda was born in Calcutta in 1863, and educated in British schools. In 1881 he came under the influence of Ramakrishna, and subsequently devoted himself to preaching a version of Ramakrishna's thought. In 'Christ, the Messenger', he argues that the Orient is superior to Western countries in religious matters. In this context he views Christ as an Oriental figure.

There is another type in Asia. Think of that vast, huge continent, whose mountain-tops go beyond the clouds, almost touching the canopy of heaven's blue; a rolling desert of miles upon miles, where a drop of water cannot be found, neither will a blade of grass grow; interminable forests and gigantic rivers rushing down to the sea. In the midst of all these surroundings, the Oriental love of the beautiful and the sublime developed itself in another direction. It looked inside, and not outside ... the Oriental ... is a visionary, is a born dreamer. The ripples of the waterfalls, the songs of the birds, the beauties of the sun and moon and stars and the whole earth are pleasant enough; but they are not sufficient for the Oriental mind. He wants to dream a dream beyond. He wants to go beyond the present. The present, as it were, is nothing to him. The Orient has been the cradle of the human race for ages, and all the vicissitudes of fortune are there... . No wonder, the Oriental mind looks with contempt upon the things of this world and naturally wants to see something that changeth not, something which dieth not, something which in the midst of this world of misery and death is eternal, blissful, undying... .

We see, therefore, in the life of this great Messenger of life, the first watchword: 'Not this life, but something higher'; and like the true son of the Orient, he is practical in that. You people of the West are practical in your own department, in military affairs, and in managing political circles and other things. Perhaps, the Oriental is not practical in those ways, but he is practical in his own field: he is practical in religion... .

So, we find Jesus of Nazareth, in the first place, the true son of the Orient, intensely practical. He has no faith in this evanescent world and all its belongings.

No need of text-torturing, as is the fashion in the West in modern times, no need of stretching out texts until they will not stretch any more. Texts are not India-rubber, and even that has its limits. Now, no making of religion to pander to the sense of vanity of the present day! Mark you let us all be honest. If we cannot follow the ideal, let us confess our weakness, but not degrade it; let not any try to pull it down. One gets sick at heart at the different accounts of the life of the Christ that Western people give. I do not know what he was or what he was not! One would make him a great politician; another, perhaps, would make of him a great military general; another, a great patriotic Jew, and so on. Is there any warrant in the books for all such assumptions? The best commentary on the life of a great teacher is his own life. 'The foxes have holes, and the birds of the air have nests, but the Son of man hath not where to lay his head.' That is what Christ says as the only way to salvation; he lays down no other way. Let us confess in sackcloth and ashes that we cannot do that. We still have fondness for 'me' and 'mine'. We want property, money, wealth. Woe unto us! Let us confess and not put to shame that great Teacher of Humanity! He had no family ties. But do you think that that man had any physical ideas in him? Do you think that this mass of light, this God and not-man, came down to earth, to be the brother of animals? And yet, people make him preach all sorts of things. He had no sex ideas! He was a soul! Nothing but a soul, just working a body for the good of humanity; and that was all his relation to the body. In the soul there is no sex. The disembodied soul has no relationship to the animal, no relationship to the body... .

He had no other occupation in life; no other thought except that one, that he was a Spirit. He was a disembodied, unfettered, unbounded Spirit. And not only so, but he, with his marvellous vision, had found that every man and woman, whether Jew or Gentile, whether rich or poor, whether saint or sinner, was the embodiment of the same undying Spirit as himself. Therefore, the one work his whole life showed was calling upon them to realize their own spiritual nature. Give up, he says, these superstitious dreams that you are low and you are poor. Think not that you are trampled upon and tyrannized over, never be trampled upon, never be troubled, never be killed. You are all Sons of God, Immortal Spirit. (pp. 208–10)

Vivekananda, 'Christ, the Messenger', in Paul J. Griffiths (ed.), *Christianity Through Non-Christian Eyes* (Maryknoll, NY: Orbis, 1990).

Hendrik Vroom

Hendrik Vroom, Professor of Philosophy of Religion at the Free University, Amsterdam, argues in Religions and the Truth *that religions are multi-centred world-views. Thus it is questionable whether it is possible to speak of a single phenomenon occurring among all religions. Rather, each faith contains basic insights through which adherents believe they experience the transcendent.*

1. It is incorrect to characterize religions in terms of a single basic conviction; there are a number of basic insights in which people believe they experience the transcendent. The truth claims of religion are therefore not monolithic and uncompromisingly opposed, but they display family resemblances, showing both similarities and differences.
2. Each tradition has an idea of the transcendent, of humanity, and of the world, which has emerged from such basic insights. The configuration which the basic insights receive in a tradition is attained in a hermeneutical process which colours the basic insights. Corresponding beliefs from one tradition cannot, therefore, simply be equated with those from another tradition.
3. Since people have different insights concerning the nature of the transcendent, man and the world, the question of truth is at stake; people claim that they know reality as it really is.
4. Conflicting views do not eliminate the fact that people agree on a number of points. Examples already mentioned concern the createdness of the world, dependence on grace, the necessity to transform one's ego, and the emphasis on a benevolent disposition towards fellow beings. This mutual concurrence is often not a matter of assent, but of criss-cross family resemblances. Religious phenomena resemble each other closely, yet they remain different. One must take into account that such similarities do not always apply to each religion as a whole, but to particular currents within a tradition which may resemble a current in another tradition... .
5. The verdict which one has about other religious traditions is implied in one's own view. It is said, for instance, that the kingdom of God comes by love and self-sacrifice, there will be little appreciation for some Islamic currents which teach the idea of holy war. It is believed, as in many Hindu and Buddhist currents, that every person must break his *karma* by way of so many lives, one will not have much confidence in Christians who see the church as an institute of salvation. One's own view naturally determines one's appreciation for other traditions... .
6. The criteria for the assessment of religious truth claims are not of such a nature that what is true and what is untrue can be established inter-subjectively. The criteria do, however, offer minimal requirements which religious claims to

truth must meet. The decisive demands are that they do justice to experience and that they disclose the fact that they speak concerning the transcendent. The problem is that religious experience pure and simple does not exist; experience is always interpreted. Traditions nurture certain interpretations. The discussion about the truth of religious insights is therefore concerned with experiences together with their interpretation.

7. When discussing beliefs, the role which doctrine plays in a tradition must be taken into account, as well as the distinction between two levels of religious knowledge. All traditions possess beliefs, even though the heart of religion everywhere is lived faith (*religio vera*). The formulation of belief springs from lived faith and cannot be separated from this experiential basis. Discussion of beliefs which one has not lived remains something outward and superficial. As a consequence, those who state that interreligious dialogue is a process are right, and those who believe that the assessment of beliefs is a matter of public, philosophical and academic study err, even though religious studies and the philosophy of religion can play an important role in such dialogue.....

8. Since people claim to know something about the nature of the transcendent in stating their religious beliefs, and about the right interpretation of the world and of man, they are not only different and (perhaps) in conflict, but can also be complementary. Just as religious traditions take stock of the reality presented by the exact sciences, they can likewise take into account each other's insights. They can, at least, apply, integrate interpretations from other traditions into their own world-view. This integration is not adaptation to a single centre of integration or basic conviction, but integration within a configuration of basic insights.

9. Since religion has a number of aspects, differences of opinion about certain beliefs can be accompanied by agreement in respect of particular moral convictions. Differences of opinion do not exclude mutual respect and co-operation. (pp. 383–5)

Hendrik Vroom, *Religions and the Truth* (Grand Rapids, MI: Eerdmans, 1989).

Keith Ward

Keith Ward, Professor of Theology at the University of Oxford, contends in 'Religion after the Enlightenment', that religions must be perceived as unified in their spiritual quest.

I have spoken of 'religion' because that term, however unsatisfactory, denotes an area of human practice and experience which is distinctive and recognizable. It is also important to locate particular religions within the whole regime of faiths which constitute that set of human practices. Indeed, the third stage of religious development to which I have referred is precisely one in which it is no longer regarded as satisfactory to live with a set of competing claimants to ultimate truth, lying alongside one another but in almost total ignorance of each other. As long as one thinks of religions as making contradictory claims to some ultimate truth, the very idea of the religious quest as lying in the pursuit of one supreme objective value is weakened. Where the values in question seem to be bluntly opposed, one could hardly speak of a quest for the same sort of thing. However, because of the rise of critical consciousness, indeed awareness of historical change and of the culturally affected character of human knowledge, we are now in a situation in which a number of developing scriptural traditions can come to new and wider understandings of themselves by consciously becoming part of a global religious outlook. Tribal religions can remain content with being the distinctive practices of one small group, ignoring all that goes on elsewhere. But to the extent that they do that, they must fail to relate fully to the way the world actually is. They must fail to see the limitations of their own way and the aspects of truth that other ways may have perceived. In the modern world, the great scriptural faiths find themselves in a very similar situation. They can insist on a self-contained finality and complete-ness for their own scriptures. But if they do, they will fail to relate to the full range of contemporary scientific knowledge of the world. They may miss aspects of truth that other traditions have discerned... .

In this new situation of global religious awareness, it is not that one must give up what is distinctive in one's own tradition, and seek some minimal highest common factor in all religions. That would show a cavalier disregard for truth and for the importance of difference in human understanding. Rather, the task is to realize how provisional and incomplete the varied interpretations of one's own conceptual schemes have been, and to see how the interaction of different conceptual schemes has been fruitful for growth and understanding in the past. If one believes that God has disclosed the divine nature and purpose in one tradition, one need not believe that this disclosure is so final that nothing can ever be added to it, in the way of understanding, or so complete that it stands in need of no interpretation when it is encountered in new cultural conditions. It is plausible to think – and it was certainly thought by many of the early Christian Fathers – that others may have seen patterns that we have missed, traced connections that we have overlooked, and can contribute to the understanding and interpretation of our own tradition, without threatening it. If the third stage may be called one of convergent spirituality, it is not one in which the different traditions will merge one with another. It is one in which each will accept the epistemic right of the others to exist and will accept that a comprehensive view will need to take into account their viewpoints; most importantly it will accept the inevitability of religious difference, and look for a positive role which such diversity can play in the growth of mutual understanding. There is thus a twofold task for religions as they move into this third stage, as I think they inevitably will. One is to reinterpret their outlook in terms of the provisional, but well-established scientific view of a vast emergent and interconnected cosmos, to take scientific knowledge and its vision of a multi-billion year time-scale for the universe with full seriousness. The other is to extend their vision to take account of the insights of other religious traditions, to place their own tradition within a more global perspective.

If this can be done, then religions may be seen, not as reactionary defences against science, and not as legitimations of ethnic or racial separatism, but as vehicles for the acceptance of a wider spiritual unity of humanity, carrying a moral vision and a power for its implementation. Within such a perspective, the various faiths can celebrate their particularity while also contributing to a wider understanding of the human spiritual quest. (pp. 146–8)

Keith Ward, 'Religion after the Enlightenment', in Dan Cohn-Sherbok (ed.), *Many Mansions* (London: Bellew, 1992).

Rowan Williams

Rowan Williams served as a Professor at Oxford University and is Anglican Archbishop of Wales. In 'Trinity and Pluralism', he argues that the doctrine of the Trinity serves as a foundation for interfaith dialogue.

The goal of any specific moment of interfaith encounter is thus – presumably – to find a way of working together toward a mode of human co-operation, mutual challenge and mutual nurture, which does not involve the triumph of one theory or one institution or one culture, but which is in some way unified by relation to that form of human liberty and maturity before God made concrete in Jesus. To put it slightly differently, and perhaps more traditionally, the Christian goal in engaging with other traditions is the formation of children of God after the likeness of Christ. For Panikkar, this formation may already be under way in other traditions; if we ask what then is the point of specifically Christian witness, the answer might well be that explicit Christianness, to use Panikkar's favoured term, is a catalyst for drawing together these processes of formation in a way that is self-aware, critical and actively concerned about sustaining common human action. Witness to the 'christic fact' as an integrating reality proposes to the world of faiths the possibility of a kind of critical human norm that can be used in the struggle against what limits or crushes humanity.... .

The Christian face to face with other traditions thus comes with queries as well as affirmations, queries shaped by the conviction that the stature of the fullness of Christ is what defines the most comprehensive future for humankind; shaped too by the form of its basic story, which is about the conflict between God and a particular kind of corrupt politicization of faith by the religiously powerful. The Christian church ought to carry in its language and practice a deep suspicion of alliances between hierarchies in faith-communities and hierarchies in absolutist political administrations – Caiaphas and Pilate, and their many more recent analogues.... .

The Christian goal in interfaith encounter is to invite the world of faiths to find here in the narrative and practice of Jesus and his community, that which anchors and connects their human hopefulness – not necessarily in the form of 'fulfilling their aspirations' or 'perfecting their highest ideals', but as something which might unify a whole diverse range of struggles for human integrity without denying or 'colonizing' their own history and expression.... .

But, supposing one partner in the conversation decides that his or her particular starting point is essentially a symbolic variant on the other partner's position or that both are variants of something more fundamental, the character of the encounter would have changed, and one's reasons for carrying on with it would be quite radically different. They would no longer be grounded in whatever feature of the native traditions had initially stimulated the engagement, whatever feature had given justification for the hope that a stranger's commitments would turn out to be familiar after all. In Panikkar's terms, the dialogue would no longer rest on the conviction that reality itself was grounded in an absolute source acting both as Logos and spirit; it would cease, that is, to be pluralist in the sense that Panikkar wants to give to the word, and by abstracting to some underlying structure separable from the historical particularity, the imagery and practices of this social group, it runs the risk of precisely the intellectualism Panikkar wants at all costs to avoid... .

If Panikkar is right in seeing trinitarian Christianity as the proper foundation for an interreligious engagement that is neither vacuous nor imperialist, the doctrines of Christian credal orthodoxy are not, as is regularly supposed, insuperable obstacles to dialogue; the incarnation of the Logos is not the ultimate assertion of privilege and exclusivity but the centre of that network of relations (implicit and explicit) in which a new humanity is to be created. This network has its symbolic form in the Christian church, but its life is not identical with the institutional reality of the church... .

Trinitarian theology becomes not so much an attempt to say the last word about the Divine nature as a prohibition against would-be final accounts of divine nature and action. To the extent that the relation of spirit to Logos is still being realized in our history, we cannot ever, while history lasts, say precisely all that is to be said about Logos. What we know, if we claim to be Christians, is as much as anything a set of negations. We know that the Divine is not simply a pervasive source and ground, incapable of being imaged, but we know that the historical form of Jesus, in which we see creation turning on its pivot, does not exhaust the divine. (pp. 9–12)

Rowan Williams, 'Trinity and Pluralism', in Gavin D'Costa (ed.), *Christian Uniqueness Reconsidered* (Maryknoll, NY: Orbis, 1990).

Sherwin Wine

Born in 1928, Sherwin Wine was ordained a reform rabbi at the Hebrew Union College, and served as rabbi at the Birmingham Temple in Detroit, Michigan. The founder of Humanistic Judaism, he argues in Judaism Beyond God *that all religions, including Judaism, must be understood as human creations. Nonetheless, he maintains that it is still possible to identify with one's own religious tradition despite rejecting any form of supernaturalism.*

The Secular Revolution subverted all the reigning epic stories that motivated religious behaviour and supported religious identity. The hero of these stories was God, however named. When Kant demonstrated at the end of the eighteenth century that it was impossible to prove either the existence or the non-existence of God, he was giving intellectual expression to a social experience. In increasing numbers, people no longer cared whether God existed or not. They had found alternative secular sources for strength and meaning. Science was not as personal as God. But it did promise more reliable power than prayer.

The new epics of the secular age shifted their attention from God to people. They became more humanistic. People were seen less as the creatures of God and more as the masters of their own story. Even if they were limited by the laws of nature, by the weakness of their own power, they had no conscious rivals to direct their lives and to interfere with their own plans. People were no longer the supporting actors in their own drama. They were the leading characters... .

Secular humanism is the philosophic consequence of the Secular Revolution. It is a set of ideas about the world and its people that pervades Western society, especially its educated and managerial classes. Since the conquest of the world by Western culture coincided with the Secular Revolution, it is a powerful force in all countries and nations.

While the surviving institution of the old religious culture is the church or synagogue, the 'temples' of secular humanism are the schools of secular studies. And its 'clergy' are the teachers and professions who use them and graduate from them.

Most secular humanists do not know that they are what they are and do not choose to use the label. Having never been united as a group with a strong group identity, they often have a clearer idea of what they do not believe than of what they do believe... . (pp. 16–17)

There is a need in the Jewish world to take the Secular Revolution seriously and to provide a clear alternative to rabbinic Judaism... . Humanistic Jews want to bring their beliefs and their behaviour together and to find their integrity. They are eager to affirm:

That they are disciples of the Secular Revolution.

That the Secular Revolution was good for Jews.

That reason is the best method for the discovery of truth.

That morality derives from human needs and is the defence of human dignity.

That the universe is indifferent to the desires and aspirations of human beings.

That people must ultimately rely on people.

That Jewish history is a testimony to the absence of God and the necessity of human self-esteem.

That Jewish identity is valuable because it connects them to that history.

That Jewish personality flows from that history – and not from official texts that seek to describe it.

That Jewish identity serves individual dignity – and not the reverse.

That the Jewish people is an international family that has its centre in Israel and its roots in the Diaspora.

That the humanistic Gentile has a positive role to play in the life of the Jewish people.

Humanistic Jews want to translate these affirmations and commitments into an effective lifestyle – for themselves and for those who share their convictions. They need a community of believers to work with and to share with in this pioneering venture. (pp. 243–4)

Sherwin Wine, *Judaism Beyond God* (Farmington Hills, MI: Society for Humanistic Judaism, 1985).

Michael Wyschogrod

Michael Wyschogrod, born in 1928, has served as Professor of Philosophy at Baruch College, City University of New York. In 'Judaism and Evangelical Christianity', he argues that despite differences between the two religions, Christians should acknowledge the election of the Jewish people by God.

The single most important contact between Judaism and evangelical Christianity is the centrality of the Bible in the two faiths. Before proceeding to qualify this point of contact – and qualify it we must – we must first pause to appreciate the significance of this point as a point of contact. Both Judaism and evangelical Christianity would be inconceivable without a Book which is the centre of the two faiths. The sacred space of the synagogue centres on the Ark in which the Torah, the parchment on which the Pentateuch is handwritten, is kept and from which it is removed to be read to the congregation during worship. In spite of the significance Judaism attaches to the rabbinic interpretation of the Bible, the reading of the Pentateuch and prophetic portion in the synagogue is not accompanied by the reading of any rabbinic interpretation, though many texts exist whose public reading as an accompaniment to the biblical lection could have been ordained. Instead, the biblical text is read in Hebrew to be heard by the congregation as the Word of God... .

The centrality of the text would be a point of contact between Judaism and evangelical Christianity even if the texts central to the two faiths were entirely different texts. But, of course, they are not entirely different texts. To a very large extent they are the same text, the Hebrew Bible. But there is also the New Testament which is sacred to Christians but not to Jews. Reduced to its simplest terms, this is the crux of the difference between Judaism and evangelical Christianity. The evangelical hears the New Testament as the Word of God and it is this basic fact which becomes a foundation of his beliefs. Since Judaism does not hear the New Testament as the Word of God, a deep division between the two faiths becomes apparent... .

But in spite of this difference there is, as we have seen, an important area of agreement. Both Judaism and evangelical Christianity hear the Hebrew Bible as the Word of God. This is surely a matter of decisive significance. (pp. 55–6)

Speaking of Israel, Karl Barth writes:

> For it is incontestable that this people as such is the holy people of God: the people with whom God has dealt in his grace and in his wrath; in the midst of whom he has blessed and judged, enlightened and hardened, accepted and rejected; whose cause either way he has made his own, and has not ceased to make his own, and will not cease to make his own. They are all of them by nature sanctified by Him, sanctified as ancestors and kinsmen of the Holy One of Israel, in a sense Gentiles are not by nature, not even the best of Gentiles, not even the Gentile Christians, not even the best of Gentile Christians, in spite of their membership in the Church, in spite of the fact that they too are now sanctified by the Holy One of Israel and have become Israel.

'They too are now sanctified', writes Karl Barth. This, it seems to me, is the challenge to Christianity, particularly evangelical Christianity. Christianity thinks of itself as the new Israel, heir to the election which the old Israel lost because it did not recognize its Messiah in Jesus. If this is so, then, after Jesus there is no longer any theological significance to the existence of the Jewish people. It is still necessary, of course, to bring individual Jews to Jesus because all men need Jesus, but the existence of the Jewish people as such is displaced by the existence of the church.

This has been the view widely prevalent in much of Christianity. The alternative is to see the church as inconceivable without Israel. In this view, Israel remains the people of election; Israel is the nucleus of the cell while the church is the substance that clusters around the nucleus. In this second definition, the church can be understood only as that body of Gentiles that has joined itself to the body of Israel and whose destiny is therefore irrevocably intertwined with the destiny of the people of

Israel. Jesus is not, then, severed from his special relationship with the people of Israel but, instead, the people of Israel is seen as the people chosen by God to carry his presence in the world. Since the election of Israel is intended as a blessing for all peoples of the earth, those who are addressed by the God of Israel can join their destinies to that of Israel as adopted sons in the household of Israel. In this interpretation, Christianity becomes the Judaism of the Gentiles. (pp. 65–6)

Michael Wyschogrod, 'Judaism and Evangelical Christianity', in Paul J. Griffiths (ed.), *Christianity Through Non-Christian Eyes* (Maryknoll, NY: Orbis, 1990).

Y

Seiichi Yagi

In the view of the Buddhist scholar, Seiichi Yagi, in 'Plurality of the Treasure in Earthen Vessels', Christian absolutism is a misguided notion which must be replaced by the acknowledgement that spiritual treasures are found in other traditions.

Religious language is an attempt to speak of what is beyond language. Seen from this point of view, Christian doctrines, Bible and apostolic *kerygma* are the treasure-in-vessels and not the treasure itself, distinct from the vessels. But, one may argue, the language of the apostolic witness is constitutive of the gospel itself, because without it the salvation event of Jesus Christ cannot be made known (cf. Rom. 10:14f.). The salvation event of Jesus is the event in history which must be told.

Of course the fact of the incarnation is the event in history. In other words, the reality of the treasure-in-vessel, Jesus of Nazareth, must be witnessed to. But, however 'heretical' it may sound, the Logos became flesh – this is the salvation event – not in Jesus alone. Jesus is the model of the treasure-in-vessel, and if one admits that, one will also admit that the language in itself is an earthen vessel for the treasure. It can become treasure-in-vessel but they cannot be confused with the treasure-in-vessel, which is beyond language. Christians are not always clear at this point, whereas Zen Buddhists are – like mystics in Christian tradition – sharply aware.

'Ugan said, "This summer I preached and preached for the sake of my brothers. Look, to see whether I have still eyebrows".' A dilemma: language is an inadequate vessel for the Ultimate, but without this vessel one cannot communicate it. The awareness of this dilemma can be found richly in Zen literature. Rinzai warned repeatedly against searching after the truth in verbal expressions. Bodhi-Dharma answered the Chinese Emperor Wu, who asked him what the ultimate formulation of the holy truth is – 'Openness to all directions. Nothing holy' – which in a way reminds us of John 3:8: 'The wind blows where it wills, you hear the sound of it, but you do not know where it comes from, or where it is going.' The Spirit-wind cannot be confined to any finite form.

In fact, the treasure is, as was said above, not actual in this world without the earthen vessels. This is the case primarily with human existence prior to its verbal expressions. When the Son of God was revealed to Paul he was qualified as the Apostle for the Gentiles and he received the formula of the Christ-*kerygma* most probably thereafter (cf. Gal. 1:16; 1 Cor. 15:3ff.). Thus we can make a distinction between the Logos incarnate and the Bible as the witness to it. The language is, as well as the ego, constitutive of, but not capable of containing the treasure fully. So also is it in the case of Zen. Buddha-nature is actual only when one becomes aware of it, that is to say, when one's bodily existence as a whole remains potential. In other words; its actuality is simultaneous with enlightenment. But the actuality of bodily enlightenment is distinguished from its verbal expression. Now precisely because of this correct 'awareness' a certain propensity seems to develop at times. Buddhists occasionally seem to tend to lay emphasis on the actuality of enlightenment rather than on its ground: *Dharma*. That then gives rise to a claim of the superiority, if not of the absoluteness, of certain enlightened individuals of the schools that hand down the enlightenment, though it is true that any enlightenment as a treasure-in-vessel is unique and individual.

We ask again in what the treasure is, keeping in mind that the reality of the treasure-in-vessel is the actuality of the treasure in the world.

If one answers that God or the universal Logos or the Ultimate is the treasure in the primary sense, one assumes naturally that there are a number of vessels, for no finite vessel can confine the infinite exclusivity to itself. Thus, if one lays all the stress on God, one tends to make light of the vessel with the result that religion becomes an unfathomable X.

If, on the contrary, one holds the treasure-in-vessel not only for the indispensable moment of the actuality of the treasure but for the treasure itself – as is the case with traditional Christianity which preaches Jesus of Nazareth not as the most important treasure-in-vessel but as the treasure, that is, as the revelation of God as the unique salvation event for all humanity – that logically grounds not only the uniqueness and individuality but at the same time also the claim of the absoluteness of Jesus and of the Bible as witnesses to Jesus.

Today, not a few Christian theologians want to avoid both extremes, absolutism and relativism. Then the solution is at hand: an absolutist–relativist view of Jesus – and therefore also of Christianity – as the treasure-in-vessel, not as the treasure in the primary sense of the word. We do not assert this on grounds of the needs of our time, which seeks such a solution. (pp. 139–40)

Seiichi Yagi, 'Plurality of the Treasure in Earthen Vessels', in Leonard Swidler and Paul Mojzes (eds), *The Uniqueness of Jesus: A Dialogue with Paul F. Knitter* (Maryknoll, NY: Orbis, 1997).

Further Reading

CHRISTIANITY AND OTHER FAITHS

Allen, E.L. *Christianity among the Religions*. London, George Allen and Unwin, 1960

Anderson, Gerald and Stransky, Thomas F. (eds) *Mission Trends No. 5: Faith Meets Faith*. New York and Toronto, Paulist Press and Grand Rapids, Eerdmans, 1981

Anderson, Norman *Christianity and Comparative Religion*. London, Tyndale Press, 1970

Arai, Tosh and Ariarajah, Wesley (eds) *Spirituality in Interfaith Dialogue*. Geneva, World Council of Churches, 1989

Bowker, John *Licensed Insanities: Religions and Belief in God in the Contemporary World*. London, Darton, Longman and Todd, 1987

Camps, Arnulf *Partners in Dialogue: Christianity and Other World Religions*. Maryknoll, NY, Orbis, 1983

Clasper, Paul *Eastern Paths and the Christian Way*. Maryknoll, NY, Orbis, 1980

Cobb, John B. *Christ in a Pluralistic Age*. Philadelphia, Westminster Press, 1975

Cogswell, James and Olivia *Dialogue with People of Other Faiths*. New York, The Division of Overseas Ministries of the NCCC in the USA, 1986

Coward, Harold *Pluralism: Challenge to the World Religions*. Maryknoll, NY, Orbis, 1985

Cox, Harvey *Many Mansions: A Christian's Encounter with Other Faiths*. Boston, Beacon, and London, Collins, 1988

Cracknell, Kenneth, *Toward a New Relationship: Christians and People of Other Faith*. London, Epworth, 1986

Cragg, Kenneth *The Christ and the Faiths*. Philadelphia, Westminster Press, 1986

Dawe, Donald G. and Carman, John B. (eds) *Christian Faith in a Religiously Plural World*. Maryknoll, NY, Orbis, 1978

D'Costa, Gavin *Theology and Religious Pluralism: The Challenge of Other Religions*. Oxford, Basil Blackwell, 1986

Dupuis, Jacques *Jesus Christ at the Encounter of World Religions*. Maryknoll, NY, Orbis, 1991

Griffiths, Paul J. (ed.) *Christianity through Non-Christian Eyes*. Maryknoll, NY, Orbis, 1990

Heim, S. Mark *Salvations: Truth and Difference in Religion*. Maryknoll, NY, Orbis, 1995

Hick, John *An Interpretation of Religion*. New Haven, Yale University Press, 1989

Hick, John and Hebblethwaite, Brian (eds) *Christianity and Other Religions*. London, Collins, 1980

Hick, John and Knitter, Paul (eds) *The Myth of Christian Uniqueness*. Maryknoll, NY, Orbis, 1987

Hillman, Eugene *Many Paths*. Maryknoll, NY, Orbis, 1989

Knitter, Paul F. *No Other Name?: A Critical Survey of Christian Attitudes Toward the World Religions*. Maryknoll, NY, Orbis, 1985

Kraemer, H. *The Christian Message in a Non-Christian World*. London, James Clark, 1956

Küng, Hans *Christianity and the World Religions: Paths of Dialogue with Islam, Hinduism and Buddhism*. London, Collins, 1987

Küng, Hans and Moltmann, Jürgen (eds) *Christianity Among World Religions*. Edinburgh, T. and T. Clark, 1986

Lochhead, David *The Dialogical Imperative: A Christian Reflection on Interfaith Encounter*. Maryknoll, NY, Orbis, 1988

Mojzes, Paul and Swidler, Leonard (eds) *Christian Mission and Interreligious Dialogue*. Lewiston, New York, The Edwin Mellen Press, 1990

Neill, Stephen *Christian Faith and Other Faiths*. London, Oxford University Press, 1970

Newbigin, Lesslie *The Gospel in a Pluralist Society*. Grand Rapids, MI, Eerdmans, 1989

Ogden, Schubert M. *Is There Only One True Religion or Are There Many?* Dallas, Southern Methodist University Press, 1992

Race, Alan *Christians and Religious Pluralism: Patterns in the Christian Theology of Religions*. Maryknoll, NY, Orbis, 1982

Richards, Glyn *Towards a Theology of Religions*. London, Routledge, 1989

Samartha, Stanley J. *One Christ, Many Religions: Towards a Revised Christology*. Maryknoll, NY, Orbis, 1991

Selvanayagam, Israel *A Dialogue on Dialogue: Reflections on Interfaith Encounters*. Christian Literature Society, Madras, 1995

Smart, Ninian and Konstantine, Steven *Christian Systematic Theology in a World Context*. London, Marshall Pickering, 1991

Smith, Wilfred Cantwell *The Faith of Other Men*. New York, New American Library, 1963

The Meaning and End of Religion: A New Approach to the Religious Traditions of Mankind. New York, Macmillan, 1962

Swidler, Leonard (ed.) *Toward a Universal Theology of Religion*. Maryknoll, NY, Orbis, 1987

Thomas, Owen C. (ed.) *Attitudes Toward Other Religions: Some Christian Interpretations*. Lanham, MD, University Press of America, 1986

Tracy, David *Dialogue with the Other*. Grand Rapids, MI, Eerdmans, 1990

Ward, Keith *Religion and Revelation: A Theology of Revelation in the World's Religions*. Clarendon Press, Oxford, 1994

Whaling, Frank *Christian Theology and World Religions*. Basingstoke, Marshall Pickering, 1986

Wiles, Maurice *Christian Theology and Inter-religious Dialogue*. Philadelphia, Trinity Press International, 1992

JEWISH—CHRISTIAN DIALOGUE

Braybrooke, Marcus *A Time to Meet: Towards a Deeper Relationship between Jews and Christians*. London, SCM, 1990

Brockway, Alan (ed.) *The Theology of the Churches and the Jewish People*. Geneva, World Council of Churches, 1987

Brooks, Roger (ed.) *Unanswered Questions: Theological Views of Jewish Christian Relations*. Indianapolis, IN, Notre Dame University Press, 1987

Burrell, David and Landau, Yehezkel (eds) *Voices from Jerusalem: Jews and Christians Reflect on the Holy Land*. New York, Paulist Press, 1992

Cargas, Harry James *Shadows of Auschwitz: A Christian Response to the Holocaust*. Indianapolis, IN, Notre Dame Press, 1987

Charlesworth, James H. (ed.) *Jews and Christians: Exploring the Past, Present and Future*. New York, Crossroad, 1990

Cohn-Sherbok, Dan *Judaism and other Faiths*. London, Macmillan, 1994
   World Religions and Human Relations. Maryknoll, NY, Orbis, 1992

Cracknell, Kenneth *Towards a New Relationship: Christians and People of Other Faiths*. London, Epworth, 1986

Croner, Helga (ed.) *Stepping Stones to Further Jewish–Christian Dialogue*. London, Stimulus Books, 1977
   More Stepping Stones to Further Jewish–Christian Dialogue: An Unabridged Collection of Christian Documents 1975–1983. London, Stimulus Books, 1985

Dietrich, Donald J. *God and Humanity in Auschwitz: Jewish–Christian Relations and Sanctioned Murder*. New Brunswick, NJ, Transaction Publishers, 1995

Eckardt, A. Roy *Elder and Younger Brothers: The Encounter of Jews and Christians*. New York, Charles Scribner's Sons, 1967

Eckardt, Alice L. and A. Roy *Long Night's Journey into Day: A Revised Perspective on the Holocaust*. Detroit, Wayne State University Press, 1987

Ellis, Marc *Toward a Jewish Theology of Liberation*. Maryknoll, New York, Orbis, 1987

Fischer, Eugene J. (ed.) *Interwoven Destinies: Jews and Christians Through the Ages*. Mahway, NJ, Paulist Press, 1993
   Visions of the Other: Jewish and Christian Theologians Assess the Dialogue. New York, Paulist Press, 1994

Fleischner, Eva *Judaism in German Christian Theology Since 1945: Christianity and Israel Considered in Terms of Mission*. Metuchen, NJ, Scarecrow Press, 1975

Gager, John *The Origins of Anti-Semitism: Attitudes Towards Judaism in Pagan and Christian Antiquity*. New York, Oxford University Press, 1983

Harrelson, Walter and Falk, Randall *Jews and Christians: A Troubled Family*. Nashville, TN, Abingdon Press, 1990

Hick, John and Meltzer, Edmund S. (eds) *Three Faiths – One God: A Jewish, Christian, Muslim Encounter*. London, Macmillan, 1989

Klenicki, Leon *Toward a Theological Encounter: Jewish Understandings of Christianity.* Mahway, NJ, Paulist Press, 1991

Klenicki, Leon and Wigoder, Geoffrey (eds) *A Dictionary of the Jewish–Christian Dialogue.* New York, Paulist Press, 1994

Littell, Franklin H. *The Crucifixion of the Jews.* New York, Harper and Row, 1975

Maduro, Otto (ed.) *Judaism, Christianity and Liberation.* Maryknoll, NY, Orbis, 1991

Novak, David *Jewish–Christian Dialogue: A Jewish Justification.* Oxford, Oxford University Press, 1989

Pawlikowski, John T. *What Are They Saying About Christian–Jewish Relations?* New York, Paulist Press, 1980

Christ in the Light of the Christian–Jewish Dialogue. New York, Paulist Press, 1982

Rahner, Karl and Lapide, Pinchas *Encountering Jesus – Encountering Judaism: A Dialogue.* New York, Crossroad, 1987

Rudin, A. James and Wilson, Marvin R. *A Time to Speak: the Evangelical–Jewish Encounter.* Grand Rapids, MI, Eerdmans, 1987

Ruether, Rosemary Radford *Faith and Fratricide: The Theological Roots of Anti-Semitism.* New York, Seabury Press, 1974

Saperstein, Marc *Moments of Crisis in Jewish Christian Relations.* London, SCM, 1989

Stendahl, Krister *Paul among Jews and Gentiles.* Philadelphia, Fortress Press, 1976

Swidler, Leonard *Bursting the Bonds: A Jewish–Christian Dialogue on Jesus and Paul.* Maryknoll, NY, Orbis, 1991

Thoma, Clemens *A Christian Theology of Judaism.* New York, Paulist Press, 1980

Ucko, Hans *Common Roots, New Horizons: Learning about Christian Faith from Dialogue with Jews.* Geneva, WCC, 1994

Van Buren, Paul A. *A Theology of the Jewish Christian Reality: Discerning the Way.* San Francisco, Harper and Row, 1980

A Theology of the Jewish Christian Reality: A Christian Theology of the People Israel. San Francisco, Harper and Row, 1983

A Theology of the Jewish Christian Reality: Christ in Context. San Francisco, Harper and Row, 1988

Wigoder, Geoffrey *Jewish Christian Relations since the Second World War.* Manchester, Manchester University Press, 1987

Williamson, Clark A. *A Guest in the House of Israel: Post Holocaust Church Theology.* Louisville, KY, Westminster, 1993

ISLAM AND CHRISTIANITY

Anderson, Norman *God's Law and God's Love: An Essay in Comparative Religion.* London, Collins, 1980

Basetti-Sani, Giulio *The Koran in the Light of Christ: A Christian Interpretation of the Sacred Book of Islam.* Chicago, Franciscan Herald Press, 1977

Brown, David *A New Threshold: Guidelines for the Churches in Their Relations with Muslim Communities.* London, BBC, 1976

Brown, Stuart *Meeting in Faith: Twenty Years of Christian–Muslim Conversations Sponsored by the World Council of Churches.* Geneva, WCC, 1989

The Nearest in Affection: Towards a Christian Understanding of Islam. Geneva, WCC, 1994

Chapman, Colin *Cross and Crescent: Responding to the Challenge of Islam*. Leicester, Inter-Varsity Press, 1995

Cohn-Sherbok, Dan (ed.) *Islam in a World of Diverse Faiths*. London, Macmillan, 1997

Cracknell, Kenneth *Justice, Courtesy and Love: Theologians and Missionaries Encountering World Religions 1846–1914*. Epworth Press, 1995

Cragg, Kenneth *Sandals at the Mosque: Christian Presence Amid Islam*. New York, Oxford University Press, 1959

The Call of the Minaret. Oxford, Oneworld, 2000

The Event of the Qur'an: Islam in Scripture. Oxford, Oneworld, 1994

Alive to God: Muslim and Christian Prayer. London, Oxford University Press, 1970

The Mind of the Qur'an: Chapters in Reflection. London, George Allen and Unwin, 1973

Muhammed and the Christian: A Question of Response. Oxford, Oneworld, 1999

Jesus and the Muslim: an Exploration. Oxford, Oneworld, 1999

Daniel, Norman *Islam and the West: the Making of an Image*. Oxford, Oneworld, 1993

Doi, A. Rahman I. *Non-Muslims under Shari'ah*. Lahore, Kazi, 1981

Esack, Farid *Qur'an, Liberation and Pluralism, An Islamic Perspective of Interreligious Solidarity against Oppression*. Oxford, Oneworld, 1997

Geisler, Norman L. and Saleeb, Abdul *Answering Islam: the Crescent in Light of the Cross*. Grand Rapids, MI, Baker, 1993

Goddard, Hugh P. *Christianity from the Muslim Perspective*. CISSC, 1994

Haddad, Yvonne Yazbeck and Wadi Zaidan Haddad (eds) *Christian–Muslim Encounters*. University Press of Florida, 1995

Hick, John and Meltzer, Edmund S. (eds) *Three Faiths – One God: A Jewish, Christian, Muslim Encounter*. London, Macmillan, 1989

Jaoudi, Maria *Christian and Islamic Spirituality: Sharing a Journey*. Mahwah, NJ, Paulist Press, 1993

Kateregga, Badru and Shenk, David *Islam and Christianity: A Muslim and a Christian in Dialogue*. Grand Rapids, MI, Eerdmans, 1980

Kimball, Charles *Striving Together: A Way Forward in Christian–Muslim Relations*. Maryknoll, NY, Orbis, 1991

Küng, Hans and Moltmann, Jürgen (eds) *Islam: A Challenge for Chritianity*. London, SCM, 1994

McAuliffe, Jane Dammen *Qur'anic Christians: An Analysis of Classical and Modern Exegesis*. Cambridge, Cambridge University Press, 1991

Mitri, Tarek (ed.) *A Christian–Muslim Discussion*. Geneva, WCC, 1995

Molla, Claude *Islam and Christianity: 150 Questions and 150 Answers*. Nairobi, Programme for Christian–Muslim Relations, 1997

Nasr, Seyyed Hossein *Ideals and Realities of Islam*. London, George Allen and Unwin, 1966

Parrinder, Geoffrey *Jesus in the Qur'an*. Oxford, Oneworld, 1995

Parshall, Phil *Bridges to Islam: A Christian Perspective on Folk Islam*. Grand Rapids, MI, Baker, 1983

The Cross and the Crescent: Reflections on Christian–Muslim Spirituality. Wheaton, IL, Tyndale House Publishers, 1989

Robinson, Neal *Christ in Islam and Christianity.* Albany, NY, State University of New York, 1991

Rosseau, S.J. Richard (ed.) *Christianity and Islam: The Struggling Dialogue.* Scranton, PA, Ridge Row Press, 1985

Swidler, Leonard (ed.) *Muslims in Dialogue: The Evolution of a Dialogue*, Lewiston, NY, Edwin Mellen, 1992

Vaporis, N.M. (ed.) *Orthodox Christians and Muslims.* Brookline, MA, Holy Cross Orthodox Press, 1986

Watt, W. Montgomery *Muslim–Christian Encounters: Perceptions and Misperceptions.* London, Routledge, 1991

BUDDHISM AND CHRISTIANITY

Abe, Masao *Zen and Western Thought.* Honolulu, University of Hawaii Press, 1985
  Buddhism and Interfaith Dialogue. Honolulu, University of Hawaii Press, 1995

Amore, Roy C. *Two Masters, One Message.* Nashville, TN, Abingdon, 1978

Batchelor, Stephen *The Awakening of the West: The Encounter of Buddhism and Western Culture.* Berkeley, CA, Parallax Press, 1994

Berrigan, Daniel and Hanh, Thich Nhat *The Raft is not the Shore.* Boston, Beacon Press, 1975

Bobilin, Robert *Revolution from Below: Buddhist and Christian Movements for Justice in Asia.* Lanham, MD, University Press of America, 1998

Bruns, J. Edgar *The Christian Buddhism of St John.* New York, Paulist Press, 1971

Calloway, Tucker N. *Japanese Buddhism and Christianity.* Tokyo, Shinkyo Shuppansha, 1957

Carmody, Denise Lardner and Carmody, John *Serene Compassion.* New York, Oxford University Press, 1996

Cobb, John *Beyond Dialogue: Toward a Mutual Transformation of Christianity and Buddhism.* Philadelphia, Fortress Press, 1982

Cobb, John and Ives, Christopher (eds) *The Emptying God: A Buddhist–Jewish–Christian Conversation.* Maryknoll, NY, Orbis, 1990

Covell, Ralph R. *Confucius, the Buddha and Christ.* Maryknoll, NY, Orbis, 1986

De Kretser, Bryan *Man in Buddhism and Christianity.* Calcutta, YMCA, 1954

De Silva, Lynn A. *Creation, Redemption, Consummation in Christian and Buddhist Thought.* Chiengmai, Thailand Theological Seminary, 1964
  The Problem of the Self in Buddhism and Christianity. New York, Barnes and Noble, 1979

Dhamasiri, Gunapala *A Buddhist Critique of the Christian Concept of God.* Colombo, Lake House Investments, 1974

Drummond, R.H. *Gautama the Buddha: An Essay in Religious Understanding.* Grand Rapids, MI, Eerdmans, 1974

Dumoulin, Heinrich *Christianity Meets Buddhism.* LaSalle, IL, Open Court Publishing, 1974

Fernando, Anthony and Swidler, Leonard *Buddhism Made Plain: An Introduction for Christians and Jews*. Maryknoll, NY, Orbis, 1985

Geffre, Claude and Dhavamony, Mariansusai (eds) *Buddhism and Christianity*. New York, Seabury Press, 1979

Graham, Dom Aelred *Conversations: Christian and Buddhist*. New York, Harcourt-Brace and World, 1969

Houston, G. W. (ed.) *The Cross and the Lotus: Christianity and Buddhism in Dialogue*. Delhi, Motilal Banarsidass, 1985

Dharma and Gospel: Two Ways of Seeing. Delhi, Sri Satguru, 1984

Ingram, Paul O. *The Modern Buddhist–Christian Dialogue*. Lewiston, New York, Edwin Mellen, 1988

Ingram, Paul O. and Streng, Frederick (eds) *Buddhist–Christian Dialogue*. Honolulu, University of Hawaii Press, 1986

Johnston, William *The Still Point: Reflections on Zen and Christian Mysticism*. New York, Fordham University Press, 1970

Kadowaki, J. K. *Zen and the Bible*. London, Routledge and Kegan Paul, 1980

Klostermaier, Klaus *Liberation, Salvation, Self-Realization: A Comparative Study of Hindu, Buddhist and Christian Ideas*. Madras, University of Madras, 1973

Lefebure, Leo *The Buddha and the Christ: Explorations in Buddhist and Christian Dialogue*. Maryknoll, NY, Orbis, 1993

Lopez, Donald and Rockefeller, Steve (eds) *The Christ and the Boddhisattva*. Albany, NY, State University of New York Press, 1987

Masutani, Fumio *A Comparative Study of Buddhism and Christianity*. Tokyo, The Young East Association, 1957

Mitchell, Donald W. *Spirituality and Emptiness: The Dynamics of Spiritual Life in Buddhism and Christianity*. New York, Paulist Press, 1991

Pieris, Aloysius *Love Meets Wisdom: A Christian Experience of Buddhism*. Maryknoll, NY, Orbis, 1988

Ross, Nancy R. *Three Ways of Asian Wisdom: Hinduism, Buddhism, Zen and Their Significance for the West*. New York, Simon and Schuster, 1987

Siegmund, Georg *Buddhism and Christianity: A Preface to Dialogue*. University of Alabama Press, 1963

Smart, Ninian *Buddhism and Christianity,* Honolulu, University of Hawaii Press, 1993

Spae, Joseph John *Buddhist–Christian Empathy*. Chicago, IL, Chicago Institute of Theology and Culture, 1980

Ssuzuki, D. T. *Mysticism: Christian and Buddhist*. New York, Harper, 1957

Tamura, Teruvasu *A Zen Buddhist Encounters Quakerism*. Wallingford, PA, Pendle Hill, 1992

Vroom, Hendrik *No Other Gods: Christian Belief in Dialogue with Buddhism, Hinduism and Islam*. Grand Rapids, MI, Eerdmans, 1996

Waldenfels, Hans *Absolute Nothingness: Foundations for a Buddhist–Christian Dialogue*. New York, Paulist Press, 1980

Walker, Susan (ed.) *Speaking of Silence: Christians and Buddhists on the Contemplative Way*. New York, Paulist Press, 1987

Yagi, Seiichi and Swidler, Leonard *A Bridge to Buddhist–Christian Dialogue*. New York, Paulist Press, 1990

HINDUISM AND CHRISTIANITY

Abhishiktananda (Henri le Saux) *The Hindu–Christian Meeting Point within the Cave of the Heart*. Bombay, The Insitute of Indian Culture, 1969
   Saccidananda: A Christian Approach to Advaitic Experience. Delhi, SPCK, 1974
Appasarny, A. J. *The Gospel and India's Heritage*. London, 1942
   The Theology of Hindu Bhakti. Madras, The Christian Literature Society, 1970
Arirajah, S. Wesley *Hindus and Christians: A Century of Protestant Ecumenical Thought*. Amsterdam, Editions Rodopi and Grand Rapids, MI, Eerdmans, 1991
Bassuk, Daniel E. *Incarnation in Hinduism and Christianity*. Atlantic Highlands, NJ, Humanities Press, 1987
Bracken, Joseph *The Divine Matrix: Creativity as Link between East and West*. Maryknoll, NY, Orbis, 1995
Braisted, John *The Theology of Ramanuja*. New Haven, CN, Yale University Press, 1974
Braybrooke, Marcus *Together to the Track*. CISCRS Books on Inter-religious Dialogue, Madras, Diocesan Press, 1971
   The Undiscovered Christ: A Review of Recent Developments in the Christian Approach to the Hindu. CISCRS Books on Inter-religious Dialogue, Madras, Diocesan Press, 1973
Brockington, John *Hinduism and Christianity*. New York, St Martin's Press, 1992
Bryant, Darrol and Flinn, Frank (eds) *Interreligious Dialogue*. New York, Paragon House, 1989
Carpenter, David *Revelation, History and the Dialogue of Religions*. Maryknoll, NY, Orbis, 1995
Chettimattam, John B. *Dialogue in Indian Tradition*. Bangalore, Dhamaram College, 1969
Clooney, Francis X. *Theology after Vedanta*. Albany, NY, State University of New York Press, 1993
Coward, Harold (ed.) *Hindu–Christian Dialogue*. Maryknoll, NY, Orbis, 1989
Davie, Ian *Jesus Parusha: A Vedanta-Based Doctrine of Jesus*. Lindisfarne Press, 1985
Devanandan, P. D. and Thomas, M. M. *Preparation for Dialogue: A Collection of Essays on Hinduism and Christianity in New India*. CISCRS Books on Inter-religious Dialogue, Bangalore, The Christian Institute for the Study of Religion and Society, 1964
Eck, Diana L. *Encountering God*. Boston, Beacon Press, 1993
Fort, Andrew O. and Mumme, Patricia Y. *Living Liberation in Hindu Thought*. Albany, NY, State University of New York Press, 1996
Grant, Sara *Towards an Alternative Theology*. Bangalore, Asian Trading Corporation, 1991
Griffiths, Bede *Christ in India*. Springfield, IL, Templegate Publishers 1966
   Vedanta and Christian Faith. Los Angeles, CA, The Dawn Horse Press, 1973
Griffiths, Paul J. *Christianity Through Non-Christian Eyes*. Maryknoll, NY, Orbis 1990

Healy, Kathleen *Christ as Common Ground*. Duquesne University Press, 1990

Hogg, A. G. *The Christian Message to the Hindu*. London, SCM, 1947

Hooker, Roger *Themes in Hinduism and Christianity*. Verlag Peter Lang GmbH, Frankfurt am Main, 1989

Klostermaier, Klaus *Hindu and Christian in Vrindaban*. London, SCM, 1969

Kulandran, Sabapathy *Grace: A Comparative Study of the Doctrine in Christianity and Hinduism*. London, Lutterworth Press, 1964

Lipner, Julius *The Face of Truth*. Albany, NY, State University of New York Press, 1986

Neill, Stephen *Bhakti Hindu and Christian*. Madras, Christian Literature Society, 1974

Panikkar, Raimundo *The Trinity and the Religious Experience of Man*. Maryknoll, NY, Orbis, 1973

The Unknown Christ of Hinduism. Maryknoll, NY, Orbis, 1981

Parrinder, Geoffrey *Avatar and Incarnation*. Oxford, Oneworld, 1997

Robinson, John *Truth is Two-Eyed*. Philadelphia, Westminster, 1979

Samartha, Stanley J. *The Hindu Response to the Unbound Christ*. CISCRS Books on Inter-religious Dialogue, Bangalore, The Christian Literature Society, 1974

Between Two Cultures. Geneva, WCC Publications, 1996

Sharma, Arvind *A Hindu Perspective on the Philosophy of Religion*. New York, St Martin's Press, 1990

Sharpe, Eric *Faith Meets Faith*. London, SCM, 1977

The Universal Gita. London, Duckworth, 1985

Smart, Ninian *The Yogi and the Devotee*. London, George Allen and Unwin, 1968

Thangaraj, Thomas *The Crucified Guru*. Nashville, TN, Abingdon, 1994

Von Bruck, Michael *The Unity of Reality: God, God-Experience and Meditation in the Hindu–Christian Dialogue*. New York, Paulist Press, 1986

Index

Solomon, Norman   18, 203–4
Sophia   187
Soter (Saviour) function   187
soul, notion of   7, 133
  no evidence for Christian belief in
    75–77
Stenger, Mary Ann   18, 204–5
Stransky, Thomas F.   33, 55, 64, 100, 193
subjectivity
  beyond subject-object duality   24
  way of deliverance   133
Suchowcki, Marjorie Hewitt   19, 206–7
Sufis   147
sunyata (ultimate reality)   131, 188
Swidler, Leonard   19, 26, 34, 43, 48, 59, 86,
    93, 104, 115, 131, 135, 137, 160, 188,
    197, 207–9, 234
symbols, and language   80
syncretism
  increasing prevalence of   5, 88
  opposed   30, 77

Tagore, R.   139
Talbi, Mohamed   19, 210–11
Taoism   8, 92–93
Tatian   63
Taylor, John V.   19, 212–13
Temple, Archbishop William   38, 163
territoriality, and religion   70–71
  colonial mentality   77–78
Tertullian   63
theism   55
theocentrism   1, 5, 205
theology
  contribution of mystical and aesthetic
    183
  examining traditional   11, 122–24
  'global'   123
  liberation   124–26
  Orthodox Christianity   6, 62–64
  and pluralism   9, 11, 97–99, 122–24, 126
  sexism, influence of   179
Theravada Buddhism   113, 119–20
Third World, shift to national status
  87–88
Thomas, Owen C.   50, 112, 216, 220
Thou, relations with eternal   52–53
Tillich, Paul   19, 104, 105, 214–15
1 Timothy
  2:4   156
tolerance   1, 9, 98, 103, 119
  going beyond   68–69

Torah   4, 43, 82, 90, 117, 187, 230
Tosefta Sanhedrin
  13:21   217
Toynbee, Arnold   19, 215–17
transcendence
  in all religions   120
  both right and wrong   49
  and immanence   78
  nature of   223
transitoriness   24
treasure-in-vessel concept   21
Trepp, Leo   19, 217
trial by imprecation   27
tribal religions   225
Trinity   188
  basis for religious encounter   7, 73, 74
  foundation for interfaith exchange   20,
    228
  rejected by Islam   146–47
  and *Saccidananda*   185–86
triumphalism, Christian   5, 7, 19, 171
  colonial mentality   77–78
  evangelism   88
  Holy Spirit's presence in the world   74
  superseding   59–60
Troeltsch, Ernst   20, 189, 218–20
tropism   187
truth
  Christian claims not superior   47
  cognitive relativism   142–43
  common core in all religions   111–12
  competing claims to   2, 92–93, 203
  criteria for judging   165
  elements in all religions   2, 30–31
  engaging in dialogue   131, 171
  experiences and their interpretation
    223–24
  and falsity   29
  and hermeneutics   208, 223
  'is one' (*Ekam sat vipra vahudha vadanti*)
    138
  Jesus's claim to be   150
  Jesus's perception of relative   100
  nonbiblical   63–64
  not monolithic   223
  partial   177–78
  personalized   29
  as pluralistic   14, 160
  progressive unfoldment of   141
  provisional pointers to   170–71
  reformulating   213
  'relational'   208